AF817323

ROUTLEDGE LIBRARY EDITIONS:
THE HISTORY OF SOCIAL
WELFARE

Volume 9

THE HISTORY OF THE ROCHDALE PIONEERS

THE HISTORY OF THE ROCHDALE PIONEERS

GEORGE JACOB HOLYOAKE

Routledge
Taylor & Francis Group
LONDON AND NEW YORK

First reprint of Tenth Edition first published in 1893 by
George Allen & Unwin Ltd.
Second reprint in 1900.
Third reprint in 1907.
Fourth reprint in 1918.
Fifth reprint in 1922.
First published in 1893

This edition first published in 2017
by Routledge
2 Park Square, Milton Park, Abingdon, Oxon OX14 4RN

and by Routledge
605 Third Avenue, New York, NY 10017

Routledge is an imprint of the Taylor & Francis Group, an informa business

All rights reserved. No part of this book may be reprinted or reproduced or utilised in any form or by any electronic, mechanical, or other means, now known or hereafter invented, including photocopying and recording, or in any information storage or retrieval system, without permission in writing from the publishers.

Trademark notice: Product or corporate names may be trademarks or registered trademarks, and are used only for identification and explanation without intent to infringe.

British Library Cataloguing in Publication Data
A catalogue record for this book is available from the British Library

ISBN: 978-1-138-20330-3 (Set)
ISBN: 978-1-315-45977-6 (Set) (ebk)
ISBN: 978-1-138-20471-3 (Volume 9) (hbk)
ISBN: 978-1-315-46885-3 (Volume 9) (ebk)

Publisher's Note
The publisher has gone to great lengths to ensure the quality of this reprint but points out that some imperfections in the original copies may be apparent.

Disclaimer
The publisher has made every effort to trace copyright holders and would welcome correspondence from those they have been unable to trace.

THE HISTORY OF THE

ROCHDALE PIONEERS

Central Stores, Toad Lane, 1868.

SELF-HELP BY THE PEOPLE.

THE HISTORY OF THE

ROCHDALE PIONEERS

BY

GEORGE JACOB HOLYOAKE

AUTHOR OF "THE HISTORY OF CO-OPERATION IN ENGLAND," "SIXTY YEARS OF AN AGITATOR'S LIFE," ETC. ETC.

1844—1892

TENTH EDITION REVISED AND ENLARGED

"From nothing, from the least,
The lowliest village (what but here and there
A reed-roofed cabin by a river side),
Grew everything ; and year by year
Patiently, fearlessly working her way
O'er brook and field, o'er continent and sea."

ROGERS' *Rome*.

LONDON: GEORGE ALLEN & UNWIN LTD.
RUSKIN HOUSE 40 MUSEUM STREET, W.C.

SOME OPINIONS OF THE PRESS.

"A tenth edition, revised and enlarged, is conclusive proof, if need there be, of the permanent value of the literary work of this veteran co-operator. The co-operative movement in England constitutes one of the best evidences of the stamina and capacity of the British working-man, and has made its mark the world over, as may be seen from the interesting account of the number of translations that have been made of Mr. Holyoake's book into foreign languages."—*Economic Review.*

"A very good account of the growth and success of a practical co-operative enterprise. Mr. Holyoake writes with much force and a certain picturesqueness of style, and his book well deserves perusal."—*Westminster Review.*

"The twenty-eight have left behind them an institution which deals justly, and provides things honest in the sight of all men. If the co-operators had learnt nothing from the vast administrative tasks which have been thrown open to them, if they had reached no higher civic standard, and gained nothing in independence and in character from the new footing which the pioneers secured for them, surely Toad Lane deserves immortality."—*Daily Chronicle.*

"The first complete edition of Mr. Holyoake's 'History of the Rochdale Pioneers,' brought down from 1844 to the Rochdale Congress of 1892."—*Co-operative News.*

"A most interesting and valuable book."—*Rochdale Observer.*

First Reprint of Tenth Edition, *November* 1893;
Second, *April* 1900; Third, *January* 1907; Fourth, *February* 1918;
Fifth, *October* 1922.

PREFACE

THE chapters of this little History were commenced to be inserted in the *Daily News* (in 1857), as the reader may infer from note to Chapter I. The breaking out of the Mutinies in India absorbed all space in that quarter, and prevented the completion of the publication in those columns; otherwise, the subsequent chapters might have had the advantage of notes of the Editor of the *Daily News* (Mr. William Weir), who had great knowledge of, and interest in, Co-operative Associations, abroad and at home.

When the chapters appeared as a book, it became known to many persons, interested in social ideas. Mr. Horace Greeley of the *New York Tribune* had an edition printed in New York. This was the first reprint. Next, Fernando Garrido, a Spanish dramatic writer and publicist, made a translation in his "Historia de las Asociaciones Obreras en Europa." Professor A. Talandier published a translation in *Le Progres de Lyons.* Great impetus, the translator reported, was thereby given to Co-operation in Lyons. The Emperor, who had social ideas, commended Co-operation to the Lyonnese, and mentioned it in an Imperial speech. M. Elie Reclus, editor of *L'Association*, told the moral of this story of the Pioneers to the Parisians, in his fable of "The Blind Man and the Lame Man." Mr. John Stuart Mill, by quoting passages from this little history in his "Principles of Political Economy," did more than any one else to call attention to the proceedings of the Rochdale Pioneers. Mr. Joseph Cowen read chapters of this narrative nightly to pitmen and other workmen who were his neighbours, which led to the formation of the Blaydon-on-Tyne Store, now occupying a street, and owning a considerable farm. Mr. Henry Pitman reprinted the book in the *Co-operator*. Mr. M'Guiness of Paris made a translation of it in the French *Journal Co-operative*.

The first principal translation in book form was one in French by Madame Godin (under the name of Marie Moret), for the information of the workmen of Guise. Professor Vigano of Milan published an Italian translation in a quarto volume. M. O. Cambier, a magistrate of Paturage, Belgium, issued a complete translation of 283 pages at Verviers and Paris, including the prefaces of 1857 and 1867, and a biography of the author. Later, Signor Lorenzi Ponti published in Milan a translation from the French of Madame Godin. Herr H. Hantschke published a translation in German, with engravings of the old store in Toad Lane and of the present central store in Rochdale, of which a presentation copy was sent me in ornate Berlinese binding.

The last translation has been that of Dr. St. Bernat of Buda-Pesth into the Hungarian language. The Sociological Society of America issued a small Manual of Co-operation. This epitome, excellently executed by ladies, included some of the following chapters. The Manual was popular, I judge, as a share of profit from it was sent to me. Foreign translations on a subject new to the public do not at first allure readers, and the translators generally lose money by their generous labour. I received no profit from any, nor stipulated for any. On the contrary, I felt under obligation to the translators for being at the expense of introducing to their countrymen an English method of industrial self-help, which otherwise might have remained much longer unknown and unregarded.

"Self-Help by the People," here first used, I believe, as a title, has been employed by Dr. Smiles to designate his popular book of brief biographies. In 1860 a condensed edition of this History was issued in Paisley, purporting to be "Abridged from the Original Publication," but what, or whose publication, was not stated. An article contributed to "Chambers's Journal" contained passages, purporting to be original, taken from the Rochdale story. The correction was at once made by the editor. Afterwards I was sorry I mentioned the matter, as other writers might have gone on quoting as their own, passages which would have advanced the knowledge of Co-operation. The *Quarterly Review* of 1863 had occasion to include this "History" in the list of books reviewed, in a very remarkable article on Co-operation, but it suppressed the name of the author. The writer of the review suggested that a single book of nameless authorship had an odd look among others that enjoyed paternity. The editor adopted an extraordinary mode of removing the singularity—he omitted the names of all the other authors reviewed, though among them were writers of the most perfect "regulation" type of thought, and the result was the only article that probably ever appeared in the *Quarterly* in which only authorless books were reviewed.

There remains, however, the satisfaction of knowing that this book has been useful. Mr. William Cooper of Rochdale, writing to the *Daily News*, December, 1863, stated that of 332 Co-operative Societies then on the Registrar's Returns, 251 had been established since 1857, when "Self-Help" was published, and he adds, "I have heard several persons ascribe the origin of their now prosperous Society to reading the History. Not fewer than 500 or 600 copies were sold in Rochdale. It was bought and read by a few working men in many towns in the United Kingdom." This History is now revised, enlarged, illustrations added, and brought down to the Rochdale Congress of 1892.

The Italians have a proverb of unusual sagacity for that quick-witted people, namely: "They who go slowly go far." Co-operation has gone both slow and far. It has issued like the tortoise from its Lancashire home in England; it has traversed France, Germany, and even the frozen steppes of Russia; the bright-minded Bengalese are applying it, as is the soon-seeing and far-seeing American; and our own emigrant countrymen in Australia are endeavouring to naturalise it there. Like a good chronometer, Co-operation is unaffected by change of climate, and goes well in every land.

G. J. H.

EASTERN LODGE, BRIGHTON,
September, 1893.

THE SOCIALISTS' INSTITUTE. THE WEAVERS' ARMS.

CONTENTS

LIST OF ILLUSTRATIONS.

THE PIONEER STORE IN ITS ORIGINAL STATE, 1844.

HISTORY OF THE ROCHDALE EQUITABLE PIONEERS.

PART I.—1844-1857.

CHAPTER I.

THE FIRST EFFORTS, AND THE KIND OF PEOPLE WHO MADE THEM.

HUMAN nature must be different in Rochdale from what it is elsewhere. There must have been a special creation of mechanics in this inexplicable district of Lancashire—in no other way can you account for the fact that they have mastered the art of acting together, and holding together, as no other set of workmen in Great Britain have done. They have acted upon Sir Robert Peel's memorable advice; they have "taken their own affairs into their own hands;" and what is more to the purpose, they have kept them in their own hands.

The working class are not considered to be very rich in the quality of self-trust, or mutual trust. The business habit is not thought to be their forte. The art of creating a large concern, and governing all its complications, is not usually supposed to belong to them. The problem of association has many times been tried among the people, and as many times it has virtually failed. Mr. Robert Owen has not accomplished half he intended. The "Christian Socialists," inspired by eloquent rectors, and directed by transcendent professors, aided by the lawyer mind and the merchant mind, and what was of no small importance, the very purse of Fortunatus himself,[1] have made but poor work of association. They have hardly drawn a single tooth from the dragon of competition. So far from having scotched that ponderous snake, they appear to have added to its vitality, and to have convinced parliamentary political economists that competitive strife is the eternal and only self-acting principle of society. True, reports come to us ever and anon that in America something has been accomplished in the way of association. Far away in the backwoods

[1] Here we must express our dissent. They failed precisely because they were aided by the purse of Fortunatus. In France, we are assured all those "Associations Ouvrières," which refused to accept money from government in 1848 are prospering, while those which accepted it have either ceased to exist, or are on the eve of ceasing to exist. Sacrifice and self-reliance are the secret of success in these as in all other enterprises.—ED. *Daily News*.

a tribe of bipeds—some mysterious cross between the German and the Yankee—have been heard of, known to men as Shakers, who are supposed to have killed the fatted calf of co-operation, and to be rich in corn, and oil, and wine, and—to their honour be it said—in foundlings and orphans, whom their sympathy collects, and their benevolence rears. But then the Shakers have a narrow creed and no wives. They abhor matrimony and free inquiry. But in the constituency till lately represented by Mr. Edward Miall, there is liberality of opinion—Susannahs who might tempt the elders again—and rosy-cheeked children, wild as heather and plentiful as buttercups. Under all the (agreeable) disadvantages of matrimony and independent thought, certain working men in Rochdale have practised the art of self-help, and of keeping the "wolf from the door." That animal, supposed to have been extirpated in the days of Ethelbert, is still found showing himself in our crowded towns, and may be seen any day prowling on the outskirts of civilisation.

At the close of the year 1843, on one of those damp, dark, dense, dismal, disagreeable days, which no Frenchman can be got to admire—such days as occur towards November, when the daylight is all used up, and the sun has given up all attempt at shining, either in disgust or despair—a few poor weavers out of employ, and nearly out of food and quite out of heart with the social state, met together to discover what they could do to better their industrial condition. Manufacturers had capital, and shopkeepers the advantage of stock; how could they succeed without either? Should they avail themselves of the poor-law? that were dependence; of emigration? that seemed like transportation for the crime of having been born poor. What should they do? They would commence the battle of life on their own account. They would, as far as they were concerned, supersede tradesmen, millowners, and capitalists: without experience, or knowledge, or funds, they would turn merchants and manufacturers. The subscription list was handed round—the Stock Exchange would not think much of the result. A dozen of these Liliputian capitalists put down a weekly subscription of twopence each—a sum which these Rochdale Rothschilds did not know how to pay. After fifty-two "calls" had been made upon these magnificent shareholders, they would not have enough in their bank to buy a sack of oatmeal with: yet these poor men now own mills, and warehouses, and keep a grocer's shop, where they take £76,000[1] a-year over the

[1] ROCHDALE EQUITABLE PIONEERS' SOCIETY, CASH ACCOUNT, DEC., 1857,

RECEIPTS.

	£	s.	d.
To Cash, balance September quarter	3311	14	1
" Repaid by the Corn Mill Society	1000	0	0
" Propositions	7	5	0
" Contributions	510	4	3½
" Received for Goods	19389	0	0
" Discounts	225	8	2
	£24,443	11	6½

counter in ready money. Their "cash sales" of £19,389, recorded in their last quarterly report, which we subjoin, show their ready money receipts to reach £1,400 a-week.

Thus the origin of the Rochdale Store, which has transcended all co-operative stores established in Great Britain, is to be traced to the unsuccessful efforts of certain weavers to improve their wages. Near the close of the year 1843, the flannel trade—one of the principal manufactures of Rochdale—was brisk. At this auspicious juncture the weavers, who were, and are still, a badly paid class of labourers, took it into their heads to ask for an advance of wages. If their masters could afford it at all, they could probably afford it then. Their workpeople thought so, and the employers of Rochdale, who are certainly among the best of their class, seemed to be of the same opinion. Nearly each employer to whom the important question was put, at once expressed his willingness to concede an advance, provided his neighbouring employers did the same. But how was the consent of the others to be induced—and the collective agreement of all to be guaranteed to each? The thing seemed simple in theory, but was anything but simple in practice. Masters are not always courteous, and workpeople are not proverbially tacticians. Weavers do not negotiate with their superiors by letter; a personal interview is commonly the warlike expedient hit upon—an interview which the servant obtrudes and the master suffers. An employer has no *à priori* fondness for these kind of deputations, as a demand for an advance of wages he cannot afford may ruin him as quickly and completely as a fall may distress the workmen. However, to set the thing going in a practical and a kind way, one or two firms, with a generosity the men still remember with gratitude, offered an advance of wages to their own workpeople, upon trial, to see whether example would induce the employers generally to imitate it. In case general compliance could not be obtained, this special and experimental advance was to be taken off again. Hereupon the Trades' Union Committee, who had asked the advance on behalf of the flannel weavers, held, in their humble way, a grand consultation of "ways and means." English mechanics are

DISBURSEMENTS.				£	s.	d.
By Cash paid for Goods				19483	0	3
" " Wages	£243	6	8½			
" " Rents	34	10	8			
" " Carriage	152	7	8			
" " General Expenses and Repairs	62	16	8½			
" " Incidental: Treasurer's salary	2	10	0			
" " Incidental: Petty Cash	1	0	0			
" " Incidental: Rates	18	16	8			
" " Incidental: Insurance	1	15	0			
" " Incidental: Building Fund	6	0	0			
				623	3	0
" Withdrawn by Members				2027	13	7
" Balance				2309	14	8½
				£24,443	11	6½

not conspirators, and the working class have never been distinguished for their diplomatic successes. The plan of action adopted by our committee in this case did not involve many subtleties. After speech-making enough to save the nation, it was agreed that one employer at a time should be asked for the advance of wages, and if he did not comply, the weavers in his employ were "to strike" or "turn out," and the said "strikers" and "turn outs" were to be supported by a subscription of twopence per week from each weaver who had the good fortune to remain at work. This plan, if it lacked grace, had the merit of being a neat and summary way of proceeding; and if it presented no great attraction to the masters, it certainly presented fewer to the men. At least Mrs. Jones with six children, and Mrs. Smith with ten, could not be much in love with the twopenny prospect held out to them, especially as they had experienced something of the kind before, and had never been heard to very much commend it.

The next thing was to carry out the plan. Of course, a deputation of masters waiting upon their colleagues would be the courteous and proper thing, but obviously quite out of the question. A deputation of employers could accomplish more in one day with employers than a deputation of all the men could accomplish in a month. This, however, was not to be expected; and a deputation of workmen on this embassy was an interesting and adventurous affair.

A trades' deputation, in the old time, was a sort of forlorn hope of industry—worse than the forlorn hope of war; for if the volunteers of war succeed, they commonly win renown, or save themselves; but the men who volunteered on trades' deputations were often sacrificed in the act, or were marked men ever after. In war both armies respect the "forlorn hope," but in industrial conflicts the pioneer deputy was exposed to subsequent retaliation on the part of mill-owners, who did not admire him; and—let it be said in impartiality, sad as the fact is—the said deputy was exposed often to the wanton distrust of those who employed him. A trades' deputation was commonly composed of intelligent and active workmen; or, as employers naturally thought them, "dissatisfied, troublesome fellows." While on deputation duty, of course, they must be absent from work. During this time they must be supported by their fellow-workmen. They were then open to the reproach of living on the wages of their fellows, of loving deputation employment better than their own proper work, which indeed was sometimes the case. Alas! poor trade deputy—he had a hard lot! He had for a time given up the service of one master for the service of a thousand. He was now in the employ of his fellows, half of whom criticised his conduct quite as severely as his employer, and begrudged him his wages more. And when he returned to his work he often found there was no work for him. In his absence his overlooker had contrived (by orders) to supply his place, and betrayed no anxiety to accommodate him with a new one. He then tried other mills, but he found no one in want of his services. The poor devil set off to surrounding districts, but his character had gone before him. He might get an old fellow-workman (now an over-looker) to set him on, at a distance from his residence, and he had perhaps to walk five or six miles home to his supper, and be back at his mill by six o'clock next morning. At last he removed his family near his new employ. By this time it had reached his new employer's ears that he had a "leader of the Trades' Union" in his mill. His employer calculated that the new advance of wages had cost him altogether a thousand pounds last year. He considered the weaver, smuggled into his mill, the cause of *that*. He walked round and "took stock" of him. The next week the man was on the move again. After a while he would fall into the state of being "always out of work." No wonder if the wife, who generally has the worst of it, with her increasing family and decreasing means, began to reproach her husband with having ruined himself and beggared his family by "his trade unioning." As he was daily out looking for work he would be sometimes "treated" by old comrades, and he naturally fell in with the only sympathy he got. A "row" perhaps occurred at the public-house, and somehow or other he would be mixed up with it. In ordinary circumstances the case would be dismissed—but the bench was mainly composed of employers. The unlucky prisoner at the bar had been known to at least one of the magistrates before as a "troublesome" fellow, under other circumstances. It is not quite clear that he was the guilty person in this case; but as in the opinion of the master-magistrate he was quite likely to have been guilty, he gave him the benefit of the doubt, and the poor fellow stood "remanded" or "committed." The chief shareholder of the *Mildam Chronicle* was commonly a mill-owner. The reporter had a cue in that direction, and next day a significant paragraph, with a heading to this effect, "The notorious Tom Spindle in trouble," carried consternation through the ranks of his old associates. The next week the editor had a short article upon the "kind of leadership to which misguided working men submit themselves." The case was dead against poor Spindle. Tom's character was gone. And if he were detained long in prison, his family was gone too. Mrs. Spindle had been turned out of her house, no rent being forthcoming. She would apply to the parish for support for her children, where she soon found that the relieving officers had no very exalted opinion of the virtues of her husband. Tom at length returned, and now he would be looked upon by all who had the power to help him, as a "worthless character," as well as a "troublesome fellow." His fate was for the future precarious. By odd helps and occasional employment when hands were short, he eked out his existence. The present writer has shared the humble hospitality of many such, and has listened half the night away with them, as they have recounted the old story. Beaten, consumptive, and poor, they had lost none of their old courage, though all their strength was over, and a dull despair of better days drew them nearer and nearer to the grave. Some of these ruined deputationists have emigrated, and these lines will recall in distant lands, in the swamps of the Mississippi, in the huts of a Bendigo digging, and in the "claims" of California, old times and fruitless struggles, which sent them penniless and heart-broken from the mills and mines of the old country. In the new land where they now dwell —a strange dream land to them—their thoughts turn from pine-forests, night fires, and revolvers, to the old villages, the smoke-choked towns, and soot-begrimed monotony in which their early life was spent. Others of the abolished deputationists of whom we speak turned news vendors or small shopkeepers. Assisted with a few shillings by their neighbours—in some cases self-helped by their own previous thrift—they have set up for themselves, have been fortunate, grown independent, and trace all their good fortune to that day which cost them their loss of employment.

CHAPTER II.

APPOINTMENT OF A DEPUTATION TO MASTERS.—GREAT DEBATE IN THE FLANNEL WEAVERS' PARLIAMENT.

So much will enable the reader to understand the hopes and fears which agitated the Rochdale Flannel Weavers' Committee, when they appointed their deputation to wait upon the masters. "Who shall go?" No sooner was this question put than the loudest orators were hushed. Cries of "We will never submit"—"We will see whether the masters are to have it their own way for ever,' etc., etc., etc.—were at once silenced. Five minutes ago everybody was forward—nobody was forward now. As in the old fable, all the mice agreed that the cat ought to be belled, but *who* was to bell the cat? The collective wisdom of the Parliament of mice found that a perplexing question. Has the reader seen a popular political meeting when some grand question of party power had to be discussed? How defiant ran the speeches! how militant was the enthusiasm! Patriotism seemed to be turning up its sleeves, and the country about to be saved that night. Of a sudden some practical fellow, who has seen that kind of thing before, suggests that the deliverance of the country will involve some little affair of subscriptions—and proposes at once to circulate a list. The sudden descent of the police, nor a discharge of arms from the Chelsea Pensioners, would not produce so decorous a silence, nor so miraculous a satisfaction with things as they are, as this little step. An effect something like this is produced in a Trades' Committee, when the test question is put, "Who will go on the deputation?" The men knew that they should not be *directly* dismissed from their employ, but *indirectly* their fate would probably be sealed. The first fault—the first accidental neglect of duty—would be the pretex of dismissal. Like the archbishop in "Gil Blas," who dismissed his critic—not on account of his candour; his grace esteemed him for *that*—but he preferred a young man with a little more judgment. So the employer has no abstract objection to the workman seeking to better his condition—he rather applauds that kind of thing—he merely disputes the special method taken to accomplish it. The reader, therefore, understands why our Committee suddenly paused when a mouse was wanted to bell the cat. Some masters—indeed many masters—are as considerate, as self-sacrificing, as any workmen are, and they often incur risks and losses to keep their people in employ, which their people never know, and, in many cases, would not appreciate if they did. Many Trades' Unionists are ignorant, inconsiderate, and perversely antagonistic. It would be equally false to condemn all masters as to praise all men. But after all allowances are made, the men have the worst of it. They make things bad for themselves and for their masters by their want of knowledge. If they do not form some kind of Trades' Union they cannot save their wages, and if they do form Unions they cannot save themselves. Industry in England is a chopping machine, and the poor man is always under the knife.

We will now tell how the Flannel Weavers of Rochdale, whose historians we are, have contrived to extricate themselves somewhat.

Our Trades' Committee numbered, as all these committees do, a few plucky fellows, and a deputation was eventually appointed, and set off on their mission. Many employers made the required advance, but others, rather than do so, would let their works stop. This resistance proved fatal to the scheme, seconded as it was by the impetuosity of the weavers themselves, who did not understand that you cannot fight capital without capital. The only chance you have is to use your brains, and unless your brains are good for something, are well informed and well disciplined, the chance is a very poor one. Our flannel weavers did not use their brains but their passions. It is easier to hate than to think, and the men did what they could do best —they determined to retaliate, and turned out in greater numbers than their comrades at work were able or willing to support. The cooler and wiser heads advised more caution. But among the working class a majority are found who vote moderation to be treachery. The weavers failed at this time to raise their wages, and their employers succeeded, not so much because they were right, as because their opponents were impetuous.

At this period the views of Mr. Robert Owen, which had been often advocated in Rochdale, were recurred to by the weavers. Socialist advocates, whatever faults they else might have, had at least done one service to employers—they had taught workmen to reason upon their condition—they had shown them that commerce was a system, and that masters were slaves of it as well as men. The masters' chains were perhaps of silver, while the workmen's were of copper, but masters could not always do quite as they would any more than their servants. And if the men became masters to-morrow, they would be found doing pretty much as masters now do. Circumstances alter cases, and the Social Reformers sought to alter the circumstances in order to improve the cases. The merit of their own scheme of improvement might be questionable, but the Socialism of this period marked the time when industrial agitation first took to reasoning.[1] Ebenezer Elliott's epigram, which he once repeated as an argument to the present writer, pointed to doctrines that certainly never existed in England :—

> " What is a Communist ? One who hath yearnings
> For equal division of unequal earnings ;
> Idler or bungler, or both, he is willing
> To fork out his penny, and pocket your shilling."

The English working class have no weakness in the way of idleness ; they never become dangerous until they have nothing to do. Their revolutionary cry is always "*more work!*" They never ask for bread half so eagerly as they ask for employment. Communists in England were never either "idlers or bunglers." When the Bishop of Exeter troubled Parliament, in 1840, with a motion for the suppression of Socialism, an inquiry was sent to the police authorities of the principal towns as to the character of the persons holding those opinions (the same who built in Manchester the Hall of Science, now the Free Library, at an expense of £6000 or £7000). The answer was that these persons consisted of the most skilled, well-conducted, and intelligent of the working class. Sir Charles Shaw sent to the Manchester Social Institution for some one to call upon him, that he might make inquiries relative to special proceedings. Mr. Lloyd Jones went to him, and Sir Charles Shaw said, that when he took office as the superintendent of the police of that district, he gave orders that the religious profession of every individual taken to the station-house should be noted ; and he had had

[1] Chartists have always complained that their most active men were won from them by the new logic of the Social Reformers. Indeed, some Social Reformers conceived a distrust of political reform as absurd as that professed by many Chartists for social reform, but the 'Doctrine of Circumstances' had one moralising effect upon the multitude—it taught them to regard with pity many opponents whose throats they otherwise would have cut with pleasure. Coleridge has owned (*The Friend*, p. 263, vol. ii.) to the pacific influence of this doctrine on his own spirit when excited by a sense of injury received. When the Bishop of Exeter called attention to the evil he discovered in the 'Doctrine of Circumstances,' he omitted to notice that if it sometimes weakened moral effort, it always diminished hatred, a fact of great political importance in a country where class rivalry is intense, and where the poor grow poorer as the rich grow richer, except where private benevolence steps in to bridge over the inequality.

prisoners of all religious denominations, but never one Socialist. Sir C. Shaw said, also, that he was in the habit of purchasing all the publications of the Society, and he was convinced, that if they had not influenced the public mind very materially, the outbreaks at the time, when they wanted to introduce the "general holiday," would have been much worse than they were, and he was quite willing to state that before the government, if he should be called upon to give an opinion.

The followers of Mr. Owen were never the "idlers," but the philanthropic. They might be dreamers, but they were not knaves. They protested against competition as leading to immorality. Their objections to it were theoretically acquired. They were none of them afraid of competition, for out of the Socialists of 1840 have proceeded the most enterprising emigrants, and the most spirited men of business who have risen from the working classes. The world is dotted with them at the present hour, and the history of Rochdale Pioneers is another proof that they were not "bunglers." No popular movement in England ever produced so many persons able to take care of themselves as the agitation of Social Reform. Moreover, the pages of the *New Moral World* and the *Northern Star* of this period amply testify that the Social Reformers were opposed to "strikes," as an untutored and often frantic method of industrial rectification; as wanting foresight, calculation, and fitness; often a waste of money. And when a strike led, as they often have done, to workmen preventing those who were willing to work from doing so, the strike became indefensible save in view of the fact that employers did the same by Unionist workmen.

As there was a general feeling that the masters who had refused their demands had not done them justice, they resolved to attain it in some other way. They were, as Emerson expresses it, "English enough never to think of giving up." Hereupon they fell back upon that talismanic and inevitable twopence, with which Rochdale manifestly thinks the world can be saved. It was resolved to continue the old subscription of twopence a week, with a view to commence manufacturing, and becoming their own employers. As they were few in number, they found that their banking account of twopences was likely to be a long time in accumulating, and some of the committee began to despair; and, as nothing is too small for poverty to covet, some of them proposed to divide the small sum collected.

At this period a Sunday afternoon discussion used to be held in the Temperance or Chartist Reading Room. Into this arena some members of the weavers' committee carried their anxieties and projects, and the question was formally proposed, "What are the best means of improving the condition of the people?" It would be too long to report the anxious and Babel disputation. Each orator, as in more illustrious assemblies, had his own infallible specific for the deliverance of mankind. The Teetotalers argued that the right thing to do was to go in for total abstinence from all intoxicating drinks, and to apply the wages they earned exclusively to the support of their families. This was all very well, but it implied that everything was right in the industrial world, and that the mechanic had nothing to do but to keep sober in order to grow rich ; it implied that work was sufficiently plentiful and sufficiently paid for ; and that masters, on the whole, were sufficiently considerate of the workman's interests. As all these points were unhappily contradicted by the experience of every one concerned, the Teetotal project did not take effect in that form.

Next, the Chartists pleaded that agitation, until they got the People's Charter, was the only honest thing to attempt, and the only likely thing to succeed. Universal Suffrage once obtained, people would be their own law makers, and, therefore, could remove any grievance at will. This was another desirable project somewhat overrated. It implies that all other agitations should be suspended while this proceeds. It implies that public felicity can be voted at discretion, and assumes that acts of parliament are omnipotent over human happiness. Social progress, however, is no invention of the House of Commons, nor would a Chartist parliament be able to abolish all our grievances at will ; but Chartists having to suffer as well as other classes, ought to be allowed an equal opportunity of trying their hand at parliamentary salvation. The Universal Suffrage agitation scheme was looked upon very favourably by the committee, and would probably have been adopted, had not the Socialists argued that the day of redemption would prove to be considerably adjourned if they waited till all the people took the Pledge, and the government went in for the Charter. They, therefore, suggested that the weavers should co-operate and use such means as they had at command to improve their condition, without ceasing to be either Teetotalers or Chartists.

In the end it came about that the Flannel Weavers' Committee took the advice of the advocates of co-operation. James Daly, Charles Howarth, James Smithies, John Hill, and John Bent, appear to be the names of those who in this way assisted the committee. Meetings were held, and plans for a Co-operative Provision Store were determined upon. So far from there being any desire to evade responsibility, as working class commentators in Parliament usually assume, these communistic-teetotal-political co-operators coveted from the first a legal position; they determined that the society should be enrolled under Acts of Parliament (10th Geo. IV., c. 56, and 4th and 5th William IV., c. 40).

CHAPTER III.

THE DOFFERS APPEAR AT THE OPENING DAY.—MORAL BUYING AS WELL AS MORAL SELLING.

NEXT, our weavers determined that the Society should transact its business upon what they denominated the "ready money principle." It might be suspected that the weekly accumulation of twopences would not enable them to give much credit; but the determination arose chiefly from moral considerations. It was a part of their socialistic education to regard credit as a social evil—as a sign of the anxiety, excitement, and fraud of competition. As Social Reformers, they had been taught to believe that it would be better for society, that commercial transactions would be simpler and honester, if credit were abolished. This was a radical objection to credit.[1] However advantageous and indispensable credit is in general commerce, it would have been a fatal instrument in their hands. Some of them would object to take an oath, and the magistrate would object to administer it; thus they would be at the mercy of the dishonest who would come in and plunder them, as happens daily now where the claim turns upon the oath.[1] Besides, some of them had a tenderness with respect to suing, and would rather lose money than go to law to get it; they, therefore, prudently fortified themselves by setting their faces against all credit, and from this resolution they have never departed.

From the Rational Sick and Burial Society's laws, a Manchester communistic production, they borrowed all the features applicable to their project, and with alterations and additions their Society was registered, October 24th, 1844, under the title of the "Rochdale Society of Equitable Pioneers." Marvellous as has been their subsequent success, their early dream was much more stupendous—in fact, it amounted to world making.[2] Our Pioneers set forth their

---

[1] A valued book, now in their Library, did not then exist, to teach them to distinguish between prejudice and a moral political economy. In the book referred to, the author says:—"Heartily do I wish that shop debts were pronounced after a certain day irrecoverable at law. The effect would be, that no one would be able to ask credit at a shop except where he was well known, and for trifling sums. All prices would sink to the scale of cash prices. The dishonourable system of fashionable debtors, who always pay too late, if at all, and *cast their deficiencies on other customers* in the form of increased charges, would be at once annihilated. Shopkeepers would be rid of a great deal of care which ruins the happiness of thousands." *Lectures on Political Economy*, by Professor Newman, p. 255.

[2] In those days the working class were justified in their jealousy of those set "in authority over them," to an extent happily less credible now. So late as February, 1849, our co-operators stipulated that a clause should be inserted in a lease of premises they were about to take, to the effect that it should not be invalid upon a conviction of nuisance against them. Their pacific objects might be sworn as a "nuisance" by enemies, and magistrates on the bench, finding them legally defenceless, might listen to prejudice against them. Such cases have occurred elsewhere.

designs in the following amusing language, to which designs the Society has mainly adhered, and has reiterated the same terms much nearer the day of their accomplishment (in the Society's Almanack for 1854). These Pioneers, in 1844, declared the views of their Association thus :—

"The objects and plans of this Society are to form arrangements for the pecuniary benefit and the improvement of the social and domestic condition of its members, by raising a sufficient amount of capital in shares of one pound each, to bring into operation the following plans and arrangements :—

"The establishment of a Store for the sale of provisions, clothing, etc.

"The building, purchasing, or erecting a number of houses, in which those members, desiring to assist each other in improving their domestic and social condition, may reside.

"To commence the manufacture of such articles as the Society may determine upon, for the employment of such members as may be without employment, or who may be suffering in consequence of repeated reductions in their wages.

"As a further benefit and security to the members of this Society, the Society shall purchase or rent an *estate or estates of land*, which shall be cultivated by the members who may be out of employment, or whose labour may be badly remunerated."

Then follows a project which no nation has ever attempted, and no enthusiasts yet carried out :—

"That, as soon as practicable, this Society shall proceed *to arrange the powers of production, distribution, education, and government* ; or, in other words, to establish a self-supporting home-colony of united interests, or assist other societies in establishing such colonies."

Here was a grand paper constitution for re-arranging the powers of production and distribution, which it has taken fifteen years of dreary and patient labour to advance half way.

Then follows a minor but characteristic proposition :—

"That, for the promotion of sobriety, a Temperance Hotel be opened in one of the Society's houses as soon as convenient."

If these grand projects were to take effect any sooner than universal Teetotalism or universal Chartism, it was quite clear that some activity must take place in the collection of the twopences. The difficulty in all working class movements is the collection of means. At this time the members of the "Equitable Pioneer Society" numbered about forty subscribers, living in various parts of the town, and many of them in the suburbs. The collector of the forty subscriptions would probably have to travel twenty miles ; only a man with the devotion of a missionary could be expected to undertake this task. This is always the impediment in the way of working class subscriptions. If a man's time were worth anything at all, he had better subscribe the whole money than collect it. But there was no other way open to them ; and, irksome as it was, some undertook it, and, to their honour, performed what they undertook.[1] Three collectors were appointed, who visited the members at their residences every Sunday; the town being divided into three districts. To accelerate proceedings an innovation was made, which must at the time have created considerable excitement. The ancient twopence was departed from, and the subscription raised to threepence. The co-operators were evidently growing ambitious. At length the formidable sum of £28 was accumulated, and, with this capital, the new world, that was to be, was commenced.

Fifteen years ago, Toad Lane, Rochdale, was not a very inviting street. Its name did it no injustice. The groundfloor of a warehouse in Toad Lane was the place selected in which to commence operations. Lancashire warehouses were not then the grand things they have since become, and the groundfloor of "Mr. Dunlop's premises," here employed, was obtained upon a lease of three years at £10 per annum. Mr. William Cooper was appointed "cashier;" his duties were very light at first. Samuel Ashworth was dignified with the title of "salesman;" his commodities consisted of infinitesimal quantities of "flour, butter, sugar, and oatmeal."[2] The entire quantity would hardly stock a homœopathic grocer's shop, for after purchasing and consistently paying for the necessary fixtures, £14 or £15 was all they had to invest in stock. And on one desperate evening—it was the longest evening of the year—the 21st of December, 1844, the "Equitable Pioneers" commenced business; and the few who remember the commencement, look back upon their present opulence and success with a smile at their extraordinary opening day. It had got wind among the tradesmen of the town that their competitors were in the field, and many a curious eye was that day turned up Toad Lane, looking for the appearance of the enemy; but, like other enemies of more historic renown, they were rather shy of appearing. A few of the co-operators had clandestinely assembled to witness their own *denouement;* and there they stood, in that dismal lower room of the warehouse, like the conspirators under Guy Fawkes in the Parliamentary cellars, debating on whom should devolve the temerity of

[1] The executive policy of democracies is in a very crude state among the people. Time and zeal are wasted woefully. A committee of thirteen working men sometimes debate half an evening away as to whether ninepence or thirteen pence shall be expended upon a broom. Money ought not to be wasted upon brooms, nor ought hard-reared zeal to be expended in the study of the petty cash book. Illustrations occur in the minutes of the Rochdale Society. "Resolved, that the two parties attending the Bank on business receive the sum of sixpence each, and the third party twopence." (June 10, 1850.) Judging by the remuneration, the transactions could not have been very responsible. "Resolved, that the shopmen be presented with an apron and sleeves each, in consideration of having to make up some bad money." (Feb. 28, 1850.) This is a very amusing instance of economical compensation. "Resolved, that we have two cisterns for treacle, two patent taps from Bradford, a shovel for sugar, and one for currants, and that the step-ladder be repaired." (May 9, 1850.) "Resolved, that the grate at the back of the wholesale warehouse be opened for air." (March 6, 1851.) "Resolved, that there be a watering-can provided for the store." (March 28, 1852.) No doubt a protracted debate, five speeches each all round, seven or eight explanations, and heavy replies by the mover and seconder, preceded these momentous resolutions.

[2] These are the articles specified in the minutes of Dec. 12, 1844.

taking down the shutters, and displaying their humble preparations. One did not like to do it, and another did not like to be seen in the shop when it was done: however, having gone so far there was no choice but to go farther, and at length one bold fellow, utterly reckless of consequences, rushed at the shutters, and in a few minutes Toad Lane was in a titter. Lancashire has its *gamins* as well as Paris—in fact, all towns have their characteristic urchins, who display a precocious sense of the ridiculous. The "doffers" are the *gamins* of Rochdale. The "doffers" are lads from ten to fifteen, who take off full bobbins from the spindles, and put them on empty ones.[1] Like steam to the engine, they are the indispensable accessories to the mills. When they are absent the men have to play, and often when the men want a holiday, the "doffers" get to understand it by some of those signs very well understood in the freemasonry of the factory craft, and the young rascals run away in a body, and, of course, the men have to play until the rebellious urchins return to their allegiance. On the night when our Store was opened, the "doffers" came out strong in Toad Lane—peeping with ridiculous impertinence round the corners, ventilating their opinion at the top of their voices, or standing before the door, inspecting, with pertinacious insolence, the scanty arrangement of butter and oatmeal: at length, they exclaimed in a chorus, "Aye! the owd weaver's shop is opened at last."

Since that time two generations of "doffers" have bought their butter and oatmeal at the "owd weaver's shop," and many a bountiful and wholesome meal, and many a warm jacket have they had from that Store, which articles would never have reached their stomachs or their shoulders, had it not been for the provident temerity of the co-operative weavers.

Very speedily, however, our embryo co-operators discovered that they had more serious obstacles to contend with than derision of the "doffers." The smallness of their capital compelled them to purchase their commodities in small quantities, and at disadvantage both of quality and price. In addition to this, some of their own members were in debt to their own shopkeepers, and they neither could, nor dare, trade with the Store. And as always happens in these humble movements, many of the members did not see the wisdom of promoting their own interests, or were diverted from doing it, if it cost them a little trouble, or involved some temporary sacrifice. Of course the quality of the goods was sometimes inferior, and sometimes the price was a trifle high. These considerations, temporary and trifling compared with the object sought, would often deter some from becoming purchasers, for whose exclusive benefit the Store was projected. If the husband saw what his duty was, he could not always bring his wife to see it; and unless the wife is thoroughly sensible, and thoroughly interested in the welfare of such a movement, its success must be very limited. If the wife will take a little trouble, and bear

[1] To pull off a bobbin is, in the language of mills, to "doff" it; hence the phrase "doffers."

with the temporary sacrifice of buying now and then an article she does not quite like, and will send a little farther for her purchases than perhaps suits her convenience, and will sometimes agree to pay a little more for them than the shop next door would charge, the co-operative stores might always become successful. (Pure quality, good weight, honest measure, and fair dealing within the establishment, buying without higgling, and selling without fraud, are sources of moral and physical satisfaction of far more consequence to a well-trained person than a farthing in the pound cheaper which the same goods might elsewhere cost.) How heavily are we taxed to put down vice when it has grown up—yet how reluctant are we to tax ourselves ever so lightly to prevent it arising. If there are to be moral sellers, there must be moral buyers. It is idle to distinguish the seller as an indirect cheat, so long as the customer is but an ambiguous knave. Those dealers who make it a point *always* to sell cheaper than any one else, must make up their minds to the risk of dishonesty, to the driving of hard bargains, or of stooping to adulterations. Our little Store thought more of improving the moral character of trade than of making large profits. In this respect they have educated their associates and customers to a higher point of character. The first members of the Store were not all sensible of this, and their support was consequently slender, like their knowledge. But a staunch section of them were true co-operators, and would come far or near to make their purchases, and, whether the price was high or low, the quality good or bad, they bought, because it was their duty to buy. The men were determined, and the women no less enthusiastic, willing, and content.

Those members of the Store who were true to their own duty, were naturally impatient that all the other members should do the same; they expected that every other member should buy at the Store whatever the Store sold, that the said member purchased elsewhere. Not content with wishing this, they sought to compel all members to become traders with the Store; and James Daly, the then secretary, brought forward a resolution to the effect that those members who did not trade with the Store should be paid out. Charles Howarth opposed this motion, on the ground that it would destroy the free action of the members. He desired co-operation to advance, he said he would do all he could to promote it; that freedom was a principle which he liked absolutely, and, rather than give it up, he would forego the advantages of co-operation. It will be seen, as our little history progresses, that this love of principle has never died out, nor, indeed, been impaired amid these resolute co-operators. James Daly's motion was withdrawn.

CHAPTER IV.

THE SOCIETY TRIED BY TWO WELL-KNOWN DIFFICULTIES —PREJUDICI AND SECTARIANISM.

In March, 1845, it was resolved that a license for the sale of tea and tobacco be taken out for the next quarter, in the name of Charles Howarth. This step evidently involved the employment of more capital; for though the members had increased, funds had not increased sufficiently for this purpose. The members, in public meeting assembled, were made aware of this fact; then, for the second time in the history of the Rochdale Store, do we hear of any member being in possession of more than twopence. One member "promised to find" half-a-crown. "Promised to find" is the phrase employed on the occasion—it was not "promised to pay, or subscribe, or advance." "Promised to find" probably alluded to the effort required to produce a larger sum than twopence in those parts. Another member "promised to find" five shillings, and another "promised to find" a pound. This last announcement was received with no mean surprise, and the rich and reckless man who made the promise was regarded with double veneration, as being at once a millionaire and a martyr.[1] Other members "promised to find" various sums in proportion to their means, and in due time the husbands could get from the Store the solace of tobacco, and wives the solace of tea. At the close of 1845 the store numbered upwards of eighty members, and possessed a capital of £181 12s. 3d.[2] At first the Store paid 2½ per cent. interest on money borrowed, then 4 per cent. After paying this interest, and the small expenses of management, all profits made were divided among the purchasers at the Store, in proportion to the amount expended; and the members soon began to appreciate this very palpable and desirable addition to their income. Instead of their getting into debt at the grocer's, the Store was becoming a savings' bank to the members, and saved money for them without trouble to themselves. The weekly receipt for goods sold during the quarter ending December, 1845, averaged upwards of £30.

[1] I have rescued and shall preserve the name of this pecuniary hero—it was William Mallalieu, a trusted servant of John Feilden, M.P., now of Todmorden, who joined the Society at its fifth meeting, September 12th, 1844. It does seem like amusement to make this note, but those concerned know it to be ludicrously true. The present writer well remembers the feeling of exultation with which the important accession of £1 was accomplished; and there was only Mr. Mallalieu in all Rochdale at that time willing and able to help the humble movement to that extent. They little expected, ten years later, to be able to put this minute upon their books—"Resolved, that A. Hill and T. Smithies wait upon the Board of the Rochdale Corn Mill Society, and give them notice that £1,500 lying in the Bank, belonging to this Society, is now at their command."—*Minutes, March 8th*, 1855.

[2] The Society paid no interest upon its shares the first year, and all profits were allowed to accumulate with a view to increasing capital. – *Vide* Minute of Committee Meeting, Aug. 29, 1844.

"The Rochdale Society of Equitable Pioneers, held in Toad Lane, in the Parish of Rochdale, in the County of Lancaster," made up its mind that a capital of £1,000 must be raised for the establishment of the Store. This sum was to be raised by £1 shares, of which each member should be required to hold four and no more. In case more than £1,000 was required, it was to be lawful for a member to hold five shares. At the commencement of the Store, it was allowed a member to have any number of shares under fifty-one. The chances of any member availing himself of this opportunity were very dreary. But the officers were ordered, and empowered, and commanded to buy down all fifty-pound shares with all convenient speed; and any member holding more than four shares was compelled to sell the surplus at their original cost of £1, when applied to by the officers of the Society. But should a member be thrown out of employment, he was then allowed to sell his shares to the Board of Directors, or other member, by arrangement, which would enable him to obtain a higher value. Each member of the Society, on his admission night, had to appear personally in the meeting-room and state his willingness to take out four shares of £1 each, and to pay a deposit of not less than threepence per share, or one shilling, and to pay not less than threepence per week after, and to allow all interests and profits that might be due to him to remain in the funds until the amount was equal to four shares in the capital.

Any member neglecting his payments was to be liable to a fine, except the neglect arose from distress, sickness, or want of employment.

When overtaken by distress, a member was allowed to sell all his shares, save one.

The earliest rules of the Society, printed in 1844, have, of course, undergone successive amendments; but the germs of all their existing rules were there. Every member was to be formally proposed, his name, trade, and residence made known to every one concerned, and a general meeting effected his election.

The officers of the Society included a President, Treasurer, and Secretary, elected half-yearly, with three Trustees and five Directors. Auditors as usual.

The officers and Directors were to meet every Thursday evening, at eight o'clock, in the committee room of the Weavers' Arms, Yorkshire Street. Then followed all the heavy regulations, common to enrolled societies, for taking care of money before they had it. The only hearty thing in the whole rules, and which does not give tic doloreux in reading it, is an appointment that an annual general meeting shall be holden on the "first market Tuesday," at which a *dinner* shall be provided at one shilling each, to celebrate the anniversary of the grand opening of the Store. At which occasion, no doubt, though the present historian has not the report before him, the first sentiment given was "Th' owd weyvurs' shop," followed by a chorus from the "doffers."

B

The gustativeness of the members appears not to have sustained an annual dinner, for in 1847[1] we find records of the annual celebration assuming the form of a "tea party," to which, in right propagandist spirit, certain Bacup co-operators were invited.

The store itself was ordered to be opened to the *public* (who never came in those days at all) on the evenings of Mondays and Saturdays only—from seven to nine on Mondays, from six to eleven on Saturdays. It would appear from this arrangement that the poor flannel weavers only bought twice a week in those times. A dreadful string of fines is attached to the laws of 1844. The value of a Trustee or Director may be estimated by the fact, that his fine for non-attendance was *sixpence*. It is plain that the Society expected to lose only half-a-crown if the whole five ran away. However, they proved to be worth more than the very humble price they put upon themselves. Under their management members rapidly increased, and the Store was opened (March 3, 1845) on additional days, and for a greater number of hours :—

Monday	from	4	to	9	p.m.
Wednesday	,,	7	to	9	,,
Thursday	,,	8	to	10	,,
Friday	,,	7	to	9	,,
Saturday	,,	1	to	11	,,

On February 2nd, 1846, it was resolved that the Store be opened on Saturday afternoons for the meeting of members ; an indication that the business of the Store was becoming interesting, and required more attention than the weavers were able to give it after their long day's labour was over. In the October of this year, the Store commenced selling butcher's meat. For the three years 1846-8, the Store was tried by dullness, apathy, and public distress. It made slow, but it made certain progress under them all. Very few new members were added during 1846 ; but the capital of the Society increased to £252 7s. 1½d., with weekly receipts for goods averaging £34 for the December quarter.

In case of distress occurring to a member, we have seen that he was permitted to dispose of his shares, retaining only one. During 1847 trade was bad, and many of the members withdrew part of their shares. Nothing can better show the soundness of the advantages created by the Society than the fact that the first time trade became bad, and provisions dear, the members rapidly increased. The people felt the pinch, and it made them look out for the best means of making a little go far ; and finding that the payment of a shilling entrance money, and threepence a week afterwards—which sum being paid on account of their shares, was really money saved—would enable them to join the Store ; they saw that doing so was quite within their means, and much to their advantage. Accordingly,

[1] An early minute, Oct. 6, 1845, I find appoints an Anniversary Tea. It was "resolved Oct. 7, 1850, that neither tea nor dinner be provided to celebrate the Anniversary" of that year. This festival must have been a modest one.

many availed themselves of the opportunity of buying their goods at the Store. The Store thereby encouraged habits of providence, and saved the funds of the parish. At the close of 1847, 110 members were on the books, and the capital had increased to £286 15s. 3½d., and the weekly receipts for goods during the December quarter were £36. An increase of £34 of capital, and £2 a week in receipts during twelve months, was no great thing to boast of; but this was accomplished during a year of bad trade and dear food, which might have been expected to ruin the Society: it was plain that the co-operative waggon was surely, if slowly, toiling up the hill. The next minute of the Society's history is unexpected and cheering.

The year 1848 commenced with great "distress" cases and an accession of new members. Contributions were now no longer collected from the members at their homes. There was one place now where every member met, at least once a week, and that was at the Store, and the cashier made the appointed collection from each when he appeared at the desk. Neither revolutions abroad, nor excitement nor distress at home, disturbed the progress of this wise and peaceful experiment. The members increased to 140, the capital increased to £397, and the weekly receipts for goods sold in the December quarter rose to £80; being an increase of £44 a week over the previous year in the amount of sales.

The lower room of the old warehouse was now too small for the business, so the whole building, consisting of three stories and an attic, was taken by these enterprising co-operators, on lease for twenty-one years.

More new members were added to the Society in 1849. The second-floor became the meeting-room of the members, and also a sort of news-room, for on August 20th, it was resolved—"That Messrs. James Nuttall, Henry Green, Abraham Greenwood, George Adcroft, James Hill, and Robert Taylor, be a committee to open a stall for the sale of books, periodicals, newspapers, etc.; the profits to be applied to the furnishing the members' room with newspapers and books." At the close of 1849 the number of members had reached three hundred and ninety. The capital now amounted to £1193 19s. 1d., and the weekly receipts for goods had risen to £179.

In the next year a very old enemy of social peace appeared in Rochdale. The religious element began to contend for exclusiveness. The rapid increase of the members had brought together numbers holding evangelical views, and who had not been reared in a school of practical toleration. These had no idea of allowing to their colleagues the freedom their colleagues allowed to them, and they proposed to close the meeting room on Sundays, and forbid religious controversy. The liberal and sturdy co-operators, whose good sense and devotion had created the secular advantages of which the religious accession had chosen to avail itself, were wholly averse to this restriction. They valued mental freedom more than any personal gain, and they could not help regarding with dismay the introduction of this fatal source of discord, which had broken up so many Friendly Societies, and often frustrated the fairest prospects of mutual improvement. The matter was brought before a general meeting, on February 4th, 1850. We give the dates of the leading incidents we record, for they are historic days in the career of our Store. On the date here quoted, it was resolved, for the welfare of the Society :—"That every member shall have full liberty to speak his sentiments on *all subjects* when brought before the meetings at a proper time, and in a proper manner ; *and all subjects shall be legitimate when properly proposed.*" The tautology of this memorable resolution shows the emphasis of alarm under which it was passed, and the endeavour to secure by reiteration of terms a liberty so essential to conscience and to progress. The founders of the Society were justly apprehensive that its principles would be overthrown by an indiscriminate influx of members, who knew nothing of the toleration upon which all co-operation must be founded, and they moved and carried :—"That no propositions be taken for new members after next general meeting for six months ensuing." From this time peace has prevailed on this subject.

Very early in the history of co-operation—as far back as 1832—the Co-operative Congress, held in London in that year, wisely agreed to this resolution :—"Whereas, the co-operative world contains persons of all religious sects, and of all political parties, it is unanimously resolved, that Co-operators, *as such*, are not identified with any religious, irreligious, or political tenets whatever ; neither those of Mr. Owen, nor of any other individual."[1]

Sectarianism is at all times the bane of public unity. Without toleration of all opinion, popular co-operation is impossible.

These theological storms over, the Society continued its success. The members increased in 1850 to six hundred ; the capital of the Society, in cash and stock, rose to £2299 10s. 5d., and the cash received during the December quarter amounted to £4397 17s., or £338 per week.

In April, 1851, seven years after its commencement, the Store was open, for the first time, all day. Mr. William Cooper was appointed superintendent ; John Rudman and James Standring shopmen.

This year the members of the Store were six hundred and thirty ; its capital £2785 ; its weekly sales £308. Somewhat less than in 1850.

The next year, 1852, the increase of members' capital and receipts was marked, and they have gone on since increasing at a rate beyond all expectation. To what extent we shall show in Tables of Results in another chapter.

---

[1] Resolution of the third London Co-operative Congress. 1832.

CHAPTER V.

ENEMIES WITHIN AND ENEMIES WITHOUT, AND HOW THEY ALL WERE CONQUERED.

THE moral miracle performed by our co-operatives of Rochdale is, that they have had the good sense to differ without disagreeing; to dissent from each other without separating; to hate at times, and yet always hold together. In most working classes, and, indeed, in most public societies of all classes, a number of curious persons are found, who appear born under a disagreeable star; who breathe hostility, distrust, and dissension: whose tones are always harsh: it is no fault of theirs, they never mean it, but they cannot help it; their organs of speech are cracked, and no melodious sound can come out of them; their native note is a moral squeak; they are never cordial, and never satisfied; the restless convolutions of their skin denote "a difference of opinion;" their very lips hang in the form of a "carp;" the muscles of their face are "drawn up" in the shape of an amendment, and their wrinkled brows frown with an "entirely new principle of action;" they are a species of social porcupines, whose quills eternally stick out; whose vision is inverted; who see everything upside down; who place every subject in water to inspect it, where the straightest rod appears hopelessly bent; who know that every word has two meanings, and who take always the one you do not intend; who know that no statement can include everything, and who always fix upon whatever you omit, and ignore whatever you assert; who join a society ostensibly to co-operate with it, but really to do nothing but criticise it, without attempting patiently to improve that of which they complain; who, instead of seeking strength to use it in mutual defence, look for weakness to expose it to the common enemy; who make every associate sensible of perpetual dissatisfaction, until membership with them becomes a penal infliction, and you feel that you are sure of more peace and more respect among your opponents than among your friends; who predict to everybody that the thing must fail, until they make it impossible that it can succeed, and then take credit for their treacherous foresight, and ask your gratitude and respect for the very help which hampered you; they are friends who act as the fire brigade of the party; they always carry a water engine with them, and under the suspicion that your cause is in a constant conflagration, splash and drench you from morning till night, until every member is in an everlasting state of drip; who believe that co-operation is another word for organised irritation, and who, instead of showing the blind the way, and helping the lame along, and giving the weak a lift, and imparting courage to the timid, and confidence to the despairing, spend their time in sticking pins into the tender, treading on the toes of the gouty, pushing the lame down stairs, leaving those in the dark behind, telling the fearful that they may well be afraid, and assuring the despairing that it is "all up." A sprinkling of these "damned good-natured friends" belong to most societies; they are few in number, but indestructible; they are the highwaymen of progress, who alarm every traveller, and make you stand and deliver your hopes; they are the Iagoes and Turpins of democracy, and only wise men and strong men can evade them or defy them. The Rochdale co-operators understand them very well—they met them—bore with them—worked with them—worked in spite of them—looked upon them as the accidents of progress, gave them a pleasant word and a merry smile, and passed on before them; they answered them not by word but by act, as Diogenes refuted Zeno. When Zeno said there was no motion, Diogenes answered him by *moving*. When adverse critics, with Briarian hands, pointed to failure, the Rochdale co-operators replied by *succeeding*.

Whoever joins a popular society ought to be made aware of this curious species of colleagues whom we have described. You can get on with them very well if they do not take you by surprise. Indeed, they are useful in their way; they are the dead weights with which the social architect tries the strength of his new building. We mention them because they existed in Rochdale, and that fact serves to show that our co-operators enjoyed no favour from nature or accident. They were tried like other men, and had to combat the ordinary human difficulties. Take two examples.

Of course the members' meetings are little parliaments of working men—not very little parliaments now, for they include thrice the number of members composing the House of Commons. All the mutual criticisms in which Englishmen proverbially indulge, and the grumblings said to be our national characteristic, and the petty jealousies of democracies, are reproduced on these occasions, though not upon the fatal scale so common among the working class. Here, in the parliament of our Store, the leader of the opposition sometimes shows no mercy to the leader in power; and Rochdale Gladstone or Disraelies very freely criticise the quarterly budget of the Sir George Cornewall Lewis of the day. At one time there was our friend Ben, a member of the Store so known, who was never satisfied with anything—and yet he never complained of anything. He looked his disapproval, but never spoke it. He was suspicious of everybody in a degree, it would seem, too great for utterance. He went about everywhere, he inspected everything, and doubted everything. He shook his dissent, not from his tongue, but his head. It was at one time thought that the management must sink under his portentous disapprobation. With more wisdom than usually falls to critics, he refrained from speaking until he knew what he had to say. After two years of this weighty travail the clouds dispersed, and Ben found speech and confidence together. He found that his profits had increased notwithstanding his distrust, and he could no longer find in his heart to frown upon the Store which was making him rich. At last he went up to the cashier to draw his profits, and he came down, like Moses from the mount, with his face shining.

Another guardian of the democratic weal fulminated heroically. The very opposite of Ben, he almost astounded the Store by his ceaseless and stentorian speeches. The *Times* newspaper would not contain a report of his quarterly orations. He could not prove that anything was wrong, but he could not believe that all was right. He was invited to attend a meeting of the Board; indeed, if we have studied the chronicles of the Store correctly, he was appointed a member of the Board, that he might not only see the right thing done, but do it; but he was too indignant to do his duty, and he was so committed to dissatisfaction that above all things he was afraid of being undeceived; and, during his whole period of office, he actually sat with his back to the Board, and in that somewhat unfriendly and inconvenient attitude he delivered his respective opinions. Whether, like the hare, he had ears behind has not been certified; but, unless he had eyes behind, he never could have seen what took place. A more perfect member of an opposition has rarely appeared. He was made by nature to conduct an antagonism. At length he was bribed into content—bribed by the only legitimate bribery—the bribery of success. When the dividends came in behind him, he turned round to look at *them*, and he pocketed his "brass" and his wrath together; and, though he has never been brought to confess that things are going right, he has long ceased to say that they are going wrong.

The Store very early began to exercise educational functions. Besides supplying the members with provisions, the Store became a meeting place, where almost every member met each other every evening after working hours. Here there was harmony because there was equality. Every member was equal in right, and was allowed to express his opinions on whatever topic he took an interest in. Religion and politics, the terrors of Mechanics' Institutions, were here common subjects of discussion, and harmless because they were open. In other respects the co-operators acquired business confidence as well as business habits. The Board was open to everybody, and, in fact, everybody went everywhere. Distrust dies out where nothing is concealed. Confidence and honest pride sprung up, for every member was a master—he was at once purchaser and proprietor. But all did not go smoothly on. Besides the natural obstacles which exist, ignorance and inexperience created others.

Poverty is a greater impediment to social success than even prejudice. With a small capital you cannot buy good articles nor cheap ones. What is bought at a small Store will probably be worse and dearer than the same articles elsewhere. This discourages the poor. With them every penny must tell, and every penny extra they pay for goods seems to them a tax, and they will not often incur it. It is of no use that you show them that it and more will come back again as profit at the end of the quarter. They do not believe *in the end of the quarter*—they distrust the promise of profits. The loss of the penny to-day is near—the gain of sixpence three months hence is remote. Thus you have to educate the very poor before you can serve them. The humbler your means the greater your difficulties—you have to teach as well as to save the very poor. One would think that a customer ought to be content when he is his own shopkeeper; on the contrary, he is not satisfied with the price he charges himself. Intelligent contentment is the slowest plant that grows upon the soil of ignorance.

Some of the male members, and no wonder that many of the women also, thought meanly of the Store. They had been accustomed to fine shops, and the Toad Lane warehouse was repulsive to them; but after a time the women became conscious of the pride of paying ready money for their goods, and of feeling that the Store was their own, and they began to take equal interest with their husbands. As usually happens in these cases, the members who rendered no support to the new undertaking when it most wanted support, made up by making more complaints than anybody else, thus rendering no help themselves and discouraging those who did. It has been a triumph of penetration and good sense to inspire these contributors with a habit of supporting that, which, in its turn, supports them so well. There are times still when a cheaper article has its attraction for the Store purchaser, when he forgets the supreme advantage of knowing that his food is good, or his garment as stout as it can be made. He will sometimes forget the moral satisfaction derived from knowing that the article he can buy from the Store has, as far as the Store can influence it, been produced by some workman, who, in his turn, was paid at some living rate for his labour. Now and then, the higgler will appear at the little co-operative stores around, and the Store dealers will believe them, and prefer their goods to the supplies to be had from the Store, because they are some fraction cheaper; without their being able to know what adulteration, or hard bargaining elsewhere, has been practised to effect the reduction.

Any person passing through the manufacturing districts of Lancashire will be struck with the great number of small provision shops; many of them dealing in drapery goods as well as food. From these shops the operatives, to a great extent, spread their tables and cover their backs. Unfortunately, with them the credit system is the rule, and ready money the exception. The majority of the people trading at these shops have what is called a "Strap Book," which, of course, is always taken when anything is fetched, and balanced as often as the operatives receive their wages, which is generally weekly, but in many cases fortnightly. A balance is generally left due to the shopkeeper, thus a great number of operatives are always less or more in debt. When trade becomes slack, he goes deeper and deeper, until he is irretrievably involved. When his work fails altogether, he is obliged to remove to another district, and of course to trade with another shop, unless at great inconvenience he sends all the distance to the old shop.

It sometimes happens that an honest weaver will prefer all this trouble to forsaking a house that has trusted him. One instance has been mentioned to the present writer, in which a family that had removed from a village on one side of the town to one on the opposite side, continued for years to send a distance of two miles and a half to the old shop for their provisions, although in doing so they had to pass through the town of Rochdale, where they could have obtained the same things cheaper. This is in every way a grateful and honourable fact, and the history of the working class includes crowds of them.

We are bound to relate that the capital of the Store would have increased somewhat more rapidly, had not many of its members at that time been absorbed by the land company of Feargus O'Connor. Many members of the Store were also shareholders in that concern, and as that company was considered by them to be more feasible, and calculated sooner to place its members in a state of permanent independence, much of the zeal and enthusiasm necessary to the success of a new society were lost to the co-operative cause.

The practice of keeping up a national debt in this country, on the interest of which so many are enabled to live at the expense of industrious taxpayers, and the often immoral speculations of the Stock Exchange, have produced an absurd and injurious reaction on the part of many honest people. Many co-operative experiments have failed through want of capital, because the members thought it immoral to take interest, and yet they had not sufficient zeal to lend their money without interest. Others have had a moral objection to paying interest, and as money was not to be had without, of course these virtuous people did nothing—they were too moral to be useful. All this showed frightful ignorance of political economy. If nobody practised thrift and self-denial in order to create capital, society must remain in perpetual barbarism; and if capital is refused interest as compensation for its risk, it would never be available for the use of others; it would be simply hoarded in uselessness, instead of being the great instrument of civilisation and national power. The class of reformers who made these mistakes were first reclaimed to intelligent appreciation of industrial science by Mr. Stuart Mill's "Principles of Political Economy, with some of their applications to *Social* Philosophy." Most of these "applications" were new to them, and though made with the just austerity of science, they manifested so deep a consideration for the progress of the people, and a human element so fresh and sincere, that prejudice was first dispelled by sympathy, and error afterwards by argument.

The principle of co-operation—so moralising to the individual as a discipline, and so advantageous to the State in its results—with wh difficulty has it made its way in the world! Regarded by the state man as some terrible form of political combination, and by the rich a a scheme of spoliation; denounced in Parliament, written against b political economists, preached against by the clergy; the co-operativ idea, as opposed to the competitive, has had to struggle, and has ye to struggle its way into industry and commerce. Statesmen might spare themselves the gratuitous anxiety they have often manifested for the suppression of new opinion. Experience ought to have shown them that wherever one man endeavours to set up a new idea, ten men at once rise up to put it down; not always because they think it bad, but because, whether good or bad, they do not want the existing order of things altered. They will hate truth itself, even if they know it to be truth, if truth gives them trouble. The statesman ought to have higher taste, even if he has not higher employment, than to join the vulgar and officious crowd in hampering or hunting honest innovation. There is, of course, a prejudice felt at first on the part of shopkeepers against co-operative societies. That sort of feeling exists which we find among mechanics against the introduction of machinery, which, for want of better arrangements, is sure to injure them first, however it may benefit the general public afterwards. But, owing to the good sense of the co-operators, and not less to the good sense of the shopkeepers of Rochdale, no unfriendliness worth mentioning has ever existed between them. The co-operators were humbly bent on improving their own condition, and at first their success in that way was so trivial as not to be worth the trouble of jealousy. For the first three or four years after the commencement of the Store, its operations produced no appreciable effect upon the retail trade of the town. The receipts of the Store in 1847, four years after its commencement, were only £36 a week; about the receipt of a single average shop, and five or ten times less than the receipts of some shops. But of late years, no doubt, the shopkeepers, especially smaller ones, have felt its effects. In some instances shops have been closed in consequence. The members of the Store extend out into the suburbs, a distance of one or two miles from the town. It has happened in the case of at least one suburban shopkeeper, that half the people for a mile round him had become Store purchasers. This, of course, would affect his business. The good feeling prevailing among the tradesmen of the town has been owing somewhat to a display of unexpected good sense and moderation on the part of the co-operators, who have kept themselves free from the greed of mere trade and the vices of rivalry. If the prices of grocery in the town rose, the Store raised its charges to the same level. It never would, even in appearance, nor even in self-defence, use its machinery to undersell others; and when tradesmen lowered, as instances often occurred, their prices in order to undersell the Store, and show to the town that they could sell cheaper than any society of weavers: and when they made a boast of doing so, and invited the customers of the Store to deal with them in preference, or taunted the dealers at the Store with the higher prices they had to pay, the Store never at any time, neither in its days of weakness nor of strength, would reduce any of its prices. It passed by, would not recognise, would in no way imitate this ruinous and vexatious, but common resource of competition. The Store conducted an honest trade—it charged an honest average price—it sought no rivalry, nor would it be drawn into any, although the means of winning were quite as much in its hands as in the hands of its opponents. The prudent maxims of the members were, "To be safe we must sell at a profit." "To be honest we must sell at a profit." "If we sell sugar without profit, we must take advantage covertly in the sale of some other articles to cover that loss." "We will not act covertly; we will not trade without profit whatever others may do; we will not profess to sell cheaper than others; we profess to sell honestly"—and this policy has conquered.

Some manufacturers were as much opposed to the co-operators' Store as the shopkeepers—not knowing exactly what to make of it. Some were influenced by reports made to them by prejudiced persons —some had vague notions of their men acquiring a troublesome independence. But this apprehension was of short duration, and was set at rest by the good sense of others. One employer was advised to discharge some of his men for dealing at the Store, who serviceably answered, "He did not see why he should. So long as his men did their duty, it was no business of his to dictate where they should deal. They had as much right as he had to spend their money in that market where they thought it would go farthest, and if they learned thrift he did not see what harm it would do them, and if they could save money they had a right to do so. Indeed, he thought it was their turn."

The co-operators have long enjoyed the good opinion of the majority of the manufacturers, and the higher classes of the town. The members of the Store are so numerous, that the masters come in contact with them at almost every turn. The co-operators work for nearly every employer in the town, and many hold the most trusty and responsible situations. The working class in general hold the Co-operative Society in high esteem, and what is more natural, since it aims at bettering their condition? Indeed, the Society exercises considerable influence in the town. As its members are spread over every part, every local or public movement is known to one or the other, and is communicated rapidly as they meet with their fellow members at the Store. Facts circulate—opinion is elicited—criticism follows—a general conviction upon particular points springs up —and thus many learn what is the right view to support, and support it with more confidence from the knowledge that numbers, upon whom they can rely, share it.

The slowness of the Rochdale movement for two or three years may be attributed to the want of confidence in any scheme originating among the working classes for the amelioration of their condition. The loss, trouble, and anxiety entailed upon the leading men of the previous co-operative societies in Rochdale, were still within the recollection of many. These reminiscences would naturally intimidate the cautious. There were others who were not aware that the former societies had been wrecked by the credit system. The "Equitable Pioneers" had most studiously avoided that shoal. In fact, so many co-operative experiments had been stranded by credit, that an almost universal opinion was prevalent, not only in Rochdale, but throughout the country and in Parliament, that co-operation was an exploded fallacy, and the poor co-operators, whose enterprise we report, were looked upon as dangerous emissaries of some revolutionary plot, and at the same time as fanatics deluded beyond all hope of enlightenment, who were bent on ruining themselves, and too ignorant to comprehend their folly or their danger. It was not until the small but unfailing stream of profits began to meander into all out-of-the-way cottages and yards—it was not until the town had been repeatedly astonished by the discovery of weavers with money in their pockets, who had never before been known to be out of debt, that the working class began to perceive that the "exploded fallacy" was a *paying fallacy*; and then crowds of people who had all their life been saying and proving that nothing of the kind could happen, now declared that they had never denied it, and that everybody knew co-operation would succeed, and that anybody could do what the Pioneers did.

CHAPTER VI.

THE GREAT FLOUR MILL PANIC.

TOWARDS the close of 1850, a new Society takes its place in our narrative—namely, the "Rochdale District Corn Mill Society." A similar one had long flourished in Leeds, a history of which would be a very instructive addition to co-operative literature.[1] The Rochdale imitation commenced its active operations about the close of 1850. This Corn Mill Society, meeting at the Elephant and Castle, Manchester Road, received encouragement from the Store. The Directors being unacquainted with the business, had, of course, to entrust it to other hands very much to its disadvantage. Our

---

[1] An account appeared in the local newspapers of 1849, of the success of the Leeds and Halifax Corn Mill Societies, which had effected a general reduction in the price of flour in those towns, thus serving the whole public, besides supplying to their own members pure flour cheaper than the public price, with added profits. These facts circulated by the newspapers led Mr. Smithies, Mr. Greenwood, and Mr Charles Howarth to initiate the discussion of a corn mill movement in Rochdale, at the Equitable Pioneers meetings.

"Equitable Pioneers" invested, in the shape of shares in the Corn Mill, from £400 to £600.

In 1851 they began to lend to the Corn Mill Society, on account of goods to come in. Unfortunately, the goods sent in—namely the flour, was of an inferior quality. This was owing to two causes—first, the Corn Society being short of capital, was obliged to buy where it could get credit, instead of where it could get the best corn ; being in the power of him who gave credit, they were often compelled to accept an inferior article at a high price. Second, there was a want of skill in the head miller—in the grinding department. The "Equitable Pioneer Society" decided to sell no flour but the "Rochdale Corn Mill Society's," and that being inferior, of course the sale fell off.[1] This is another of those little crevices in the walls of a popular experiment through which the selfishness of human nature peeps out. Of course a man who pays a dearer rate than his neighbour for any article taxes himself to that amount ; but, in a public movement, this is one of those liabilities which every man who would advance it must be prepared to encounter. When the support of the purchasers at the Store began to drop off by this refusal to take the flour, it brought on a crisis in the Co-operative Society. By the end of the third quarter of 1851, the Corn Mill had lost £441.[2] This produced a panic in the Store, which was considered, by its investments, to be implicated in the fall of the Corn Mill. It was soon rumoured that the Store would fail, and some of the members proposed that the Corn Mill business be abandoned. Others suggested that each member of the Store should subscribe a pound to cover the loss, and clear out of it. But as the Corn Mill held its meetings at the Pioneers' Store, and its leading members belonged to the Store, Mr. Smithies considered that their honour was compromised if they were defeated ; and insisted, with much energy, that the name of "Pioueers" must be given up, unless they went on altogether. Had the Mill been brought to the hammer at this time, there would not have been realised ten shillings in the pound. This was the point to try their faith in co-operation. The members did not fail. Some brought all the money they could collect together to enable the difficulties to be conquered ; a few, as usual in these cases, fell back. In the first place, amid those who distinguished themselves to avert the disaster of failure, all agree to name Abraham Greenwood, whose long and protracted devotion to this work cost him his health, and nearly his life. How much has depended, in the fate of the Store, on the honesty of its officers, may be seen from the disasters of the Corn Mill, arising from defects of character in some of its servants. One miller systematically went to Manchester, instead of

[1] The deficiency of capital is always aggravated by miscalculation. After contracting for the machinery of £750, the millwright sent in a bill of extras of £140—a dressing machine at £44 was overlooked ; the result was that when the mill was ready no money existed with which to purchase grain.

[2] The joy with which the Directors hailed the production of their first sack of flour was turned into dismay at this result.

to Wakefield, to buy his grain. By acting in concert with some seller, he got a commission in Manchester, and the Store suffered for it. The first great loss of the Mill was probably occasioned in this way. The next miller had a weakness for "toddy," and his successor was liable to faint perceptions of truth; so between the man who *would* not know what he was doing, and the man who *did* not know what he was doing, and the man who did not know what he was saying, the affairs of the Corn Mill got somewhat confused.

Another very usual error among the working class muddled every thing further. Thinking it economical to accept volunteer book-keepers, they had their books kept by those who offered—who officiated in turns—and the books were duly bungled for nothing. The confusion was cheap but inextricable, and the perplexity of everything grew worse confounded. The directors acted with good sense and vigour as soon as they comprehended their position. The defective manager for the time being was dismissed, Mr. A. Greenwood, the president of the Society, acting in his place. A paid book-keeper was appointed—debts were commenced liquidation by small instalments, when an unexpected disaster overtook them. One morning news was brought to town that the bailiffs were in possession—to the dismay of the struggling co-operators and secret satisfaction of the prophets of failure, who could not help felicitating themselves on so portentous a sign. The landlord, of whom the Corn Mill was rented, had neglected to pay the ground landlord his rent, and for three years' ground rent, amounting to £100, he had put in a distraint upon the property of the co-operators, who were not morally responsible. This enemy was in due time routed—perseverance triumphed, and successive dividends, from fourpence to one shilling in the pound, cleared off the loss of £450, and the day of substantial profits at length dawned.

When the Store was first opened, one shopkeeper boasted that he could come with a wheelbarrow and wheel the whole stock away, which was quite true. He had the command of ten times more capital. He threatened that he would sell cheaper, and break up the Store. It was quite true that he could sell cheaper, but the weavers held together, and he did not break up the Store. There were many unfriendly traders of this way of thinking. It often happens that men who do not exactly mean ill towards you become your enemies artificially. They begin by predicting that you will fail, and without exactly wishing you should fail, are sorry when you do not. As an abstract matter, they would perhaps be glad of your success; but having committed themselves to a prediction, they are disgusted when you falsify it, and they will sometimes help to bring about your ruin for no other reason than that of fulfilling their own prediction. In 1849, when the public Savings' Bank in Rochdale so disgracefully broke, and many thousands of pounds of the hard earnings of the poor were swept away,[1] the poor and ruined people turned to the Store

[1] Out of £100,403 deposits, an officer had appropriated to his own use £71,717. The

for protection. Since 1849 there has been no Savings' Bank in Rochdale.

Many of the weavers who, up to this time, had preferred investing their money in the bank, had now to look out for another place in which to deposit their savings. They felt that they had misplaced their confidence in the Savings' Bank, which was an institution without an adequate responsible security, or in which they had no controlling influence over the application of the money. As the Store offered both these advantages, and a higher rate of interest, many of their bank dividends [1] found their way to the Store, and future savings also.

They had more confidence in the "Equitable Pioneers" than in the false Government bank. The failure of the Savings' Bank led to an accession of members and capital to the Store. This growth of confidence brought great discredit on the prophets to whom we have referred. No sooner, however, did the Corn Mill panic get rumoured about than they recurred with sinister emphasis to their old predictions, and their rumours brought about a run upon the Store. The humble Directors said nothing, but quietly placed their cashier behind the counter with orders to pay every demand. One man, who had twenty-four pounds in the Store, the whole of which he had made from the profits, began with a demand for sixteen pounds. He had some sort of sympathy for his benefactors, and thought he would leave a little in their hands.

"Are you about to commence some sort of business?" asked the cashier.

"No," said the man, "but I want my money."

"Well, you are aware that notice is required?"

"Oh, yes, and I am come to give notice." He "would have his money."

"Well," said the cashier, "we avail ourselves of the notice when we are likely to be short; but we can dispense with notice now. You'd better 'tak brass now.'"

And they made the man "tak brass" then, and much to his astonishment, he was obliged to carry his money away in his pocket, and he went away half suspecting he had been playing the fool.

Eighteen months after, this man brought his money back: he had kept it in some stocking foot all that time (that celebrated "patent safe" of the poor), losing the interest. He himself then told the cashier the story of his taking it out; in consequence of being assured that the Store would break. He now tells the story to his comrades, far and near, and nobody has more confidence in the Store than he.

Next a woman appeared: she *would* have her money out then. It was at once offered to her—then she would not have it. She de-

amount still due to the depositors (1877) is £38,287. Sir A. Ramsay has lately presented a petition to the House of Commons on the subject.

[1] 12s. 6d. in the pound is all yet paid.

manded her money because she had been told she could not get it; and when she found that she could have it, she did not want it. More sensible and quickwitted than the dullard man who carried his sixteen pounds home to his stocking foot, when *she* found there was no risk, she left her money. Another woman refused to draw her money out whether it was in danger or not, though a shopkeeper said to her:—"It will be sure to break, and you had better draw it out."

From the depositors the panic extended to traders; but the panic among them did not last long. At that time, corn was bought for the Mill one week, and paid for the next. The payments, at this time, were made at Wakefield, one week under the other. One week the buyer-in missed the paying. The old gentleman who was, in this case, the creditor, was told by millers about him that the Store had broken—he might depend upon it. He took an express train to Rochdale and a cab from the railway station, rushed down to the Store, and demanded his money. He was quietly asked for his invoice, and his money was at once paid him; and he was told if he knew any others wanting money on account of goods supplied to the Corn Mill, to be kind enough to send them in. The old gentleman went away very much astonished; he felt that he should never have another order; and he afterwards stated to the superintendent at the railway station he had ever since regretted the unfortunate journey he was induced to make.

About this time, the bank in Rochdale, with whom our "Equitable Pioneers" did business, did them a frank piece of service, which they have always remembered with appreciation. Some tradesmen being at the counter of the bank, a person remarked that he thought the Store was running down, evidently fishing from the bankers some confirmation of his suspicions. The answer given by one of the firm was, that he did not see why it should, as the Board had left £2000 in their hands for a long time, which they had never touched. This observation established confidence in influential quarters; and as the depositors who applied for their money at the Store invariably carried it back with them in their pockets, it soon restored confidence among their own order. The humble Directors of the Store, like all other honest men, had more pride and pleasure in paying money than in receiving it, and their firm and judicious conduct re-established the credit of the "Equitable Pioneers."

Here from one to two thousand working men had done what Sir John Dean Paul failed to do—kept an honest banking house. In point of morality, how infinitely superior are these Rochdale co-operators to that Lord of the Treasury who finally poisoned himself on Hampstead Heath! Surely these men are as fit for the franchise as Paul and Sadleir, as Hugh Innes Cameron and Humphrey Brown. What standard of electional fitness does the Government take, who gives the franchise to fraudulent bankers and knavish lords of the Treasury, and withholds it from honest working men?

The September quarter of 1852 showed a clear balance of gain for that quarter of £100 upon the Corn Mill. The energy of Mr. Greenwood and his colleagues had turned upwards the fortunes of the Corn Mill.

In the origin of their flour operations a curious circumstance occurred. Determined to supply all things genuine, they supplied the flour so. It might be inferior, as we have related it was, but it was pure ; but being pure, it was browner than the usual flour in the market. It was rejected for its difference of colour. A friend of the present writer, disgusted with the spurious coffee of London, made arrangements to supply the common people with a genuine cup. To this end he opened a house in Lambeth, and ground up the real berries pure. But no one would drink his coffee, and he had to shut up his house. Accustomed to adulterated coffee until their taste was formed upon depraved compounds, the people rejected the pure beverage. So it happened to our Corn Mill. The unadulterated flour would not sell. The customers of the Store knew neither the colour nor taste of pure flour. Then there was a cry against the co-operators. It was said they could not compete with the usual millers; and if they adulterated, the only way open of rendering their flour popular, there would be another cry out against them for adulterating it, and being as bad as other traders. For a short time they made their flour white in the usual way, but it was so much against their principles to do it that they discussed the folly of the preference with their purchasers at the Store, and the pure flour, of whatever colour, was taken into favour, and from that day to this it has been sold genuine.

CHAPTER VII.

SUCCESSIVE STEPS OF SUCCESS—THE ROCHDALE STORE ON A SATURDAY NIGHT.

The Equitable Pioneers' Society is divided into seven departments : —Grocery, Drapery, Butchering, Shoemaking, Clogging, Tailoring, Wholesale.

A separate account is kept of each business, and a general account is given each quarter, showing the position of the whole.

The grocery business was commenced, as we have related, in December, 1844, with only four articles to sell. It now includes whatever a grocer's shop should include.

The drapery business was started in 1847, with a humble array of attractions. In 1854 it was erected into a separate department.

A year earlier, 1846, the Store began to sell butchers' meat, buying eighty or one hundred pounds off a tradesman in the town. After awhile, the sales were discontinued until 1850, when the Society had a warehouse of its own. Mr. John Moorhouse, who has now two assistants, buys and kills for the Society three oxen, eight sheep, sundry porkers and calves, which are on the average converted into £130 of cash per week.

Shoemaking commenced in 1852. Three men and an apprentice make, and a stock is kept on sale.

Clogging and tailoring commenced also in this year.

The Wholesale department commenced in 1855, and marks an important development of the Pioneers' proceedings. This department has been created for supplying any member requiring large quantities, and with a view to supply the co-operative stores of Lancashire and Yorkshire, whose small capitals do not enable them to buy in the best markets, nor command the services of what is otherwise indispensable to every store—*a good buyer*, who knows the markets and his business, who knows what, how, and where to buy. The wholesale department guarantees purity, quality, fair prices, standard weight and measure, but all on the never-failing principle—cash payment.

After registering the Society under the 13 and 14 Vict., chap. 115,[1] the Society turned its attention to a wholesale department, an operation which would have been impossible but for the legal protection of this Act, an Act which has called forth more expressions of gratitude to Parliament than any Act I have heard commented upon by working men. The Pioneers' laws say (we quote three of their rules):—

14.—The Wholesale department shall be for the purpose of supplying those members who desire to have their goods in large quantities.

16.—The said department shall be charged with interest, after the rate of five per cent. per annum, for such capital as may be advanced to it by the Board of Directors.

17.—The profits arising from this department, after paying for the cost of management and other expenses, including the interest afore-

[1] An act which is itself an answer to those who would apply the maxim of *Laisser faire* (Let things alone) to politics, a maxim which, however advantageous in political economy, cannot, observes Professor Newman, be applied to politics without blundering or disingenuousness.—*Political Economy*, p. 188.

said, shall be divided quarterly into three parts, one of which shall be reserved to meet any loss that may arise in the course of trade until it shall equal the fixed stock required, and the remaining two-thirds shall be divided amongst the members, in proportion to the amount of their purchases in the said department.

In 1854, a conference was held in Leeds, to consider how the co-operative societies of Lancashire and Yorkshire could unite their purchases of produce and manufactures among themselves. Mr. Lloyd Jones lent his valuable counsel on this occasion, and at Rochdale, where a second Conference with this object was held in August, 1855. Of course the cardinal question was, *who* should find capital to carry out the idea of a wholesale department. Some stores were willing to contribute a proportional share, others had hardly cash to carry on their own operations; other stores, with a prudence very old in the world, proposed to see how the plan was going to succeed before joining in it. This is a cautiousness commendable in some cases, but were all to act upon it no advance would ever be made. The Equitable Pioneers accepted the initiative with their usual pluck. As many of the stores had the notion in their heads that all the Rochdale Pioneers took up succeeded, several stores joined, and put in a little money; but the principal capital was supplied by our enterprising friends, the Rochdale Equitables. As the law we have quoted shows, they stipulated for five per cent. on their advances. Differences, though not dissensions, arose. The Equitable Pioneers' Society felt dissatisfaction that stores not contributing a fair share of capital to work the wholesale trade should yet receive an equal dividend of profits in proportion to their trade with the department. As the Equitable Pioneers found nearly all the capital, they were by many thought entitled to nearly all the profit. On the other hand, it was urged that the five per cent. on their capital was all they had a right to, and they had no claim to the profits made by the trade of other stores. The Store of the Pioneers dealt with the wholesale department, and had, in common with other stores, their profits upon the amount of their own trade. It was true that many stores only bought articles that yielded little profit, while the Rochdale Store bought so generally and largely as to create the chief profits itself, besides risking its capital, which seemed at first to be in danger. For in the March quarter of 1856, £495 10s. 4d. were lost through purchasing sugars, syrups, treacle, soaps, etc., when prices were high, which prices came down before the goods could be sold. A committee of inquiry at a later date reported that several stores had increased their purchases from the wholesale department of goods, which yielded even more profit than the purchases of the Pioneers' Store. Mr. William Cooper, the Secretary, defended the proceedings and position of the department, and it was ultimately agreed that the District Stores had dealt fairly by the wholesale department on the whole, although they had not supported it by capital to the extent the promoters could have wished. Still many remained dissatisfied, although they were unable to show what was wrong, and at an adjourned quarterly meeting, so late as October, 1856, it was "Resolved, that the wholesale stock be dispensed with." Owing to the energy of Mr. Samuel Stott and others, this resolution never took effect. The department being founded by an enrolled rule, it could not be dispensed with without an alteration of the rules, and before an alteration in the rules can take place the three-fourths of the whole members specially convened must consent to it. The opponents of the department despaired of getting this wide ratification of their partial dissatisfaction, and the department continued. The loss of £495 10s. 4d. has by the end of the March quarter of 1857, in one year's operation, been reduced to £141 14s. 1d. In half a year more, the loss will be cancelled, and profits beyond the interest on capital accrue. The stores, to their credit, continue to trade with the department, just as though they were receiving a dividend in addition to the interest on the capital, which they will shortly do; were they to receive no dividend, it would be to their advantage to trade with the department. The most important officer of a store is the purchaser. He must be acquainted with his business and the markets. No honesty, if he has not tact and knowledge, will prevent him from damaging the prosperity of a store by bad purchases. Small stores cannot always find a man, nor support him when they do. But a wholesale department, by keeping a few such, can serve all stores, can enable the smallest to command genuine articles equally with the greatest, and to command them even cheaper, as well as better, as large, united, wholesale, purchases can be made more advantageously, of course, than small ones. It is clear, however, that this admirable and well-devised department must have fallen but for the wise provision of the Act of Parliament upon which Mr. Stott and his colleagues fell back. This useful law gives stability to a society, it prevents short-sighted sections from destroying general purposes, and enables the errors of a few to be revised and rectified by the decision of a veritable majority of all concerned.

The members of the Store attracted from a distance make their purchases—some once a fortnight, and have their goods sent home; others unite together and employ a carter to deliver them. The desire to obviate this inconvenience, and the difficulty of serving the great increase of members at Toad Lane (the Central Store), Branch Stores have been lately opened. In 1856, the first Branch was opened in the Oldham Road, about a mile from the centre of Rochdale. In 1857, the Castleton Branch, and another in the Whitworth Road, were established, and a fourth Branch at Pinfold.

An idea of the appearance of a Branch Store may be gathered from the next page. On each side the door a narrow upright sign, the height of the entrance, gives the following information :—

EQUITABLE PIONEERS' CO-OPERATIVE STORES.

Enrolled according to Law.

—

Objects.

To improve the social and domestic condition of its members.

—

Five per cent. interest paid on shares.

—

Remaining profits divided amongst

[*Copied from the Doors of the School Lane Branch.*]

purchasers in proportion to the money expended.

—

No second prices.

—

All purchases paid for on delivery.

—

Dividends declared quarterly.

The "owd weyvurs' shop," or rather the entire building, was (in 1849), as we have related, taken on lease by the Store, in a state sadly out of repair. One room is now pleasantly fitted up as a news-room. Another is neatly fitted up as a library.[1] Every part has undergone neat refitting and modest decoration, and now wears the air of a respectable place of business.

The Corn Mill was, of course, rented, and stood at Small Bridge, some distance from the town—one mile and a half. The Society have since built in the town an entirely new mill for themselves. The engine and the machinery are of the most substantial and improved kind. It is now spoken of as "the Society's New Mill in Weir Street, near the Commissioners' Rooms." The capital invested in the Corn Mill is £8,450, of which £3,731 15s 2d. is subscribed by the Equitable Pioneers' Society. The Corn Mill employs eleven men.

The Almanack of 1855 announced the formation of a "Manufacturing Society," enrolled pursuant to the 15 and 16 Vic., chap. 31. Every Branch of the (we are entitled to say now) Great Store's proceedings are enrolled pursuant to some Act or other. This was their first formal realisation of the design announced eleven years before, of attempting the organisation of labour. Now they avail themselves of the Industrial and Provident Societies' Act for carrying on in common the trades of cotton and woollen manufacturing. The capital in this department is £4,000, of which sum £2,042 has been subscribed by the Equitable Pioneers' Society. This Manufacturing Society has ninety-six power looms at work, and employs twenty-six men, seven women, four boys, and five girls—in all, forty-two persons.

In 1854, the Store commenced to issue an almanack, in which their announcements to members were made, and from which the reader might gather the historic sympathies of the co-operators from the memorable men and dates selected. Now a considerable portion of dates is occupied with their Store, and Corn Mill, and other meetings. Advertisements of the different operations of the Society are given; a little history of its origin is crowded into one corner; the ancient objects of the Society are repeated in another place; such principles and extracts from the laws as are suitable for the information of strangers find due place upon the same broad sheet. In 1855 they announce their Central London Agents:—"The Central Co-operative Agency, No. 356 Oxford Street." In 1856 they add, "and the Universal Purveyor (William Islip and Co.), No. 33 Charing Cross." In 1853 the Store purchased, for £745, a warehouse (freehold) on the opposite side of Toad Lane, where they keep and retail their stores of flour, butcher's meat, potatoes, and kindred articles. Their committee-rooms and offices are fitted up in the same building. They rent other houses adjoining for calico and hosiery,[2] and shoe

[1] *Vide* Almanack, 1854.

[2] In 1855 the drapery stock was ordered to be insured in the Globe for £1000.

stores. In their wilderness of rooms the visitor stumbles upon shoemakers and tailors, at work under healthy conditions, and in perfect peace of mind as to the result on Saturday night. Their warehouses are everywhere as bountifully stocked as Noah's Ark, and crowds of cheerful customers literally crowd Toad Lane at night, swarming like bees to every counter. The industrial districts of England have not such another sight as the Rochdale Co-operative Store on Saturday night.

At seven o'clock there are five persons serving busily at the counter, others are weighing up goods ready for delivery. A boy is drawing treacle. Two youths are weighing up minor articles and refilling the shelves. There are two sides of counters in the grocer's shop, twelve yards long. Members' wives, children of members, as many as the shop will hold, are being served ; others are waiting at the door, in social conversation, waiting to go in. On the opposite side of the Lane, three men are serving in the drapery department, and nine or ten customers, mostly females, are selecting articles. In the large shop, on the same side of the street, three men are chopping and serving in the butcher's department, with from twelve to fifteen customers waiting. Two other officers are weighing flour, potatoes, preparing butter, etc., for other groups of claimants. In other premises adjoining, shoemakers, cloggers, and tailors are at work, or attending customers in their respective departments. The clerk is in his office, attending to members' individual accounts, or to general business of the Society. The news-room over the grocery has twenty or more men and youths perusing the newspapers and periodicals. Adjoining, the watch club, which has fifty-eight members, is collecting its weekly payments, and drawing lots as to who shall have the repeaters (manufactured by Charles Freeman, of Coventry), which the night's subscription will pay for. The library is open, and the librarian has his hands full in exchanging, renewing, and delivering books to about fifty members, among whom are sons, wives, and daughters of members. The premises are closed at ten o'clock, when there has been received during the day for goods £420, and the librarian has lent out two hundred books. In opposite districts of the town, the Society has now open four Branch Stores for the convenience of outlying members, where, on a lesser scale, the same features of sales are being repeated.

But it is not the brilliance of commercial activity in which either writer or reader will take the deepest interest ; it is in the new and improved spirit animating this intercourse of trade. Buyer and seller meet as friends ; there is no overreaching on one side, and no suspicion on the other ; and Toad Lane on Saturday night, while as gay as the Lowther Arcade in London, is ten times more moral. These crowds of humble working men, who never knew before when they put good food in their mouths, whose every dinner was adulterated, whose shoes let in the water a month too soon, whose waistcoats shone with devil's dust, and whose wives wore calico that would not wash now buy in the markets like millionaires, and, as far as pureness of food goes, live like lords. They are weaving their own stuffs, making their own shoes, sewing their own garments, and grinding their own corn. They buy the purest sugar, and the best tea, and grind their own coffee. They slaughter their own cattle, and the finest beasts of the land waddle down the streets of Rochdale for the consumption of flannel weavers and cobblers.[1] When did competition give poor men these advantages? And will any man say that the moral character of these people is not improved under these influences? The teetotalers of Rochdale acknowledge that the Store has made more sober men since it commenced than all their efforts have been able to make in the same time. Husbands who never knew what it was to be out of debt, and poor wives who, during forty years, never had sixpence uncondemned in their pockets, now possess money sufficient to build them cottages, and go every week into their own market with coins jingling in their pockets; and in that market there is no distrust, and no deception; there is no adulteration, and no second prices. The whole atmosphere is honest. Those who serve neither hurry, finesse, nor flatter. They have no interest in chicanery. They have but one duty to perform—that of giving fair measure, full weight, and a pure article. In other parts of the town, where competition is the principle of trade, all the preaching in Rochdale cannot produce moral effects like these.[2]

As the Store has made no debts, it has incurred no losses; and during thirteen years' transactions, and receipts amounting to £303,852, it has had no law suits.

Children are not generally sent to shops when adults can be spared for the errand, as it is very well known children are put off with anything. The number of children who are sent to the Store to make purchases is a proof of the honourable family confidence it has inspired. A child is not sent to the Store with a message to go to a particular man with grey whiskers and black hair, and get him to serve, and to be sure and ask him for the "best butter." Everybody has grey whiskers and black hair at the Store; the child cannot go to the wrong man, and the best butter is given to every one, old and young, without its being asked for, for the best of all reasons—they keep no bad.

The meetings of the Store were quite a family feature during the first few years. Afterwards, when the members much increased, the meetings assumed a more commercial character. Of course the Store will not now hold its eighteen hundred members. They are numerous enough to make a large public meeting; and the Public Hall, at Rochdale, has to be engaged when a general meeting is held. The perfect freedom of intercourse maintained, the equality of all, which

[1] Last year, the Society advertised for a Provision Agent to make purchases in Ireland, and to devote his whole time to that duty.

[2] The Arbitrators of the Societies, during all their years of office, have never had a case to decide, and are discontented that nobody quarrels. The peaceableness of the co-operators amounts to what elsewhere would be termed "contempt of court."

has ever been undisturbed, both in the board room and on every occasion of intercourse, have imparted an air of independence of feeling and manner to the whole. Eighteen hundred workmen are brought into weekly intercourse with each other, under circumstances which have raised the tone of society among them all.

The Directors of this important and encouraging movement are the same modest and unassuming men they were thirteen years ago; shining in oil, or dusted with flour, or flannel jackets and caps, they in no way answer the expectations of strangers in appearance, however they surpass expectation in moral and commercial capacity.

The following Tables show the progress of the Store from 1844 *to* 1857—*a period of thirteen years.*

Year.	No. of Members.	Amount of Capital.			Amount of Cash Sales in Store. Annual.			Receipts per Week in December Quar.			Amount of Profit. Annual.		
		£	s.	d.	£	s.	d.	£	s.	d.	£	s.	d.
1844	28	28	0	0									
1845	74	181	12	5	710	6	5	30	0	0	32	17	6
1846	80	252	7	1½	1,146	17	7	34	0	0	80	16	3½
1847	110	286	5	3½	1,924	13	10	36	0	0	72	2	10
1848	140	397	0	0	2,276	6	5½	80	0	0	117	16	10½
1849	390	1,193	19	1	6,611	18	0	179	0	0	561	3	9
1850	600	2,299	10	5	13,179	17	0	338	0	0	889	12	5
1851	630	2,785	0	1½	17,638	4	0	308	0	0	990	19	8½
1852	680	3,471	0	6	16,352	5	0	371	0	0	1,206	15	2½
1853	720	5,848	3	11	22,760	0	0	524	0	0	1,674	18	11½
1854	900	7,172	15	7	33,364	0	0	661	0	0	1,763	11	2½
1855	1400	11,032	12	10½	44,902	12	0	1,204	0	0	3,106	8	4½
1856	1600	12,920	13	1½	63,197	10	0	1,353	0	0	3,921	13	1½
1857	1850	15,142	1	2	79,788	0	0	1,491	0	0	5,470	6	8½

Total sales in thirteen years, £303,852. Total profits, £19,888 16s. 11½d.

The Capitals of Three Departments. 1856-7.

Store.	Corn Mill.	Manufacturers.	Total of Capitals.
1856—£12,920 1857— 15,142	£8,450 8,450	£4,000 5,500	£25,370 29,092
Weekly Receipts of the same, 1856-7.			Total Annual Returns.
1856—£1,353 1857— 1,491	£850 1,184	£360 300	£133,276 153,088

These Returns will be much higher for 1858, as the Balance Sheet for the first quarter shows an increase of more than £10,000 for the year, for the Store alone.

CHAPTER VIII.

ANECDOTES OF THE MEMBERS—THE WORKING CLASS STAND BY THE STORE AND THEY "KNOW THE REASON WHY."

It is as instructive as it is gratifying to notice the kind of replies frequently made by persons who have been served by the Store. One woman who had about £50 in the Store to her credit, was told the "Store would break," by persons who wished it would do so. She answered, "Well, let it break; I have only paid one shilling in, and I have *fifty pounds* in it. It'll break with it's own if it do break." These anecdotes are common. Many poor people, whose confidence was sought to be tampered with, have answered alarmists, who have tried to shake their trust—"Well, if it do smash it may smash with all it has of mine, for it has paid me out more than ever I paid in." These answers not only show good sense, but gratitude and generosity of sentiment. In all service of the people there will be ingratitude displayed. Every man finds it so, sometimes among his private and chosen friends; no doubt, it will be so with the public, whom you serve at random. In publicism in all human relations a man who will not be cast down needlessly must learn to look on both sides. He will in every crowd find many whom he cannot respect, and who do not deserve respect; and numbers of poor, yet devoted, trusting, toiling, manly, impassable, grateful men and women, whom you might worship in the fulness of the sentiment of admiration with which they inspire you.

Another fact ought not to escape notice, which none but those having considerable experience are aware of—*viz.*, it is seldom that the people whom you expect to help forward a movement do it. Exactly those on whom you most rely—commonly those whom you elect for appeal—deceive you, or fail to help when you expect, and when the crisis requires it.

The effects of the Store in improving the finances of its members was seen in the instance of one known as Dick, who has lived in a cellar thirty years, and was never out of debt. He one morning astonished his milkman by asking him to change him a £5 note. The sly dog never had one before, and he felt a pardonable pride in displaying his first possession. Dick has now twenty pounds of "brass" in Store. And most of those who have the largest balances standing to their credit are persons who have never paid many shillings in. The whole is the accumulation of their profits.

The following cases, designated by the numbers belonging to the particular member, were taken by the present writer from the books of the Store in 1853, and communicated to the *Leader* newspaper:—

"No. 12 joined the Society in 1844. He had never been out of a shopkeeper's books for forty years. He spent at the shop from twenty shillings to thirty shillings per week, and has been indebted as much as £30 at a time. Since he has joined the Pioneers' Society he has paid in contributions £2 18s.; he has drawn from the Society as profits £17 10s. 7d., and he has still left in the funds of the Society £5. Thus he has had better food and gained £20. Had such a Society been open to him in the early part of his life, he would now be worth a considerable sum.

"No. 22 joined the Society at its commencement. He was never out of a shopkeeper's debt for twenty-five years. His average expenditure with the shopkeeper was about ten shillings per week, and was indebted to him forty shillings or fifty shillings generally. He has paid into the Society £2 10s.; he has drawn from the Society £6 17s. 5d.; he has still left in the funds of the Society £8 0s. 3d. He thinks the credit system made him careless about saving anything, and prevented his family from being as economical as they would have been had they been compelled to pay ready money for their commodities. In this he agrees with No. 12. Since he (No. 22) has joined the Society, he has enjoyed other advantages, having a place accessible, where he can resort to, instead of going to the public-house or beer-shop for information and conversation.

"No. 114 joined the Society in 1848. Paid in fifteen shillings has drawn out £11 14s. 11d., has still in the funds of the Society £7 2s. 11d. Gained in two years £18.

"No. 131 joined the Society at its commencement in 1844. He says he was never out of debt with a shopkeeper for fourteen years. He spent on an average about nine shillings per week with the shopkeeper, and generally owed him from twenty to thirty shillings. He has paid into the Store as contributions at different times £1 18s. 4d.; and has drawn from it £1 12s. 1d.; and has still in the funds of the Society £3 1s. 10d. He thinks the credit system one reason why he was always poor, and that since he joined the Society his domestic comfort has been greatly increased; and had he not belonged to the Society in 1847, he would have been obliged to apply to the parish officers for relief.

"Thus the members derive all the advantage of a sick as well as a benefit society. It is thus that the Society give to its members the money which they save."[1]

A mother who had always sent her child to the neighbouring shop, at length began to send her child to the Store, which was more than a mile away from her house. The child asked the mother why she should be sent so far away for things instead of going into the shop next door. The mother explained to the child that the profits made at the Store would come to them. The child understood the lesson, and would come down in a morning to fetch the food for breakfast, and the family at home would wait till she returned; and, as Sir

[1] These instances were quoted by *Chambers's Journal* at the time of their appearance.

James Graham would express it, both mother and child knew the reason why. A butcher's wife expressed her new experience thus:—"Instead of having to take her 'strap' book with her, she now had money in her pocket and money in the Store." One member has £50 in the Store, all of which he has made by profits, he having drawn out for his own use all that he ever paid in. In one case a woman withdrew £5 from her savings in the Store, not so much because she had special occasion for the money, as for the pleasure of having £5 in her possession. She had traded at shops for nearly half a century, and she declared it was the first time she had ever had £5 of her own in her hands in her life.

A husband who dealt at the Store, and had accumulated money in it, had a wife who did not believe in co-operation, and was easily persuaded that the Store was unsafe, and she took the opportunity of drawing her savings from the Store and placed them, for more safety, in the Savings Bank. Before long the Savings Bank broke. The poor woman's faith was made whole by the mishap. She gathered up the tardy dividends of the bank and placed the residue in the Store, where since they have remained.

George Morton, an old man above sixty, says that had there been no Store, he does not know how he could have lived without going to the poor-house. The profits he has received from the Store on goods purchased has nearly kept him out for the last eleven years—that is, from 1845 to 1856. He has, during that time, received in dividends £77 3s. 6d., and has remaining in the Society £11. He has never paid into the Society more than £5 16s. 7½d. altogether.

Of the confidence in the dealings of the Store, Mrs. Mills, a widow, gives this testimony. She came to the Store for a steak, but as the Store butchers had none, and she wanted it for a sick person, she went into the public market and bought a pound and a half. On reaching home she weighed her purchase, and found that the pound weighed fourteen ounces, and the half-pound only seven ounces. She now says that when there is no steak at the Store, "they lump it;" meaning that they make shift until the Store is replenished. This authentic anecdote gives no bad idea of a Rochdale sickness, to which a pound and a half of steak seems congenial. The vegetarians might take a turn there.

Speaking of beef—the other day I was standing at the upper window of the Store, when the Store butchers, who had just come from the Society's abbatoirs, drove up with an immense waggon full of "prime joints." Upon looking over the chief butcher's bill, I found he reported himself as having "killed four cows and a half," which led me to inquire by what co-operative process he was enabled to kill half a cow at a time. The explanation was this. Some butcher in the town wanted half a cow for that day's market, the Store wanted four cows and a half only, so the fifth cow was divided and both parties served, which the butcher called "killing half a cow."

"The Tillicoultry Co-operative Society" admits no member who is immoral in his conduct. A female householder is admitted a member, but is refused a vote. The Baking Company of the same place has a similar ungallant and uncivil rule.[1]

The Rochdale Store renders incidental but valuable aid towards realising the civil independence of women. Women may be members of this Store, and vote in its proceedings. Single and married women join. Many married women become members because their husbands will not take the trouble, and others join it in self-defence, to prevent the husbands from spending their money in drink. The husband cannot withdraw the savings at the Store standing in the wife's name unless she signs the order. Of course, as the law still stands, the husband could by legal process get possession of the money. But a process takes time, and the husband gets sober and thinks better of it before the law can be moved.

Many single women have accumulated property in the Store, which thus becomes a certificate of their conjugal worth. And young men, in want of prudent companions, consider that to consult the books of the Store would be the best means of directing their selection. The habits of honourable thrift acquired by young men, members of this Store, renders it unlikely that they would select industrious girls in marriage for the purpose of living in idleness upon their earnings or savings, as happens elsewhere.[2]

What quality is it that makes a poor woman pay her way? Ladies do not always do it; many bankruptcies in London are occasioned by their neglect; the poor woman who has been born with that faculty, or who has acquired it, is a treasure and a triumph of good sense and social cultivation. The difficulty of bringing about this result many working class husbands can tell. The art of living within your income is a gift. The woman who has it, will do it with £1 a week; she who has it not, will be poor with £20. Peter Noakes, tired of finding himself always in debt, wants to get his wife one week in advance with the world. He wants to stand clear on the shopkeepers' books. He knows that the small tradesman cannot pay his way unless his customers pay theirs. He therefore saves, by carefulness and secret thrift, a little money, and one week delights his wife by giving her double wages, that she may pay in advance for her things. What is the result? Next week he finds her running into debt as usual. He complains, and then she tells him the everlasting story of a thousand working-class homes, "What could she do? Mr. Last's bill for Tommy's boots had never been paid, the account for Billy's jacket had stood over till she was ashamed of it, little Jane's shoes were out at the toes, and poor Polly, she was the disgrace of the family for want of a new frock, and as for Mrs. Noakes herself,

---

[1] *Vide* rules 1845-6 of the above societies.

[2] *Vide* letter of S. H. Musgrave, read by Sir Erskine Perry at the public meeting to consider the laws relating to the property of married women, held at 21 Regent Street, London, 31st May, 1856.—*Law Amendment Journal*, No. 14, p. 94.

her own bonnet was not fit to be seen, she would rather stop in the house for ever than go out in that old fashioned thing any longer." Poor Peter is overwhelmed—he had never thought of these things. In fact, Mrs. Noakes tells him "he never does think of anything. He gets up and goes to work, and comes home and goes to bed, and never thinks of anything in the house." What can Peter do? He does the only thing he ought—he allows that his wife ought to know best, confesses that he is very stupid, kisses her in confirmation of his repentance, and promises to save her another week's wages, and she shall try what can be done the next time. In the course of a few weeks, Peter, by over-work and going without customary half-pints of beer, saves up another week's wages, when, alas! he finds that the shoemaker has sent in another bill, and the tailor another account—that Master Tommy's trousers have grown too short for him, young Billy's jacket is out at the elbows, Jane's shoes let in water, Miss Polly (bless her sweet soul!) is still the disgrace of the family, and Mrs. Noakes, although Peter thought she never looked so young nor so pretty as she did last Sunday, declares her bonnet "perfectly hateful; indeed, there is not such another fright as herself in the whole neighbourhood, and if Peter was like anybody else, he would be ashamed to see his wife go out in such a condition." And the little book still goes to the shop, Peter eats cheese tough as guttapercha, she buys tea that has been used to boiling before it was sold to her, the coffee tastes grievously of burnt corn, Tommy's boots are a long time being mended, Mrs. Noakes never has sixpence to bless herself with, her money is all condemned before it comes in; Peter, degraded and despairing, thinks he may as well drink a pint as a half-pint—things can't be worse at home. He soon ceases to take interest in public affairs. How can he consistently help the public who cannot help himself? How can he talk of independence, who is the slave of the shoemaker and the tailor? How can he subscribe to a political or social society, who cannot look his grocer in the face? Thus he is doubly destroyed. He is good neither for home nor parish. So ends many domestic experiments for paying in advance. When children are sick, or the husband is out of work, a wife will submit to any amount of privation. If she would submit to half as much from pride of independence as she will from affection, thousands of families, now always poor, would be in possession of moderate competence. But to starve your household when you can help it, to prevent them being starved one day when you cannot help it, implies good sense, strength of will, and courageous foresight, which many women certainly display, but which is yet so rare a quality that one cannot but marvel and applaud the Rochdale co-operators, who have taught so many families the art of getting out of debt, and inspired them with the pride of keeping out.

Let the enemies of co-operation ponder on this fact, and learn wisdom; let the friends of co-operation ponder on this fact and take courage; the fact that the members in a short period learn provident habits by connection with these societies—habits which, in some cases, forty years of competition have failed to teach.

CHAPTER IX.

RULES AND AIMS OF THE SOCIETY.

THE founders of the Society were opposed to capital absorbing all profit arising from trade, and to hit upon a plan that should give proportionally the gain to the persons who make it, was a problem they had to solve. After meeting several times for the purpose of agreeing to laws, Mr. Charles Howarth proposed the plan of dividing profits on purchase—that is, after paying expenses of management, interest on capital invested, at a rate of five per cent., the remaining profits to be divided quarterly among the members in proportion to their purchases or dealings with the Society. This plan continues the feature of the Rochdale Store.

The division of profits is made quarterly from the net proceeds of all retail sales in every department, after paying :—

1. Expenses of management.
2. Interest on loans.
3. Reduction in value of fixed stock.
4. Dividends on subscribed capital.
5. Increase of capital for the extension of business.
6. Two and a half per cent. (of the remainder after the above are provided for) applied to educational purposes.

The residue thus accruing is divided among the members of the Store in proportion to the amount of their respective purchases during the quarter.

The Pioneers prudently established early in their career a "Redemption Fund," which consists of the accumulation of entrance fees of one shilling from each member. The last two pounds drawn from the Society by a retiring member are liable to a forfeit of one shilling each pound. The trade of non-members of the Society affords some profit. These sums go to the Redemption Fund, which is a reserve to meet the depreciation of the fixed stock. In all financial reports of the Society a broad allowance is always made for depreciation of stock, and the fixed capital at stock-taking is always estimated below its real value, so that if the Society broke up, it is calculated that every subscriber of £1 invested in the Society would receive twenty-five shillings as his dividend.

A new member must now hold five £1 shares in the capital. He pays one shilling deposit on these on entrance, and threepence a week afterwards, or three and threepence a quarter, until the £5 are paid up; but these payments are assisted by all the profits he makes by dealing at the Store, and any interest, which is fixed at 5 per cent., accruing to him as successive pounds are made up. All profits and interest are not paid to the member, but carried to the credit of his shares, until the £5 are paid.

The Board of Directors may suspend any member whose conduct is considered to be injurious to the Society, and a general meeting may expel him, after which he has great difficulty in obtaining re-admission, if he desires it.

Any co-operative society can buy to any extent through one of its members, who, however, must become a member of the "Equitable Pioneers' Society."

A member, being in distress, may withdraw any sum he may have in the funds of the Society above £2, at the discretion of the Board of Directors. In the great distress period of 1849, many applications were made to be allowed to draw all out except £1. Though it is rarely that any Director puts a question as to the personal affairs of an applicant, yet narratives were volunteered of so painful and remarkable a character, that the Directors learned to esteem that co-operation which had placed in their hands a wholesome power of relief. To this day these Directors recur to the experience of that year when defending the Society. Members may withdraw any sum above £5 according to the following scale of notice:—

£2	10s.	at once on application to the Board.				
2	10	to	£5	at	2	weeks' notice.
5	0	,,	10	,,	3	,,
10	0	,,	20	,,	4	,,
20	0	,,	30	,,	5	,,
30	0	,,	40	,,	6	,,
40	0	,,	50	,,	7	,,
50	0	,,	60	,,	8	,,
60	0	,,	70	,,	9	,,
70	0	,,	80	,,	10	,,
80	0	,,	90	,,	11	,,
90	0	,,	100	,,	12	,,

No member can hold more than £100 [1] of shares in the Society except by way of annuity, nor, under any circumstances, shall his interest in the funds exceed £30. The Directors can obtain loans, but not exceeding four times the amount of the paid up subscriptions of the members for the time being.

All disputes are settled—

1. By the Directors, or
2. By appeal at a general meeting.
3. By arbitration.

[1] A recent Act of Parliament has increased this amount to £200.

Complaints and suggestions relative to the qualities or prices of goods, or conduct of servants of the Society, are required to be made in writing to the Directors, who record their decision thereupon ; if not satisfactory, the question is referred to a special general meeting, whose decision is final.

The question of liability to Income Tax occupied the attention of the Store for several years. Its apparently final solution may be useful information to other Stores. In August, 1850, the Board applied to editors of newspapers, who are the popular lawyers of the poor, to learn whether co-operative societies were liable when the individual members have not the requisite amount of income. Answers so obtained could not have the force of law, but they had the quality of direction. The Society paid Income Tax regularly, but as the separate income of each member was far below the amount at which the Government commences its assessment, the Society appealed against it. Still the local Commissioners forced its payment. They were told, indeed, that each member might demand a form of Exemption, and claim the amount of his assessment back again. But this, on the part of a thousand members, involved too much trouble, as the Exemption claims must have been filled up for them in most cases. One year the members went to the Appeal office in a body, but the Commissioners refused to admit them, and required one representative to be appointed. It ended in the old order to pay being enforced. Opinions of Members of Parliament were obtained, who said the Society was liable, and the opinions of lawyers, who said they were not liable. As their numbers and importance increased, their confidence grew, and, in 1856, they resolved to make a stand against the exaction, and, if need be, carry it to trial. An adjourned meeting of the Board, held in October, appointed Messrs. Smithies and Ellis "to appeal against the Income Tax." These officers, who were trustees of the Society, presented themselves on Appeal day, and argued that the Society was exempt, being enrolled under the Industrial and Provident Societies' Act, which forbid any member receiving more than £30 annually in any or all forms from the Society. The case was adjourned to another day, when it was to be heard first. The day came, but Messrs. Smithies and Ellis were edified by the opportunity of hearing numerous cases disposed of without their case being called on. They were told to come the following day. On the "following day" they were told they should receive notice when required to appear, as the Commissioners were in correspondence with London. Messrs. Smithies and Ellis had the happiness never to be sent for. However, the Income Tax Collector could not refrain from making his accustomed demand, and insisted that it must be paid, giving the Society the gratifying assurance that, if illegal, they could get it back again. The Society, however, were not to be gratified in this way. They thought it audacity on the part of the collector to make the demand, so long as the case was undecided, and attempt to use his legal position to intimidate uneducated men. Mr. William Cooper reported the case to the Pioneers' Board, who put on their minutes, December 4th, 1856, this very English resolution :—"Resolved, that we do not pay the Income Tax until we are made." The next Saturday, the collector again called and demanded the money. He was told the decision of the Board. He replied, in professional terms, that "he wanted no unpleasantness, but the Society had no alternative but to pay, and that, if his demand was not paid in a few days, he should seize the goods of the Store." On the Board being informed of that, they resolved, Dec. 18th, 1856, "That the Income Tax Collector take his own course." He has not taken his course to this day, nor have the Commissioners made any sign of having a course to take.

One most honourable feature of the Society, which proves the earnest desire of the members for self-improvement, is the reservation of a portion of their funds for educational purposes. The 2½ per cent. of their quarterly profits assigned for division among the members, together with the fines accruing from the infraction of rules, constitute a separate and distinct fund, called the "Educational Fund," for the intellectual improvement of the members of the Store, the maintenance and extension of the Library,[1] and such other means of instruction as may be considered desirable.

GENERAL FINANCIAL ACCOUNT OF THE EDUCATIONAL FUND.

Receipts.	£	s.	d.	*Disbursements.*	£	s.	d.
Donations - - - -	1	2	6	Paid for Books - -	308	11	9
2½ per cent. from Educational Fund -	424	18	11½	,, Bookbinding -	20	12	3½
Catalogues and Fines	17	19	11	,, Book Case - -	25	9	11
Sale of Newspapers -	2	14	3	,, Wages - - -	28	5	4½
Sundry Receipts - -	3	7	9	,, Catalogues, etc.	6	0	6
				,, Newspapers[2] -	17	5	2½
				,, Sundry Disbursements -	2	8	8
				Cash on hand - - -	41	9	8
	£450	3	4½		£450	3	4½

Their News-room is as well supplied as that of a London club, and the Library contains 2,200 volumes of the best, and among them, many of the most expensive books published. The Library is free. In their News-room, conveniently and well fitted up, a member may read, if he has the time, twelve hours a day, also free.

[1] A minute of Sept. 20th, 1853, orders a motion to be made at the quarterly meeting, for awarding £40 to the Library.

[2] The News-room has become chargeable on the Education Fund only within the last six months (1857). The quarterly meeting passed a resolution that the News-room should be free to members, and supported from the Education Fund.

From 1850 to 1855, a school for young persons was conducted at a charge of twopence per month. Since 1855, a room has been granted by the Board for the use of from twenty to thirty persons, from the ages of fourteen to forty, for mutual and other instruction. on Sundays and Tuesdays.

Any readers of these pages, who may contemplate forming stores in their own neighbourhood, will, on application to the Secretary of the Equitable Pioneers' Society, Toad Lane, Rochdale, obtain the laws at present in force, and other printed documents from which executive details may be learned, not necessary to be included in this history; but a personal visit to the Store ought to be made by all who would initiate similar establishments. Many Members of Parliament, political economists, and some distinguished publicists, have made journeys of late years to the Rochdale Store. The officers receive with courtesy, and give information with enthusiasm to, all inquirers. Indeed, they are often found travelling thirty miles from their homes to give evening explanations to some workmen's meeting desirous of information in practical co-operation, and of forming societies themselves. It will greatly promote the extension of co-operative societies if the Rochdale Pioneers will train officers who may be transplanted to the towns commencing stores, to organise and conduct them. This co-operative colonisation will save both waste and failure in many places.

Though an element of self-sacrifice for the good of others—a feeling that justice rather than selfishness should pervade industrial intercourse, if it is to be healthy—animates these co-operators, who are neither dreamers nor sentimentalists. This may best be shown by a quotation from a letter by one of their leaders, to whom we elsewhere refer—Mr. Smithies. "The improved condition of our members is apparent in their dress, bearing, and freedom of speech. You would scarcely believe the alteration made in them by their being connected with a co-operative society. Many well-wishers to the cause think that we rely too much upon making ourselves capitalists; but my experience among the working classes for the last sixteen years has brought me to the conclusion, that to make them act in union for any given object, they must be bound together by chains of gold, and those of their own forging."

In 1855, a co-operative conference was held at Rochdale. A Committee was appointed to carry out certain resolutions agreed to. Abraham Greenwood, President, James Smithies, Secretary, published a declaration of the principles on which the proceedings of the said Committee would be regulated. We shall quote them to the credit of co-operation. They were these:—

I. That human Society is a body consisting of many members, the real interests of which are identical.

II. That true workmen should be fellow-workers.

III. That a principle of justice, not of selfishness, must govern our exchanges.

We think these three sentences honourably illustrate how much higher is the morality of co-operation than that of competition. When did any commercial firm ever issue, and, what is more, act up to, a manifesto like this?

The co-operative conference of 1855, held in Rochdale, was called by the Equitable Pioneers; the delegate from London was Mr. Lloyd Jones,[1] who has as continually aided, as he has serviceably defended, these associations. On this occasion, the Rochdale Society, in addition to the manifesto of its own principles and public aims, which entitled it to distinction above all other societies, took the opportunity of paying a just tribute to the labours of others, to which they had themselves been indebted, as well as the public:—

"They were convinced that the Society for Promoting Working Men's Associations had, during the period of its active existence, conferred great benefits on the Co-operative cause by gathering all sorts of valuable information, and spreading it throughout the country amongst the various Co-operative bodies; by urging on the attention of Parliament, through members favourable to the cause, the legal hindrances to the movement; and by helping to procure such alterations of the laws relating to Friendly Societies as to give freer action and greater security to the men who have embarked in the Co-operative undertaking. Not only have they done these things, but they have likewise drawn up model laws suitable for either distributive or productive associations, so as to facilitate the safe enrolment of all Co-operative bodies, and to secure the highest degree of legal accuracy with the smallest possible cost; in addition to which, they have at all times given legal advice freely to such of the Societies as stood in need of it—a matter, it must be acknowledged, of great value to bodies of working men.

"The Rochdale Equitable Pioneers feel deeply the value of the services rendered to Co-operation by the Council of the Society for Promoting Working Men's Associations; and, as the fullest and most acceptable acknowledgment, they considered that the best thing they could do would be to attempt to continue the work which the Society for Promoting Working Men's Associations had begun, and perfect, if possible, the design which they were unable to complete."

Never was testimony more nobly deserved than this thus borne to the services rendered to working men by the gentlemen known in London as "Christian Socialists," Professor Maurice, Mr. Vanstittart Neale, the Rev. Charles Kingsley, Mr. Furnival, Mr. Ludlow, and others. Guided by their wisdom and sustained by their

[1] Mr. Lloyd Jones, being the manager of the Manchester branch of the Co-operative Central Agency of London, and subsequent traveller for that firm, has frequently visited the working and co-operative societies of the North of England, and addressed the members at their anniversary meetings. On these occasions, and at the several co-operative conferences held in London, Manchester, Rochdale, Leeds, and Bury, he has exercised an important influence in the development of the co-operative idea. The "Wholesale department" of the Rochdale store, so important a step in organisation was carried out under his advice.

wealth, efforts for "Promoting Working Men's Associations," for which the people will be more grateful as they acquire more knowledge to appreciate their sympathy, their generosity, their patient and costly services, the Working Men's College of London is the crowning tribute of their catholic love of the people.

The Rochdale Store has done business for several years with "The Universal Purveyor," instituted by J. L. St. André,[1] author of the "Prospects of Co-operative Associations in England," a volume remarkable for comprehensive views of industrial organisation. In the words of one who knew him, "M. St. André, whatever may be his enthusiasm, or his over-estimate of what can be done with men as they are, appears to have the merit of a sincere desire to draw associations together in a spirit of unselfish co-operation, and at the same time *to place them in a healthy connection with the external world*."[2]

We record, and rightly, the names of inventors and discoverers—we record the names of those who signalise themselves on the field of battle—it is no less useful to record the names of those who have discovered, or perfected, or, at least, improved the art of self-help among the people, and conquered in the field of industry by providence and good sense, where so many fail and perish. Every name represents the continuity of small duties well fulfilled—a quality more valuable to society than the emulation of sublime virtues. Every member of this Store has been a co-worker equally with the officers, but we can only enumerate those who have taken the lead in the most successful experiment conducted by the people. Their perseverance must give a new idea of the capacity of the working class.

The first general meeting of the founders of the Store was held in the Social Institution, Rochdale, on Sunday, August 11th, 1844. The first resolutions upon their minutes are as follows :—

Resolved, 1st—That the following persons be appointed to conduct the business of the Society now established—Mr. John Holt, Treasurer, Mr. James Daly, Secretary, Mr. Miles Ashworth, President, Messrs. Charles Howarth, George Ashworth, and William Mallalieu, be appointed Trustees.

2nd—That Messrs. James Tweedale, James Smithies, James Holt, James Bamford, and William Taylor, be appointed Directors.

3rd—That John Bent and Joseph Smith, be appointed Auditors.

(Signed) Miles Ashworth, Chairman.

ARBITRATORS OF 1844.

Mr. James Wilkinson, shoemaker, High Street; Mr. Charles Barnish, weaver, Spotland; Mr. George Healey, hatter, Sudden-

[1] And sustained by the Rev. Charles Marriott, Fellow of Oriel, one of those Churchmen who commend the priestly character by uniting a clear faith to works of human interest.

[2] "The Co-operative Principle not opposed to a true Political Economy,' by the Rev. Charles Marriott, B.D., Fellow of Oriel—pp. 35-6.

brow; Mr. John Garside, cabinetmaker, High Street; Mr John Lord, weaver, Cronkey Shaw.

The present arbitrators (1858) are—[1]Thomas Livsey, Esq., Alderman, Rochdale, late Chief Constable; [2]John Garside, cabinetmaker; Rev. James Wilkinson, Unitarian Minister; John Lord, publican; Samuel Tweedale, foreman.

First among the arbitrators of the Co-operative Manufacturing Society, and of the Corn Mill Society, of which we have yet to speak, stands the name—universally esteemed among the working classes of Lancashire—of Jacob Bright, Mayor of Rochdale.

OFFICERS' NAMES FROM OFFICIAL PUBLICATIONS OF THE STORE, ETC.

John Holt (Treasurer), Benjamin Rudman, James Standring. Names appended to the Laws of 1844.

John Cockcroft, Henry Green, John Kershaw. Names attached to the Laws of 1848.

William Cooper and Abraham Greenwood. From Laws of 1855.

George Adcroft (President), James Hill, Robert Taylor, John Whitehead, Robert Hoyle, Thomas Hollows, James Joyce Hill, George Morton, James Mittall, John Clegg. Names attached to Corn Mill Rules.

Abraham Hill, Treasurer; John Tweedale, Robert Woolfenden, Trustees; Robert Law, Thomas Hill, James Whittaker, Directors; Samuel Ashworth, Superintendent. Store officers from the Almanack of 1854.

Samuel Fielding, David Hill, John Hollows, Trustees; Peter McKenzie, Robert Whitehead, William Ellis, Adam Grindrod. Directors. Store officers from the Almanack of 1855.

James Manock, Trustee; John Smith, Secretary; Thomas Glegg, Isaac Tweedale, John Worsnip, Directors; Emeryk Roberski,[3] Superintendent. Store officers from Almanack of 1856.

Edward Farrand, Clerk. Corn Mill advertisement. *Vide* Almanack, 1856.

William Whitehead, Secretary. *Vide* Manufacturers' advertisement, 1856.

John Aspgen, Librarian; William Holt, Samuel Newton, Robert Glegg, Samuel Glegg, Robert Howarth, Thomas Halliwell, Committee of Library. *Vide* Almanack, 1856.

John T. W. Mitchell, Secretary; John Kenworthy, Trustee; Jonathan Crabtree, Thomas Fielding, Thomas Cheetham, Samuel Stott, Directors. Store officers from the Almanack of 1857.

James Glegg, George Watson, Matthew Ormerod, William

1 The most radical and popular chief constable of the day.

2 Known among old social reformers as "Father Garside."

3 An intelligent young Polish exile, exiled through the Hungarian struggle, to whom employment was given in the Store, and who rose to be superintendent. He has lately emigrated to Australia.

Briggs, William Hoyle, Abraham Howard, Edmund Kelly, Thomas Whittaker. Library Committee from Almanack of 1857.

These names are given here in the order of time in which they appear in the public documents cited, and with the office annexed the person happened to hold in the list quoted. Each name is given but once, though most of them occur again and again, some in connection with every office. For instance, Mr. James Smithies, to whom the members, some time ago, presented a valuable watch and chain, in testimony of their regard, has held offices during twelve years. Mr. Abraham Greenwood, mentioned in connection with the Corn Mill, has been an officer nine years. Mr. William Cooper has been an officer in the Store from the commencement. To the last-named persons I have been mainly indebted, and especially to Mr. W. Cooper, the present Secretary, for the sources of the leading facts of these pages.

CHAPTER X.

THE OLD CO-OPERATORS—WHY THEY FAILED.—THE NEW CO-OPERATORS—WHY THEY SUCCEED.

"THAT were a noble achievement which should originate a system of more wages and less work, that the labour of the handicraftsman might be lighter on his hands, and his earthly blessings and little comforts be increased; and that were a still more worthy achievement which should teach him to fill his intervals of time with the study of philosophy, and the pursuit of literature and science." Thus wrote Dr. Chalmers.

"This that they call organisation of labour is, if well understood, the problem of the whole future, for all who would in future govern man." Thus wrote Thomas Carlyle.

"It appears from actual experiment, that a thousand subscribers of from one penny upwards will yield a weekly revenue of £5. In Great Britain there are 6,000,000 adult males. Take of these, including such females as choose to subscribe, 4,000,000; these will yield £20,000 weekly, or £1,040,000 a-year. Now, £1,040,000 a-year, with compound interest, would amount,

	£	s.	d.
In 10 years, to - - - - - - - -	18,232,413	14	11
In 20 years, to - - - - - - - -	65,522,599	8	3
In 30 years, to - - - - - - - -	188,181,161	18	8
In 40 years, to - - - - - - - -	506,325,883	12	8
In 50 years, to - - - - - - -	1331,511,365	15	1
In 60 years, to - - - - - - -	3471,129,995	18	4

Now this sum would buy all the property of the kingdom. Do not suppose for a moment that 4,000,000 of working men will soon be found steadily subscribing their penny or twopence a-week for this object; but these figures show what a fund there lies in the smallest co-operation of the millions, and which the devotion of the sums expended merely on spirits and tobacco might accomplish for mankind." So calculates the Leeds Redemption Society, and seeks to win by figures those whom argument fails to reach.

"Wait no longer on the banks of the great and ever-growing river of poverty for the golden boat of the capitalists to carry you over, till you perish. Awake to the fact you may become capitalists yourselves—that you can and must help yourselves." Thus exhorts the *People's Journal*, in its genuine sympathy for the working classes.

Upon how many thousands of our countrymen have these words of wise direction fallen, as upon "stony ground." The more, therefore, the esteem with which the public will regard the men of Rochdale, upon whom they have not fallen in vain.

That co-operation was the secret whereby the poor could make money was known to old co-operators, though the Rochdale Society has been the most skilful in turning it to *progressive* account; for as early as 1831, one William Shelmerdine, storekeeper of a society, meeting at 7 Rodger's Row, Deansgate, Manchester, reported that their members, with a stock of only £46 12s., and subscriptions of £26 10s., had made, in twelve months, £20 2s. of profits. Eight members founded the Society, and thirty-six had joined it by the end of the year.

The second Co-operative Congress was held in Birmingham, in October, 1831. The first appears to have been held in Manchester, in May, in the same year. In this year, the *Lancashire and Yorkshire Co-operator* appeared—a small fortnightly penny paper, calling itself the advocate of the useful classes, and bearing this sensible motto:—

> **"Numbers without Union are powerless—**
> **And Union without Knowledge is useless."**

The true warning is here, though twenty-six years of experience has not supplied the necessary wisdom to profit by it.

At the third London Co-operative Congress, 1832, there was reported the existence of a "Rochdale Friendly Co-operative Society," which sent, as a delegate to London, one William Harrison. It had a secretary of the gentle name of T. Ladyman, whose address was 70 Cheetham Street, Rochdale. The Society was formed October, 1830. In 1832 it had fifty-two members. It employed ten members and families. It manufactured flannel. It had thirty-two volumes in its library. It had never discussed the "principles of exchange;" and there were two societies in its neighbourhood.

In 1832, there existed in Birkacre a society, whose secretary was Ellis Piggot, Printer's Arms, Salford, which had 3,000 members and £4,000 of funds. This society were silk and calico printers.

At the third London Co-operative Congress there were sixty-five societies represented, of which nine were in London. Of the delegates or secretaries, the following names are still known:—W. Lovett, B. Cousins, T. Whitaker.

Why have so many stores one after the other disappeared? Some have not known how to turn their prosperity to a progressive account, and have grown tired of a monotonous success. There have been of late years failures around Rochdale; the leading cause assigned is the system of credit.

The Oldham Mechanics' Store, and the Bolton Store, were broken up through the strike of the amalgamated ironworkers; but it was said they paid twenty shillings in the pound. The Brighton Store did not acquit itself so well on its failure, which was attributed to its giving credit to its members. Mr. Smithies, who is certainly the most competent and practical authority we can follow, said, writing in 1855:—"Nearly all the Stores—there is hardly one exception—are now on the ready-money principle. We find that those Co-operative Societies which commenced by giving credit, but have since adopted the ready-money plan, have all improved since doing so. I look upon the strap book," says he, "as one of the greatest evils that can befal a working man. He gets into debt with the shopkeeper, and is, for ever after, a week behind; and, as we express it here, eats the calf in the cow's belly."

Hence arose that just terror of credit which the Store from the first betrayed. In their first book of laws—the laws of 1844—the grand fine, the lion fine of the list there given, was to be inflicted on any officer, who, on any pretence, should either purchase or sell any article except for ready-money; which prohibition, as usual when they are emphatic, is given twice over.

The Liverpool Co-operative Store, rising every year in importance and usefulness, gives credit to the amount of two-thirds of the paid-up shares of the members. The Store connected with Price's Patent Candle Manufactory acts upon a similar rule. This, of course, is a safe form of credit, but it involves a great additional amount of book-keeping, and stops short of that moral discipline which ready-money payments exercise upon the poor and naturally improvident.

In Rochdale, each workman in the manufacturing department is required to become a capitalist. Either by weekly subscription or other payments he is required to hold five shares in the Society. Each of these artisan shareholders receives 5 per cent. upon the amount he has invested. After the payment of this interest, and the wages of the workmen at the usual average of the district, and all trade expenses, the surplus of profit is divided according to the wages received by each workman. The amount of profit over 5 per cent. interest, which is first paid to the shareholders, is divided equally between the shareholders and the workmen. One half goes to the shareholder[1] according to the number of his shares; the other half goes to the workman or workwoman according to the wages paid to him or her. The dividend in the Rochdale Co-operative workshops, paid January, 1857, was one shilling and sixpence upon every pound of wages received by workman or workwoman.

An important difference in the division of co-operative profits in Padiham and in Rochdale should be noticed. In Padiham, workmen who had made small savings, and other minor capitalists, subscribed a fund among them, bought machinery, and employed workmen. The chief profits were reserved by the subscribers of the capital for themselves. The workmen they employed had better situations and somewhat higher wages than at other mills. This arose from most of the proprietors being workmen, and having sympathy with the persons they employed. In other respects, the Padiham Cotton League Company, under the Joint Stock Companies' Act, paid their profits wholly to the capitalists or shareholders. All the societies enrolled under this act are understood to pursue this rule. It is no part of their plan to acknowledge the labourer's right to a share of the profits his labour creates, which is the Rochdale principle.

By precautions and good sense, the Rochdale Co-operators have succeeded, notwithstanding the impediments the prejudices of their class put in their way. During the period known among them as "the Corn Mill Panic," Mr. Coningham, M.P., to whom the country is indebted for valuable personal reports of the Working Men's Associations of Paris, consented to make an advance of capital to assist in the exigence of the Corn Mill, but on being very naturally required to submit their securities to the examination of his solicitor, the Board objected to "having anything to do with a lawyer," yet their securities were ample and good, and they knew it.

Confidence among the members was sought the first year of the existence of the Store by establishing and showing plainly that checks upon the honesty of the officers existed. Drawers conveniently constructed are now used by each salesman, provided with brass or tin coins according to the nature of his sales, of which he hands to each purchaser an amount exactly representing the cash expended.

The Treasurer and Secretary of the Store, the Corn Mill, and manufacturing departments, balance their cash accounts weekly. This rule, which enables errors to be corrected as they may arise, has operated very beneficially.

Security is now taken from £10 to £200 from each officer employed, according to his measure of responsibility. Each officer in charge of a shop till gives £10 security. Where other guarantee is not provided, the Society holds the deposits of the officer in the Society, and if he has not a sufficient amount paid in, he is required to make up

[1] Though capitalists were twice paid (a bad example to set) they rose up and took away from the workman his share, as soon as they proved numerous enough.

such amount by periodical payments. For sums so lying in the hands of the Society, interest is paid as in the case of shares. This is a very efficient regulation of securities, for no man will find it answer his purpose to rob himself. The early Boards of Directors assisted the shopmen in their duties. Economical in all their improvements, it was not until 1854 that they lowered the floor of their flour store, for the convenience of children and the aged members coming to make purchases.

Numerous stores have at times sprung up around the Rochdale one, and in consequence of its example; but none have been conducted with the same ability, nor have achieved more than a tithe of its success. This is owing to no fault in the principle, but to deficiency on the part of those who apply it, to want of sense, of union, of patience, and enterprise. There are numerous instances in which the Stores have not only succeeded, but, in the opinion of the members, have succeeded too well. They have made more money than they know what to do with. Not knowing how to employ their savings advantageously, they have been returned to the members, who have commenced saving again. Their Directors have lacked the talent of expanding their operations, and making their capital reproductive. The Rochdale weavers appear to have been born with a special talent for co-operation.

One cause of the striking success of these co-operators is, no doubt, to be found in the great economy of their trade expenses. The proportion of the salaries they pay to their receipts is very small.[1] It would be impossible to maintain the same rate in the metropolis, where rents and wages are higher, and the rate of poor men's provisions, in leading articles, the same. In answer to a question put to him on this point, Mr. W. Cooper writes me—"I see no reason why the people of London cannot carry on a Co-operative Society as well as people who live in the provinces. In a small town, some dozen or twenty persons will meet, and agree that if a Co-operative Provision Store could be commenced it would be a good. These twelve or twenty *do* commence one. They work on together, determined to make the thing do. When it has worked on awhile, people who doubted begin to see that it can be carried out, and they join too. I see no reason why a number of earnest men in London cannot act in the same way." In answer to other questions, the same informant writes—"At the commencement of a co-operative store or manufacturing society, it is essential that the members be visited or brought together often, so that contributions may be collected to establish and carry on the society, and that the members may become acquainted with the objects, position, and requirements of the society. With

The cost of distribution at the central Store is 1¾ per cent. upon the returns, and with the branch shops, about 2¼ per cent.; so that for 2 per cent. all working expenses of rent, rates, wages, etc., are defrayed.—John Holmes's paper, read before the British Association for the Advancement of Social Science, at Birmingham, which we commend to the reader.

this kind of management a store easily acquires sufficient capital to work its business with, because the members have gained confidence, and pay in subscriptions on their own account without being much looked after."

To get people together in this personal and continuous manner is the difficult problem in London. Making some allowance for higher expenses in proportion to profits, the thing might be done if a number of the working-class could be got to act together, and *keep together*, for this end. It requires to convert a number of them to a clear view of their own personal interest, to be promoted in no other way, and a deep sense of duty towards their order, whose character is elevated by such successes. Compare Rochdale with Liverpool for instance. In Rochdale, a little bridge that spans, like a rocking horse, an imaginary stream, in which there is nothing liquid but the mud, situated in an invisible part of the town, is the only picturesque object in it. There is, indeed, a church with a flight of steps to it, so narrow, steep, and interminable, that you can never get to it, or if you do, it is a question as to whether you will ever get back. The remainder of the town is made up of roads that lead to nowhere, ornamented with factories apparently built before the dawn of architecture. There is not a building in Rochdale upon which it will do any eye good to look. The town is in the shape of a teacup, with a gutter at the bottom and a burying-ground upon the rim. In such a place, if people are disposed to act together, there is nothing in the way of striking attraction around them to prevent them. The people are immensely before the town, which like many other manufacturing towns in the North, has grown into importance anyhow ; but will, no doubt, yet assume the magnificence which is gradually being imported into Bradford, Leeds, and other places, which, twenty years ago, were quite as unpromising as Rochdale. Now pass to Liverpool, with the bright and busy Mersey—its migratory population—its magnificent buildings—its open halls, surpassing in variety those of London. Plainly, it requires more devotion among the few to carry a store to success in Liverpool than it does in Rochdale. Then if you compare the ordinary provincial town, fixed, stolid, and tame, with London and its countless attractions, the difficulty is greater. The people are "too clever by half" to be useful. Will a dozen men stick to a plan of reform year after year, never failing on the weekly night of meeting to be at their posts, amid the charms of the metropolis? Dickens is making a speech at Drury Lane, or reading his "Christmas Carol" at St. Martin's Hall—Thackeray is lecturing on the "Four Georges" at the Surrey Gardens, with Mr. Spurgeon to succeed him—Robson is coming out in a new character—Mr. Saunders has a new play at the Haymarket—Cardinal Wiseman is preaching in the next street—Dr. Cumming is to prove that the end of the world will occur on Saturday, and the People's Subscription Bands play in the Parks on Sunday—Neal Dow is at Exeter Hall, and George Dawson at the Whittington Club—there are Cremorne, Rosherville, and Kew—the National Gallery and the British Museum, and the Houses of Commons and Lords, South Kensington Museum, and public meetings, where you may hear speakers never to be heard before, and often never again—and countless other allurements. A man must have self-denial as well as interest, who steadfastly grinds coffee berries and watches the sale of tea and sugar, and sits for years upon Candle and Treacle Committees, amid this confluence of celebrities and novelties, though it be duty and religion to do it. This is why popular movements in London, which depend upon the working and middle classes, make such uncertain progress. Unless a man be wise enough to choose a side and discharge its obligations as a sacred duty, undertakes to win others to act in concert with him and pursues his object with the fidelity of a soldier, nothing can be depended upon. In fine, it requires working men in London to be as superior to the average of their class in the metropolis as the Pioneers of Rochdale are superior to the average of their own class in Lancashire, and then co-operation may carry its moral discipline and physical comfort among the poor of London.

The Leeds Corn Mill Society—the Padiham Co-operative Manufacturers—the Galashiels Co-operators—present features of success worthy to be placed side by side with the Rochdale Store. Whether in being originated and conducted by purely working men—whether in the variety and development of their operations—whether in propagandist spirit—they are to be compared or placed before the Rochdale Pioneers, are matters I leave for others to determine. The public will be glad to hear more about these experiments than these pages can communicate.[1]

Just as the farmers, some years ago, could not be prevailed upon to make returns of their crops, lest their interests should be prejudiced in Parliament by the fact, so the Co-operators in some districts, having the fear of the Income Tax Commissioners before their eyes (the Rochdale issue of this question not being known, or not being considered settled), or distrust of Government, object to make reports. Mr. T. Barker, of Todmorden, in an unfilled return sheet before me, assigns this reason for its incompleteness. Todmorden, Walsden, Bridge End, Alma Works, and Commercial, are mentioned in his return. Mr. Smithies, of Rochdale, whom I had requested to get certain forms filled up for me, despairs on these grounds of succeeding.

Working men are often injudiciously treated by employers in this way. Where the men dressed with some taste, and maintained an appearance of social comfort, masters would infer that they were doing too well, and would reduce their wages. This had a disastrous influence on the men, who came to regard careless habits and indigence of dress as means of keeping up wages. How were working

[1] For the History of the People's Flour Mill Society of Leeds, the reader can consult the paper mentioned in the note on p. 59. It may, probably, be had of the author, James Holmes, Leeds, or the printer, David Green, 38 Boar Lane, Leeds.

men to be raised from improvidence while those who ought to incite them to improvement suggested to them the policy of keeping themselves poor, in order to avoid being made poor. A master whose pride or ignorance was put to the blush by superiority in the manners of his men, would reduce their wages in order to lower their tone. This, however, has changed now; and masters are prouder of being enabled to say, "all my men are worth money," than that "half of them are in debt." Throughout mankind the tendency is universal to help those who can help themselves. The poorest man that exists will, if he reflects, find himself unconsciously acting on this feeling. The very beggar will not give to the beggar if he has reason to think that what he gives him will do him no good. There is no benevolence, high or low, that will many times repeat the act of pouring the water of charity into a sieve. This fact, so common to every man's experience, should teach the working class that if they display the habits of thrift, others may display the disposition to help. Moral statistics will assure the intelligent workman that where one employer reduces the wages of his men because of their social aspirations, there are more who make it a pretext to reduce them because they see no resulting improvement.

Writers who speak with the authority of political science have testified to the utility of these efforts of self-help. One to whom the working classes are indebted both for instruction and defence, remarks :—"We think, moreover, that these Co-operative Associations may be one of the most powerful of the many influences now at work for the education of the lower orders of the people; that wisdom will be gained, if not wealth, from the industry, self-control, and mutual forbearance needed to conduct them.[1]

This is the place where one may usefully cite words which one of the sincerest friends of the people has written, and which cannot be too widely known among them, as this grave truth is not to be disputed.

"I lately heard the case of a letter-printer, who used to employ in his trade the savings of his workmen with mutual advantage. At one time he had thus in his hands as much as a thousand pounds, the property of one of the workmen. A master manufacturer at Manchester assured me that he would gladly employ in his business any sums which his men would entrust him with, but that it was out of the question, although, personally, he was on excellent terms with them. To invest money in their master's business would be binding themselves to his interests, and separating themselves proportionably from that of their own order. Such a step might even expose them to resentment, and, at any rate, their party feeling was too alive. They had an indefinable suspicion that the master would be able to take advantage of it. Many of them, perhaps, did not like the master to know how rich they were."[2]

[1] W. R. Greg, "Investments of the Working Classes," p. 120.
[2] Professor F. W. Newman's lectures on "Political Economy," pp. 321-2

Perhaps no sentence written about the people is more likely to serve them than the following words by Mr. J. S. Mill:—"In Europe the time, if it ever existed, is long past, when a life of privation had the smallest tendency to make men better workmen or more civilised beings." This sentence strikes at the root of that intellectual apathy about the condition of the people which has checked, and still checks, so many endeavours for their elevation. The gentlemen of England are, as a class, probably less indolent and sensual than the poor. Opulence, and the means of physical ease, have not robbed them of enterprise. No spur of privation remains to stimulate them, but the spur of intellect, of art, of high cultivation, excites them, occupies them, interests them—a new pride possesses them, and a lofty consciousness of nobler powers than those which poverty simulated, now carries them on to a destiny undreamed of, and, indeed, undesired before. When this truth is applied to the common people, when it is no longer an article of parish faith, that "privation" is the sole incentive of labour, the social policy of our rulers will be changed, and the systematic elevation of the people begin.

When, a few years ago, Mr. Carlyle began, with his noble insight, to write of "Captains of Industry," he was considered to have visions of the most hopeless class of chieftains ever pictured in romances. But his ideas, grafted on the age, have taken root. Modern employers, if they wished, might found chieftainships, nobler far than those of feudal days, and will, no doubt, do it yet. The Crossleys, Akroyds, and Salts of the North, are already taking proud places in the industrial history of the people. A few years ago, the "hives" of Lancashire and Yorkshire, Halifax, Bradford, Leeds, and Manchester, were dreary as penal settlements—as Oldham, Ashton-under-Lyne, Hyde, Stockport, and crowds of smaller towns, are still. Of late years, however, the warehouses of Manchester, and Bradford, and Leeds have assumed an air of magnificence. Buckingham Palace does not look half so imposing as does the regal structure erected by Sir John Watts, of Manchester. Towering in variegated marble, head and shoulders above all surrounding structures—occupying the site of sixty-three former tenements—it stands the Monarch of Warehouses. The factory worker grows taller by looking up at it—the most insensible inspire pleasure in walking by it. Must not the beef-built, square-headed, shrewd Bradford man, grow somewhat refined, and even proud, if he has a spark of national spirit in him, as his way home lies by noble structures every day rising up on his path, and raising the industrial glory of his native town and land? Are we not all far away, proud to think that trade is not all mammon worship and gross materialism. Is it not a relief to see the careful saving merchant, wooing the arts, and obtain from the brain of the designer glorious structures, in which to enjoy his patiently earned wealth? Let not the pallid, often stunted, hot-air-stewed factory hands of Hyde, on precarious nine shillings or fourteen shillings a-week, nurse a sense of perpetual despondency. Their turn is coming. When the noble warehouse has, for some time, been admired, public attention will be turned to the factory, and next to the "factory hand," and will be found quite ready to admire both, if they will bear admiring; and then it will never do for the proud and rich employer to say, "Oh, I keep dainty rooms to store my cottons in; but as for the people who make them, any murky, sooty, unventilated, and dreary den will do for them." The day is coming when no employer in the North will like to say this. Mr. Titus Salt has been the first to feel this, and Saltaire; the noble factory and dwellings he has erected point to what will one day be done. Workmen think it a privilege to get an engagement in Mr. Salt's mill. The town of Bingley has been deserted by men who prefer Saltaire. The workmen's rooms, in which the factory operations are carried on, are nobler, higher, healthier, pleasanter rooms, than were the drawing-rooms of the gentlemen of the North fifty years ago. Any workshop in Saltaire is pleasanter than any room in the house you pass at Bury, where the late Sir Robert Peel was born.

A man, whose soul is affluent as well as his circumstances, will supplement his stately warehouse by a stately and healthy factory; from being an artist in his premises, he will, to use Mr. Thornton Hunt's words, become "an artist in flesh." He will covet that his men shall, in their way, look as well and bear themselves as gracefully as his machines, and then that they shall dwell in homes as tasteful, as salubrious, and as suitable as those accorded to spinning-jennies: he will covet that the ring of his money shall echo with the contentment of those who aided to earn it. Thus, were the advocate silent, and the plea of humanity disregarded, and social rights ignored, a principle of artistic consistency will, one day, enforce universal co-partnership in the produce of industry and the conquests of science.

CHAPTER XI.

AN ILLUSTRATIVE CHAPTER.

DURING the progress of this little book through the press, some new incidents in the career of the Store and its departments have arisen, which deserve brief notice.

(1857.) The Store has been attacked in local newspapers, and on placards, by anonymous writers, who appear to seek the destruction of the Society by sowing disunion and creating distrust of its financial security. The attacks were commenced during the recent panics. In the December quarter the Board reported that although unfavourable reports had been circulated respecting the Stores, the number of members on the books was greater by forty-eight than at the commencement of the quarter—making a total of 1,848. Had the placard writers here referred to succeeded in their design, considerable injury would have been done to a large body of the working class at a time when firms were daily breaking. Had the credit of any commercial house been attacked in the same way, a jury would have given considerable damages, had the case been brought before them: and we think the Board of Directors would do well to regard themselves as entitled to the usual protection of commercial houses, and to make an example of the first responsible assailants to whom they can trace similar wanton aggressions. There is fear that enemies to the success of the Pioneers, enemies on competitive grounds, will, now that the Pioneers have become really formidable, seek to destroy them by disunion. It requires great good sense and mutual powers of forbearance to sit silent and see statements published which appear to the public more than half true, and which you know to be wholly false. The temptation to go into controversy in self-defence is very great; and the ease with which controversy slides into personalities we all know—then time is wasted, temper lost, and only scandal gains, and the enemy triumphs. Any shrewd opponent may naturally calculate that amid 2,000 persons, some will be found who may, by taunts of want of courage, or want of truth, be seduced into a disastrous newspaper or placard war. It is said of the first Napoleon, that in the early part of his Italian campaign he was followed by numerous letters, some criticising him, some abusing him, and all perplexing him very much to answer. After a good deal of time had been consumed in replies, which time might have been much better employed upon maps and strategy, and actual war with the enemy, it occurred to him to throw all his letters into a capacious basket, and let them lie there for six weeks: at the end of which period he found that time and events had answered them nearly all. We suggest some such plan as this to the Board of Directors of the Rochdale Store. We recommend them to refer all matters of controversy to a committee of three clear-headed, dispassionate men, whose duty it should be to give very brief explanations of any point really misunderstood; and if any controversy seemed called for, to enter upon it only once a year, and to lay by all placards, newspapers, letters and articles, until December, and then reply, to what time and success may not have confuted, and what the public may not have forgotten (which will be found to be nine-tenths of the whole), and then let silence and peace prevail for twelve months more.

LETTER FROM THE SECRETARY OF THE PIONEERS' SOCIETY.

Equitable Pioneers' Co-operative Stores,
Nos. 8, 16, and 31 Toad Lane,
Rochdale, April 17th, 1858.

SIR,—By this post I send the report of the R. D. C. C. M. S. (Rochdale District Co-operative Corn Mill) for March, 1858, from which you will see that the Society is making progress—as is the co-operative principle as a whole. I think I told you that our next step forward will be to extend the operations of the "Manufacturing Society" here, and, while I write, a Committee is sitting to consider proposals which have been made in response to an advertisement for a capitalist to build us a mill, which we purpose to fill with machinery and work. The working classes may at times lose by having over confidence, but do not they lose much more who never have any confidence? The five thousand members of the Co-operative Societies within ten miles of Rochdale, representing twenty-five thousand persons, could not derive the benefits they now receive unless they had confidence in each other and in the principle of co-operation.

WILLIAM COOPER.

To Mr. G. J. Holyoake.

THE OPINION AND ADVICE OF LORD GODERICH, M.P.[1]

(*A later Letter from the Secretary of the Store.*)

We (writes William Cooper of Rochdale), received a long letter from Mr. Holmes, of Leeds, this morning, April 26th, 1858, which shows that they are aiming at Co-operative Stores to distribute their groceries in preference to the agency principle, which they adopted to distribute the flour made at their own mill. In the course of his letter Mr. Holmes remarks:—"The other day your West Riding Member, Lord Goderich, being in the town, visited our mill, and met the Board in a conference. We had a very interesting meeting and conversation. His lordship told us *we*, Leeds and Rochdale (or rather Rochdale and Leeds, for we cheerfully give way to Rochdale superiority), were the objects of frequent conversations both in the House and out of it; that our success was most welcome to some good statesmen, who see if the people are doing well, all else must be well. Our prosperity was pointed at as proving the people can, and will, manage their own affairs. If we fail, the reputation of the principle will be seriously damaged, and when our contentions and difficulties are mentioned, it ties their hands. He told us it was not ourselves alone we should consider; we were now held up and closely watched by other societies, and other people would follow us if we succeed, or be disheartened if we fail. We had a most kind and strong exhortation to go on, economise, save, and extend—to be shrewd, wise and peaceful. It would take me long to tell you all, but he promised us good service should we need it, and he be able to do us good. By the way, I could recommend

---

[1] Since Marquis of Ripon.

you to send reports to Lord Goderich, Mr. Conningham, M.P., Mr. Slaney, M.P., and other good friends in London. It affords them pleasure, and their sympathy is deserving of return."

I make you this copy of Mr. Holmes's letter, which will interest you, as showing you that our progress bears some fruit.

WILLIAM COOPER.

To Mr. G. J. Holyoake.

The cordial interest taken by Lord Goderich in the welfare of the working classes is well known, not only in the West Riding but throughout England. We choose to close this brief history of the first thirteen years of the Rochdale Pioneers with the above transcript of Lord Goderich's wise and influential words of encouragement and advice.

CHAPTER XII.

AN OLD PIONEER'S ACCOUNT OF THE ORIGIN OF THE STORE.

MR. JOHN KERSHAW, the last but one of the Pioneers, sent to Mr. Abraham Greenwood various MSS. (1891-2) records relating to the period preceding the formation of the Equitable Pioneers, which he wished should reach my hands. Many things are new, all told by him with the vividness of a witness, and the circumstantiality of one who took part in them. The story adds to our knowledge of the old Pioneers, and is confirmatory of all that has been published of them. The pictures given of Rochdale life and meetings of working men, are scenes from the past well worth preserving.

"I began," Mr. Kershaw writes, "to work as a tearboy at the Gate Printworks before I was seven years old, and went to work in the pit before I was eight years old. So you will see there was not much time for my schooling had any schoolmaster been about."

The Rochdale Pioneers began their work when distress was wide spread. The hand-loom weaver seemed to be the worst off of any of the working class. Improved machinery had driven him to the lowest point at which he could live. The condition of things in Rochdale would be incredible did it not rest upon authority. Sharman Crawford, the member for the borough, declared in the House of Commons in the debate Sep. 20, 1841, that in Rochdale there were 136 persons living on 6d. per week,[1] 200 on 10d. per

[1] Mr. Kershaw took it from Mr. Lloyd Jones' "Life of Robert Owen." Mr. Lloyd Jones took it from the late John Noble's "National Finance." I verified it by going to Hansard's Parliamentary Debates. It seems incredible now how any human being could live on the sums named. Dr. Abernethy advised a fat alderman "to live on six-

week, 508 on 1s. per week, 855 on 1s. 6d. per week, and 1,500 were living on 1s. 10d. a week. Five-sixths of those he spoke of had scarcely any blankets, eighty-five families had no blankets, forty-six families had only chaff beds, with no covering at all. No wonder the country was full of agitations, and in Rochdale, where there was intelligence as well as unrest, all agitations seemed to rage. There was a great local agitation against the new Poor Law. There was one for the Charter. Temperance had its advocates. The Socialists had their society. The Anti-Corn-Law agitation was rife in the town. The Ten Hours Bill was fiercely discussed. Two social facts stood out very clear—labour was cheap, but bread was dear. Yet bread was almost the only article of food the people were able to get.

"In 1842, at an Anti-Corn-Law meeting, a proposal was made to close factories to compel Parliament to repeal the Corn Laws. The chairman was about to put the motion, when an elderly gentleman, who seemed to have more forethought than the rest, said it would never do, as the work-people would soon be starving, and very soon there would be rioting. Another speaker said that employers would reduce the wages lower than they were."

In the summer of 1843, Rochdale was placarded, announcing a discussion on "The best means of obtaining the People's Charter." Mr. Kershaw says "I attended that discussion; so did Charles Howarth, James Smithies, and James Daly. It was there I first heard the principles of the Pioneers announced; Charles Howarth taking the lead, was well supported by Smithies, Daly, and others. Mr. Howarth showed, as I thought, very clearly that it was the only lever whereby the working class could permanently improve their social and political condition. His scheme and its details were so well studied out and clear that it commanded assent. It was said at this meeting that a co-operative society had been in existence in Rochdale not more than two years before, and that it had gone down. Howarth at once showed us the reason why. He seemed thoroughly acquainted with the cause, and was well prepared with a new principle which would keep continually infusing new life into the movement. A few days before Christmas, 1843, a circular was issued calling a delegate meeting to be held at the Weavers' Arms, Cheetham Street, near Toad Lane. Each trade was invited to send two delegates. The colliers sent me (John Kershaw). The promoter of this meeting was a strong trade unionist, and a unionist chairman was at once appointed. His address pointed out what the colliers had just done in getting their wages increased nearly double the amounts they were receiving a few weeks before. He praised the

pence a day and earn it." But a prescription of sixpence a week would have killed the patient. However did 136 Rochdale persons—not fat and full like Abernethy's alderman, but lean and hungry—contrive to live on a penny a day and nothing for Sunday?

colliers to the skies, as it were. It appeared from what he said that he thought all other workers could do the same, if they took the same means."

After a deal of talk, a collier (Mr. Kershaw) was asked to show how they had managed to get advances in their wages without a strike. He said he could not recommend them all to do just what the colliers had done, for if all branches of industry did the same, they would be worse off after the advance than they were before. This seemed to puzzle the meeting not a little, which could not see how they would be worse off with higher wages, and asked the speaker to explain. He said: "Suppose you were all getting £1 a week, and with it you could just pay your way. Then suppose you got an advance of 4s. a week, but at the same time the price of all the articles you needed to buy cost you 5s. a week more, you would be worse off after the advance than you were before." The plan of the colliers was this—the Haddershaw Moor Colliery just employed thirty coal getters at that pit. For every quarter each got (a quarter contains fifteen loads) the collier was advanced 2d. per quarter, and the masters advanced the coal 2d. per load or 2s. 6d. per quarter. That is for every 2d. they paid the collier they charged the public fifteen twopences. The collier got 2d. and the coalowner 2s. 4d. "I say," said the speaker, "that if everything is raised upon the same principle we shall all be worse off after the advance than we were before." Whereupon a great tumult arose in the meeting, and the colliers were called everything that was bad, and were even charged with conspiring with the masters to rob the public.

No one seemed to perceive that all employers could not charge the public 2s. 6d. for every 2d. extra they paid the workmen. The collier speaker himself did not appear to see that if he had 4s. extra wages he would not have to spend 4s. for the coal he burnt in his house every week, probably not 1s., and he would be 3s. the better. In every trade the same argument applied. The poor collier had got into his head the nonsense employers always talk. They always say the higher your wages the worse you will be off, and the only way to improve your condition is to work for nothing. Those who smile to-day at the poor colliers' muddle-headedness should remember that political economists in those days talked the same nonsense, and they talk the same thing still in the House of Commons, when they say that any advance in wages will drive trade to other countries. The wages of all men are double now what they were that day, and according to that theory all trade should have left the country long ago.

Hearing how the increased price of coal had come about, a tumult arose, and the colliers were accused for having incited the masters to raise the price of coal. When it did subside Mr. Kershaw cried out:

"Hold on a bit, there are some of you talking of what you know nothing about. If anyone is more to blame than another for what has been done, that man is I, for I gave the colliers the advice upon which they acted. Up to the present time I have not uttered a single word to any master, nor has any master said anything to me upon that subject. But the masters were not slow to take advantage of what we had done. It is well known that our wages have been doubled and the price of coal has risen in the market."

Then a new charge was made, that the colliers had neglected their duty to the public in not exposing the conduct of the masters in raising the price of coal so exorbitantly beyond what they had given to the men. The denunciation of this neglect was loud and fierce. This roused Mr. Kershaw's indignation, and he replied with great force and directness. He said "the colliers owed no obligation whatever to the public. The public cared nothing about the colliers, and why should the colliers care anything about the public? All the public cared for in connection with colliers was cheap coal. Cheap coal was all their aim.

"Only a few months before this time, I was," Mr. Kershaw said, "getting a two-feet seam of coal, doing all the bye work, paying the banksman; in fact, delivering it into the boats. All I was paid was thirteenpence a ton, but never did any of the public come and say, 'Here, Kershaw, you were not properly paid for that coal that was got so cheap. Here's sixpence for you.' No; it was cheap coal they wanted. It did not matter to them what became of the collier."

Mr. Kershaw relates "that in going home Howarth and he discussed the colliers' duty to the public." Mr. Kershaw maintained that they owed no obligation to the public and the public cared nothing for the producer, which was amply proved by the fact that the hand-loom calico weaver was driven out of his trade; when, if the public would have given ½d. per yard more for hand-loom woven calico than they gave for steam-power weaving, the hand-loom calico weaver would have held his own. No, the public preferred the cheaper article, and the hand-loom weaver was driven from the industrial field. Mr. Howarth well knew that the hand-loom flannel weaver could maintain his ground if the public would give 1d. a yard more for hand-woven flannel, but the public cared for cheapness, and not for the lives of the workers. The result was that the hand-loom flannel weaver was going after the hand-loom calico weaver. Mr. Howarth acknowledged he had never seen the question in that light.

At the meeting above described, some trade unionist opposed co-operation and some co-operators were against trade unions, Mr. Kershaw remarking, "All you can justly say of trade unions is they are a never-ending contention between employer and employed, without producing any corresponding benefit." He did not see then, very few workmen did, that organised unionism would one day become a powerful defender of workmen, and the regulator of wages.

"The question arising, what could be done to amend things,

it was said that Charles Howarth had a plan, but as the night was far advanced it was arranged to hear it explained another evening. Howarth came well prepared. The trade unionists were there with a considerable opposition. They said co-operation had been tried and had failed; the shop had been closed two years ago. Charles Howarth showed very clearly why and how it had gone down, and always would go down, he said, so long as the rich, in the character of shareholders, ran away with all the profits. Under his scheme the larger the family the greater would be its gain, while the investments of the richer members would receive a fair remuneration, profits remaining among members according to their purchases."

Mr. Kershaw asked the question, "Suppose all working men were in earnest, and paid threepence a week until they were able to start a co-operative store, and then allowed all the profits to accumulate and be relaid out productively—that is, in establishing co-operative workshops—how long would it take to get the land and workshops of the country under the control of the working people?" Charles Howarth and Macnaught (who was present) took pencil and paper to calculate the result. Macnaught was the first to raise his head, and said that in fifteen years, if all working men went into the project, they might get command of the workshops if their contributions and store profits were laid out productively." At the next adjourned meeting, a week later, Charles Howarth, proceeding upon his own and Macnaught's calculation, brought a tract ready written, showing how working men might become their own employers in fifteen years. The paper was read, earnestly discussed, and it was resolved to print it. Each man, who could, paid 5s. down there and then. The meeting was a thin one, but £3 was given to Howarth that he might get as many printed as he could for that sum and bring them to the next meeting. The largest quantity were consigned to Mr. Kershaw, with the understanding that he would distribute them and collect them in the way tract collectors did. He did this for several weeks, allowing each tract to remain a fortnight before calling for it. Every alternate week he might be seen collecting these tracts and re-delivering them at houses where they had not been before. At one house, at Clegg Hall, he met with a very strong rebuff. On collecting the tract he asked whether it had been read. The answer was mostly "Yes." He then asked what was thought about it, and frequently a little debate followed; but at Clegg Hall, when the occupant, a man about fifty years old, was asked what he thought about it, he said, "Such folks as Kershaw and his friends were unfit to live. It was such men who made things as bad as they were. It was all their fault that times were so bad." He deprecated any new agitation for amending social and industrial evils, lest it should make matters worse—a doctrine which, if it was generally acted upon, would make oppression of long life, and reform or improvement of any kind impossible.

Those who were in the wrong would never find it out, nor be disquieted in doing wrong; and those who found doing wrong agreeable to their interests would be guaranteed an easy time of it. The burglar is ensured a charmed life when people, whose houses he is looting, are advised not to interrupt him, nor call in the police, lest he should be irritated and matters made worse. The poor workman Mr. Kershaw encountered was of this way of thinking. The simple-minded Clegg Hall man had probably learned this kind of chatter from people far more astute than he. It is a commonplace of governments, capitalists, monopolists, and all who have some interest to defend, or some improvement or act of justice to resist. The Government say, "You need not agitate, the time has not yet come; you only make irritation and indispose people to do what you want." When, after a lapse of time, those who act upon this advice ask the fulfilment of the implied promise, they are told "their demand is perverse; nobody is asking for the change"—thus making the silence they asked for an argument for refusing the very thing which they were told agitation prevented them conceding. In the same way as a partisan of an interest or an injustice is officiously saying, to any who ask redress, "You indispose those in office to concede what you request by perpetually agitating for it." If you listen to them they sharply tell you "nobody cares for the improvement you seek or they would be asking for it." It is agitation that makes opinion, and it is opinion alone which compels those to do justice whose interest it is to withhold it. This kind of argument could not impose upon the intelligent Rochdale co-operators of that day; and Mr. Kershaw at once said, "I know things are bad, since I cannot earn 10s. a week, and that is not sufficient to maintain a family upon. That state of society which compels a man to work for so little wants altering," and he for one was determined that it should be altered, so that an honest man should be able to earn sufficient to live upon by honest means. It transpired afterwards that the Clegg Hall man was a steady workman, who had been imposed upon by those who knew better, and he was afraid that agitation would make things worse with him than they were.

At another meeting the subject discussed was the "habits of the people," when Mr. Pennington said, "the man who lost a quarter of a day's work, or spent or wasted a sixpence unnecessarily, was a fool to himself, a rogue to his family, and a knave to his fellowmen." These honest men who had industry in their blood, who coveted sixpences, and had to economise them, were justly indignant that other people, because they had a little capital, were able to amass pounds out of their unrequited labour and they be unable to help it. Accordingly they decided to become the pioneers of a new co-operative store.

There was then a building in Toad Lane, three storeys high; the topmost storey a Bethel school; the middle a day school; the ground floor unoccupied. It had been a warehouse, and had a pair of large doors as an entrance. These would have to be removed, and proper shop doors and windows be put in. Charles Howarth and others were appointed to go and see the landlord. As soon as he was told the name of the society, and what they proposed doing, he said he could not think of letting the room to them. At this point Charles Howarth sprang to the front and said: "Will you take me for a tenant, and I will pay you a quarter's rent in advance?" "Yes," said the landlord, "I will do that." So it was agreed that the new society should have the place for three years, Howarth being the tenant, and paying the rent each quarter in advance. It was decided to open only at nights. Samuel Ashworth and William Cooper volunteered to act as shopmen, and if the business did not pay the first three months they would take nothing for their services, but if it was able to pay a dividend, they were to receive threepence an hour, which, if they were on duty three hours, would be ninepence a night, and the salary of a permanent night shopman would be 4s. 6d. a week. The Store was opened on the evening of St. Thomas's day, 1844.

New societies who think they are not going to succeed because their first dividends are small, may take courage from Kershaw's story.

At the end of the first quarter the Rochdale Society did pay a dividend of 3d. in the pound, after reducing the value of the fixed stock to what they thought it would bring under the hammer. The second dividend was 4d., the fourth 7d., the fifth 9d., the sixth 11d., the seventh 1s. 2d., the eighth 1s. 4d., the ninth 1s. 6d.; 1s. 8d. was the largest dividend they ever calculated upon getting; but for many years afterwards it ranged from 2s. to 2s. 6d.

They arranged their rules so that they could devote one-tenth of their profits to educational purposes. But when sent to Mr. Tidd Pratt, the Registrar, he refused to certify them. The contest with him lasted for some months. The rules were altered again and again. The Society tried to edge in education in several different ways; but he always struck it out. "We were not allowed to educate ourselves, but the Society was very loth to part with its education clause. We had considerable correspondence with Mr. Tidd Pratt on the subject, but he would never give way." These were the days when the law prohibited workmen from educating themselves and the Government refused them the franchise on the ground of their want of knowledge.

[The major portion of the following part first appeared in 1878. twenty-one years later.]

PART II.—1857-1892.

"Others, we doubt not, if not we,
The issue of our toil shall see ;
And children gather as their own
The harvest which the dead have sown—
The dead, forgotten, and unknown."

To

THE REV. WILLIAM NASSAU MOLESWORTH, M.A.,

A CLERGYMAN WHO, TEACHING CHRISTIANITY BY EXAMPLE

AND LEAVING CONVICTION TO CONSCIENCE,

WENT AMONG HIS CO-OPERATIVE PARISHIONERS, GIVING THEM WISE COUNSEL

AND FRIENDLY HELP,

IRRESPECTIVE OF THEIR WILFULNESS IN PIETY OR POLITICS,

THIS STORY OF THEIR CAREER FROM 1857 TO 1878

IS RESPECTFULLY INSCRIBED.

CHAPTER XIII.

THE WEAVERS' DREAM.

THIRTY-TWO years ago certain working men in a third-rate town in Lancashire dreamed, like Bunyan, a dream. Their subject was different from his. The famous Bedford tinker dreamed of the kingdom of Sin—the Rochdale weavers dreamed of the kingdom of Labour. Both dreamers, however, had one vision—that of the pilgrimage out of an evil and hopeless land. The weavers were weary of dwelling in the unrequited grounds where toil had no reward; and turned their eyes towards the Enchanted Lands of self-secured competence. Both knew there was a rugged pilgrimage before them, and the flannel weavers of the town in question resolved, like Christian of Bunyan's immortal story, to set out without delay.

We do not pursue any further the allegory between the two sets of pilgrims: a different and simpler comparison will be sufficient for our purpose. In 1844, co-operation was no unknown thing. It was worse than that. As sometimes happens at the police courts, it had, like the prisoner at the bar, "been seen there before." Co-operation was an old offender; it had been tried and condemned many times. Many workmen had lost by it; more had suffered disappointment by it. It was regarded as an exploded scheme. To use a nautical phrase, the vessel was not seaworthy; in fact, co-operation was little better than a leaky, rickety cockboat, in which few would sail out into the sea of industry. It was doubtful whether it would ever get into port, and was sure to be a long time about it, if ever it did arrive. However, a few resolute mariners, who could not be much worse off if they went to the bottom, made up their minds to the attempt.

A year, as the reader [1] knows, was spent in preparing for the voyage. The sides of the old hulk were caulked, and the old rigging repaired in 1844. She had been on the water then sixteen years, the leaky old craft having been launched at Brighton in 1828. Her condition was very frequently discussed, and unfriendly onlookers shook their heads. Others tried to keep up the spirits of the sailors. An outsider or two did take a small share in the adventure, but the cargo was almost entirely supplied by the crew which were to man her; and at the end of twelve months she was launched again, with half £28 worth of provisions, consisting chiefly of oatmeal, salt, and bacon; and general preparations were made for a very rough passage. The Equitable Pioneers had pretty hard work to balance themselves. They were finely tossed about. One minute they were seen on the crest of an ugly wave, and the next lost in a nasty trough of

[1] Meaning the reader of the First Part of this narrative.

sea. The townspeople were on the look-out on the shore. The crew had been a little shy of getting into so insignificant a cockboat. Everything was mean, shabby, poverty-stricken, and worm-eaten about the affair, excepting the bravery of the Rochdale sailors, who sustained their national renown for pluck and daring. Some of the spectators wished them "God speed," but these were too poor to aid, and mostly too desponding to believe in their own kind-hearted hope: Others jeered, for never was a more absurd, battered, leaky old barque seen, which went by the name of "The Weavers' Dream."

In more prosaic, but not truer terms, it may be told that co-operation was a distrusted and doubtful thing, when the flannel weavers of Rochdale began business in Toad Lane on £28 of capital, the produce of much hard saving. Gradual gains were made. Years of vicissitude and progress followed. The "Pioneers' Store," as it was called, increased; members multiplied; new departments of business were opened. Panics occurred, and again it was predicted that the "Weavers' Dream" would end as dreams usually do, in fantastic nothingness.

This was not to be so. The old craft made many voyages, and always with an increasing profit on its freights. Storm clouds darkened its passage, the crew were often driven upon the rocks, but each year they repaired, strengthened, and new-painted their vessel; and at times new ones were launched, amid expressions of confidence unknown before, and rejoicings that none ever thought to witness. At length 1861 arrived, and cotton famine clouds blew from the South and threatened the wreck of everything. A slave war monsoon blew across the Atlantic, and withered in a night all the vast industry of the northern counties. Then was to come the wreck of co-operation and the crash of stores. Then, at last and for ever, the weavers were to awaken from their long and infatuated dream!

The great tornado came—panic and famine, and all the furious winds of war and disaster—but nothing moved the adventurous Pioneer vessel from its moorings. It had become a stout ship by this time. It had been remasted, new rigged, had a quarter deck laid down, and been fitted with machinery of the latest improvements in co-operative navigation. It made its usual voyages during the tempest as though nothing was happening; and, while many other ships foundered, it always came safe into port. And when other vessels were in difficulties, from stress of weather or want of provisions, it would put off and gallantly render help. Of course its timbers had been well strengthened, and the commanders had provided themselves with good maps, on which the rocks were laid down pretty accurately. The captain knew where to coast about and when to put out on the open sea. The crew consisted of stout-hearted, experienced sailors. How it came about that they alone made prosperous voyayes in dangerous seas will be told herein, in due course, for the entertainment and instruction of future co-operative navigators.

CHAPTER XIV.

THE FAMOUS TWENTY-EIGHT.

ROCHDALE is a town which has been in its time equally distinguished for poverty and pluck. The distress and discontent which existed there before the days of the Reform Bill of 1832 are, happily, no longer, even in the recollection of the present generation of inhabitants, who have ceased to be reminded of it in their daily personal experience.

In the old hungry Corn Law days, from 1825 to 1830, things went ill with the working classes of Rochdale. At public meetings of working people in the town statements were made of lowness of wages and domestic wretchedness, which would be deemed incredible now. Delegates were sent to neighbouring towns to report upon their condition, and deplorable stories they told. No one would imagine that such persons had the capacity of co-operation in them, or that it was in the power of any industrial device to do them substantial service. The creditable thing is that Rochdale men, though in desperate circumstances, were not wanting in public spirit. They had constables who were not pleasant-minded persons and were guilty of some offensive official irregularities, and though they had the power of retaliation on those of the workmen who objected to such proceedings, the weavers resolved to bring them to account, and out of their scanty means subscribed enough to "have the law" upon them, and succeeded. The old parish records contain, no doubt, particulars of the affair. Mr. Francis Place preserved the only published account of it I have seen. The creditable incident is worth recalling. Scores of local officials, magistrates included, have elsewhere "gone wrong" since that day, without being called to account, as was done by the unappeasable weavers of Rochdale.

Twenty years have now nearly elapsed since the first part of this history appeared. The two dozen and four adventurous operatives who began the Store in Toad Lane, have come to be spoken of as the "famous twenty-eight." Most of them are now gathered to their fathers, and the public will be willing to hear final details of them.

A correspondent to whom I have been heretofore indebted for information says that "in a recent conversation with a member of the Rochdale Educational Committee, he was informed that the old shop in Toad Lane, in which the Pioneers commenced business, was known as 'The Pioneers' Store' for years before it was occupied by them, in consequence of being used as a storeroom for the Pioneer regiment, stationed in Rochdale, before the barracks were removed to Bury. The place behind the shop is still known as Barracks' Yard, and there may be some truth in this. If so, it may be that the Pioneers took their name from that circumstance, or it may be a mere coincidence."

My belief is that this was merely a coincidence. In social and trade union literature before that date, there were publications bearing the name of the *Pioneer*, and pioneering was in the mind of the early Socialists; it was a common ambition amongst them to be going forward and doing something. The fact, however, is worth recording, as it has never before been mentioned.

In the minds of many outsiders, Chartists and the co-operators were so mixed together in the rise of co-operation in Rochdale, that only time and testimony can separate them, and satisfy every one to whom the credit of the movement was really owing. There never was a doubt entertained among persons living on the spot, or acquainted with the facts, that the Socialists were the persons who first thought of starting co-operation, who counselled it, who originated it and organised it, kept it going, and carried it out. The fact is, the Chartists were impediments in the way of it. They were the most troublesome opponents the co-operators had to contend with. The Chartists were opposed to co-operation. They took little interest in it. They treated as apostates those who did. For a long time they did not understand it, and when they did they distrusted it. But sixteen years after, when co-operation had succeeded and become a thing of pride and repute, they made attempts to prove they were the persons who commenced it. Many years after co-operation acquired notice and power, their able and cultivated leader, Mr. Ernest Jones, opposed it in a public discussion at Padiham about 1851 with Mr. Lloyd Jones. It has been the fate of other movements than that of co-operation to be strenuously opposed throughout all its struggling days, and then to be claimed by its greatest adversaries as their own discovery and as being the cause which they had advocated and befriended. It is always a good sign when these pretensions are advanced by opponents, since it shows that the principle has triumphed, and its most strenuous adversaries are covetous of the honour of being associated with it. But it is the business of history to discern to whom the credit of origination belongs, and give it to whom it is due.

In 1861, the Chartist claim was put forward in the *Rochdale Spectator* with confident pertinacity by Ambrose Tomlinson. A Chartist Society existed in Rochdale in 1843. Mr. Tomlinson denied that the co-operative movement grew out of the flannel weavers' strike of 1843-4. He said that it commenced with the Chartist Society, who met in Mill Street, the fact being the Mill Street Chartists opposed the movement in its infancy, and, because several of their members joined the Society formed under the name of the Equitable Pioneers, they were denounced by their Chartist brethren as "deserters." In those days the doctrine was—"The Charter, the whole Charter, and nothing but the Charter." These oft-repeated phrases still ring in the ears of those who mingled in working-class movements of those times. To co-operators, to advocates of the Ten Hours Bill, to Corn Law repealers—three separate parties who then occupied public attention—the Chartists everywhere said—"If you will not help us to get what we want, we will prevent you getting anything." And they did it as far as they were able. The Chartists did not succeed in carrying their measure by that unfriendly policy, and did not deserve to succeed. Each movement has a right to do the best for itself, but when it seeks to frustrate the success of those going in the same direction in order that it may win first, it merely helps the common enemy of all, and enables it to be said derisively—"See how these Reformers are fighting amongst themselves."

Mr. Ambrose Tomlinson, an active Rochdale Chartist of those days, gives an account of what occurred among his comrades, in words nearly as follows:—"The co-operators, the few originators of the movement, who were all Chartists, became so enamoured of co-operation, that they nurtured it in one corner of Mill Street Chartist room. The Chartist council held their meetings in the opposite corner of the same room; but on many successive occasions the Chartist council corner became very thin of attenders. At this juncture those of the Chartists who had attended the council meetings reproached the Chartist co-operators who had resolved to attend the co-operative meetings, and neglect Chartist business. The few sturdy co-operators took umbrage, and resolved to meet together at the Labour and Health beer-house, kept by Mr. Tweedale at that time, not one hundred yards from the Chartist room in Mill Street. The use of that room at the Labour and Health was secured by Ann Tweedale, a female co-operator, who was sister to the landlord. She afterwards became the wife of Benjamin Standring, inducing him to become a co-operator soon after their marriage. The co-operators met there for only a very few weeks before they joined the Chartists at their place of meeting again. They again became attached as friends, when the Chartists took the Socialists' room from the Socialists, at the time of the failure of the Harmony Hall scheme. The co-operators went with the Chartists from Mill Street Chartist room to the room situate at the top of Yorkshire Street. The co-operators remained with the Chartists until the September following. During that time they were contriving plans for the future of co-operation, drawing up rules, making preparations for commencing; then they resolved to look out for more suitable premises for carrying on business, when they got possession of the building in Toad Lane, formerly known as Bethel School Room."[1]

One is glad to hear again of the beer-house with the pretty name of "Labour and Health." But let us hope that the attendance was not too enthusiastic there—because when that is the case "labour" sometimes loses its "health" in those quarters. No doubt the

[1] *Co-operative News*, December 16, 1876.

Chartist opposition to the early Pioneers in Rochdale seems a small thing in 1877, now the Pioneers have grown to many thousands and the Chartists have become nearly extinct—but it was a very different thing in 1844 and long afterwards, when the Chartists were ten or twenty times as numerous as the Socialists. Every earnest party in which principles are masters of its leaders, instead of leaders being masters of their principles, has its mad days when its advocates think their principles should take precedence of all others. Indeed, they sometimes contend that all other principles are injurious. Sanity is known by seeing what your place is and working in it.

The Socialist flannel weavers, after their unsuccessful strike, founded the Equitable Pioneers' Society, and commenced subscribing practically to create a fund with which to begin a small provision store. At first they met where the weavers had done, in the Bethel School Room, Toad Lane. Ultimately their meetings were removed to the Social Institution, top of Yorkshire Street, and the Equitable Pioneers' Society dates its establishment from this place. Mr. John Holt, who had been the treasurer at Mill Street, became the treasurer of the Store Society, and continued to hold that office until shortly before his decease. The rules of the Equitable Pioneers' Society were drawn up at the Social Institution, and the older heads among the Socialists were those who framed them and organised the Society. Mr. Tomlinson [1] handed to the Editor of the *Rochdale Spectator* the book of the Society existing immediately before the Equitable Pioneers' Association was formed. The names it contained are worth preserving for historical reference :—

"George Morton, Mount Pleasant; and then follow Charles Ratcliffe, Regent Street ; Robert Whitehead, John Dawson, Richard Farmer, Richard Brierley, Thomas Kershaw, Mary Bromley, Mount Pleasant ; Ann Tweedale, Mount Pleasant ; Charles Holroyd, Lower Fold ; Samuel Shore, Healey ; John Cain, Richard Street ; Benjamin Rudman, Shawclough ; Abner Riley, Calder Brow ; Abraham Birtwistle, Water Street ; Fred. Greenwood, Moss ; Miles Ashworth, Spotland Bridge ; James Nutall, Bank Side ; Samuel Ashworth, Spotland Bridge ; John Holt, Shawclough."

The next matter in the book is the list of parties who received the money from Mr. George Howe, watchmaker, Walk, when he refused to continue secretary. The names are the same as those above. The next account is that in which Mr. Alderman Livsey receives as treasurer of the co-operators various sums, amounting in the whole to £8 13s. 6d. This money was received by Mr. Livsey on the 7th February, 1843.

The capital with which the Pioneer Society first commenced business was, as everybody knows now, £28 ; and, by coincidence, the number of members which commenced the Society was also 28.

In 1865, 21 years after the formation of the Store, the then sur-

[1] February, 1861.

vivors, 13 in number, were prevailed upon by Mr. Smithies to meet together and be photographed in a group, for the gratification of friends of the great Store.[1] For the convenience of readers who may meet with the group, I give here the following description of the Pioneers in it, as told me by William Cooper, retaining his own language, not devoid of force and individuality:—

"A short sketch of the thirteen persons who were amongst the early members of the Rochdale Equitable Pioneers' Society, now on a photograph taken at the latter end of the year 1865.

"The photograph being placed before you, commence at the left hand with those sitting in the front.

"No. 1. James Standring, at the time of the Society's formation a flannel weaver by trade; an Owenite or Social Reformer; was secretary in Rochdale for the Ten Hours Factory Act agitation. When the flannel weavers turned out in 1843-4 for an advance of wages, and failed in accomplishing their object, he procured a copy of the Friendly Societies Acts, to see whether the remnant of the union amongst the weavers could take advantage of its provisions to form manufacturing or other associations for their self-employment, protection, and benefit.

"No. 2. John Bent, tailor by trade, belonged to the Socialist body, was one of the first auditors of the Society.

"No. 3. James Smithies, wool-sorter and book-keeper, a Social Reformer, was one of the first directors. Has at various times held office as president, secretary, trustee, and director in the Society. Has always laboured to promote the spread of co-operation, and to preserve in it the just and fraternal spirit.

"No. 4. Charles Howarth, a warper in a cotton mill by trade, belonged to the Socialist body. Was one of the first trustees of the Rochdale Equitable Pioneers' Society. He mostly drew up the rules by which the Society was to be governed, and proposed that the rule or principle of dividing profits on purchases in proportion to each member's trade, should be adopted. He has at sundry periods held office on the committee as secretary. During the Ten Hours Bill agitation he was one of the delegates who went to London to confer with members of Parliament and watch the Bill while before the House of Commons. Being a mill worker, he was in close contact with the employers, some of whom had no liking for legislation as between them and their employes. On one occasion he was called into the office by his employers, and they made a proposal something in this way:—He must remain in the office, and they would send for the hands one by one out of the mill, and put the question to them whether they wanted the Ten Hours Bill, with a reduction in wages corresponding with the shorter time. By this means they said it could be ascertained whether a majority of their workpeople were in

[1] The last communication I received from Mr. Cooper contained this cartoon; underneath the sitters is the name of each written by Mr. Cooper. I have it framed and it hangs in my chambers before me now.

favour or against the Ten Hours Factory Act. Charles Howarth agreed so to do, providing they would consent first for him to have a meeting with the hands in one of the rooms of the mill, to explain and address them on the subject. The employers did not assent to this, so there was no meeting and no calling of the workpeople into the office.

"No. 5. David Brooks, a block printer by trade; a Chartist in politics. Was the first appointed purchaser of goods for the Society. He was an honest enthusiast, who spared neither time, labour, nor means to promote the success of the Society.

"No. 6. Benjamin Rudman, a flannel weaver by trade; a Chartist in politics. A man of few words, but a steady supporter of the Society.

"No. 7. John Scrowcroft, hawker by trade; nothing in politics; a Swedenborgian in religion. In the early days of the Society members often came to the Store and had conversations. Politics, religion, or other subjects, were at times talked over, and occasionally there would be a night set apart—not a business meeting of the Society—by those members who choose to attend, to debate on a stated question. Of course, religion was sometimes the topic for the evening. Some of the members who were religious thought it a sin to debate their faith, and they proposed to prohibit such matters being open to criticism; but John Scrowcroft was thoroughly sincere in his religion, and said it was as much a proper subject for debate as any other question. Indeed, he was certain his was the true faith, and the more religion was examined and discussed the greater number would come to believe it. The motion to 'muzzle did not get itself carried.'

"Commencing at the left with those standing in back:—

"No. 8. James Manock, flannel weaver by trade; Chartist in politics; has served on the committee at various times as trustee, director.

"No. 9. John Collier, engineer by trade; a Socialist. Has been a committee-man of the Society several times. He speaks in the broad Lancashire style, and no wonder, as he is a great-grandson of the famous John Collier ('Tim Bobbin'), of Milnrow, near Rochdale, who wrote books in verse and prose in the years 1744 and 1750 in Lancashire dialect, full of wit and droll humour, in which the 'Witch' and the 'Parson' come in for a fair share of satire. John Collier ('Tim Bobbin') was buried in Rochdale Old Churchyard, 1786, with the following epitaph on his gravestone, said to have been composed by himself about ten minutes before he died:—

"'Here lies John, and with him Mary,
Cheek by jowl and never vary;
No wonder that they so agree,
John wants no punch, and Moll no tea.'"[1]

[1] Rochdale old church, as visitors to the town are aware, stands on an abrupt hill, overlooking the borough; and at the foot of the hill runs the Roach. It is among the dead on the plateau above where "Tim Bobbin" lies, and old townsmen believe it was

"No. 10. Samuel Ashworth, flannel weaver by trade; Chartist in politics. Was appointed the first salesman in the Store.

"No. 11. William Cooper, flannel weaver by trade; a member of the Socialist body. Was appointed the first cashier in the Store.

"No. 12. James Tweedale, a clogger by trade; a Socialist. Was one of the first directors in the Society.

"No. 13. Joseph Smith, woolsorter by trade; a Social Reformer. Was appointed one of the first auditors of the Society."

Mr Cooper on another occasion, with that sense of justice always a pleasant feature in him, desired me to remark that the photograph does not give all the persons then living in Rochdale who were among the early members of the Rochdale Equitable Pioneers' Society. Partly by oversight and partly by misunderstanding three are left out:—

"Miles Ashworth, flannel weaver by trade; Chartist in politics. Was the first president of the Society."

"James Maden, flannel weaver by trade, teetotaler; nothing in particular in politics or religion."

"John Kershaw, warehouseman by trade; Swedenborgian and half Chartist."

Mr. James Smithies, no less considerate and conservative of the repute of co-operative workers, sent me at my request the following notice of David Brooks, No. 5 of the series explained by Mr. Cooper:—

"Mr. David Brooks, a block printer by trade, whose name has never been mentioned in connection with the Rochdale Co-operative Society in its earliest stages of existence, rendered services of no mean order. He was the first purchaser appointed by the Society, an office which required much care and ability, besides being the butt at which the scorn and contempt of the shopkeepers was directed. He never flinched from the post assigned to him, although the foreman of the works at which he was employed was a shopkeeper; yet he still served the Store with a fidelity rarely, if ever, surpassed by a true believer in the emancipation of the working classes by their own exertions. He frequently left his own employment, at which he could then earn 7s. to 8s. per day, to work for love of the cause, until the Society could afford to pay him something like 3d. per hour for his labour. For four to five years he was superintendent and purchaser. Although, like many a flower, 'born to blush unseen,' his services

on his grave that Mr. Bright made his first public speech in the town. He was then a young man. He had come down from One Ash, his father's house, to protest against levying a church rate. "Tim" must be very proud, if he knew it, that that voice should first be heard over his head, which one day all the world would hear.

Tim Bobbin's gravestone was put down and the verses on it composed long after his death, by a distant relative. The stone, and the inscription on it, has since been renewed by subscription. Mr. John Bright did not speak from it at the Church Rate meeting. The authority to whom I am indebted for this information, stood by Mr. Bright on the top of one of the monuments in the old churchyard, from which he addressed the assemblage. Mr. Bright could not have addressed them from Tim Bobbin's stone, because it was not then raised above the level of the churchyard, and he would have been lost in the crowd, had he stood there. However, if the dead hear at all, Mr. Bright was quite near enough for Tim to be aware of what was going on.

have never been acknowledged: or rather say, until the present panic, which almost annihilated the block printing business, brought the old boy so low in his finances that a notice was given that an application would be brought before the quarterly meeting to make him a present of ten pounds, to assist him to stave off his enemy, poverty; but a generous committee did better, they found him employment at one of the Branch Stores, where he was numbered among the servants of the Society, contented to serve where he once commanded."

Mr. Smithies does not mention that it was he who made the honourable motion which brought acknowledgment and succour to Mr. Brooks in the day of his decay of means and power.

It would be well were Mr. Walter Morrison's suggestion acted on, and the old Toad Lane Store purchased by the Pioneers, and held in its old Store state, as a memorial of the early days of their career, and used as a news-room: and portraits, so far as can now be done, painted of the old Pioneers, and preserved in the hall of the old Toad Lane Store. This would be a graceful memorial, quite in the power of the great Society to preserve, and it would have infinite interest a century hence to all visitors from afar and students of the science of co-operative economy. From the public spirit of the Pioneers, it may come to pass, as it is in the power of the Store, to remain, if it chooses, the Pioneer Store of the great movement. Let us hope that the wealthy and historic Society which has grown out of Toad Lane will endeavour to possess and preserve in its original state the humble building in which the organisation of Co-operation was commenced. One of the Oldham Societies has a "conversation room;" the lower part of the Toad Lane building might serve that purpose, where questions might be continually debated, and the business meeting of the Society elsewhere would be greatly facilitated by the members being personally informed of the questions to be decided. Other parts of the building might contain the reference library, which business requires to be separate from the great library at the central stores.

The following are the names of the original Twenty-Eight:—

James Smithies.
Charles Howarth.
William Cooper.
David Brooks.
John Collier.
Samuel Ashworth.
Miles Ashworth.
William Mallalieu.
George Healey.
James Daly.
James Tweedale.
Samuel Tweedale.
John Kershaw.
James Maden.

John Scrowcroft.
John Hill.
John Holt.
James Standring.
James Manock.
Joseph Smith.
William Taylor.
Robert Taylor.
Benjamin Rudman.
James Wilkinson.
John Garside.
John Bent.
Ann Tweedale.
James Bamford.

No complete list has been given before of the "original Twenty-eight." One list wanted four names—they are given above. Mr. George Adcroft, president of the Store, in 1847, three years after its formation, has gone with me over the names of all the early members, and has decided that James Wilkinson, shoemaker, was one; John Garside, cabinetmaker, was another; George Healey, hatter, was the third, and Samuel Tweedale was the fourth, belonging to the "Twenty-eight." There were two Tweedales among them, James and Samuel. James was a clogger, and lived at the top of Wardleworth Brow, and kept a cloggers shop there. Samuel Tweedale was a weaver at King's the quaker, Oldham Road. Samuel gave the first little lecture they had in the Toad Lane Store. It was on "Morals in their relations to every day life." It was on a Sunday night. He was considered the "talking man" of the Store. He afterwards went to Australia. Among the "Twenty-eight" there were eight Jameses and seven Johns.

CHAPTER XV.

LEGAL IMPEDIMENTS TO ECONOMY.

When the Rochdale Society began, and for many years subsequent, such associations were not recognised by law. The members had no defined rights, and were under unlimited responsibility: yet they were incompetent to deal with outsiders, or even with themselves. Indeed, the cash box might disappear with impunity. The Society could not hold land above a small quantity; members could only hold a very limited sum in the funds even after the law did begin to befriend them: nor could they devote their savings to self education. Indeed, it would take pages to explain all the legal disabilities then existing. By whose generous exertions all this came to be altered is related elsewhere.[1]

Nobody understood better or cared more for the legal position of co-operation than the Rochdale Pioneers. The townsmen who had Mr. Thos. Livsey for an alderman, Mr. Cobden for a member, and Mr. Bright for a neighbour, ought to be in advance of other towns, and they were. The Pioneers, assisted by eminent friends of social reform in London, Mr. E. V. Neale, Mr. Thos. Hughes, Mr. F. J. Furnivall, and Mr. J. M. Ludlow, procured the necessary amendment of the law; and when it was done, they had the grace to distinguish who had served them and to place on record their thanks to each. On Christmas Day, 1862, an annual conference of 100 delegates from the co-operative societies of Lancashire and the neigh-

[1] History of Co-operation in England, Vol. II., Constructive Period.

bouring counties was held in Oldham. Seventy-five societies were represented. Mr. Abraham Greenwood, of Rochdale, presided. Mr. William Cooper of Rochdale, secretary of the conference committee, stated that when the previous conference met at Rochdale, on the 25th of December, 1861, the Hon. Robert A. Slaney, M.P., who had, up to that time, had the charge of their Bill in the House of Commons, was on the Continent, owing to failing health. The committee (on the approval of Mr. Slaney and the advice of Mr. Bright, who accompanied a deputation for that purpose) solicited the Government to bring in the Bill. They declined to bring it in as a Government measure, but intimated that they should not oppose it if it was brought in by a private member. Mr. Bright then recommended the committee to solicit Mr. Estcourt to introduce the Bill to Consolidate and Amend the Industrial and Provident Societies Acts. He cordially took charge of the Bill in the Commons, and the Hon. Robert A. Slaney, M.P. (who, we regret to say, soon after died), arrived just in time to second the Bill in its first reading. The committee sent three separate deputations to London, at various stages of the Bill while before Parliament, to explain it and interest Members in its favour. Besides these special deputations, their tried friend, Mr. E. V. Neale, living in the neighbourhood of London, was at call to act on behalf of the committee on other needful occasions. The Rev. W. N. Molesworth generously undertook to use what influence he had with Members of Parliament, on their behalf. During this time there was much written correspondence going on between those conducting the Bill through Parliament and the committee.

Mr. Edward Hooson, of Manchester, moved—

"That this Co-operative Conference presents its grateful acknowledgments to John Bright, Esq., M.P., for the valuable advice he tendered to the promoters of the 'Bill for the Amendment of the Industrial Provident Societies Acts;' for the great service of his personal assistance at every stage of the Bill; for arranging the interviews of the deputation with the Board of Trade, and for his indispensable offices in soliciting Mr. J. S. Estcourt to take charge of the Bill in the House of Commons—services not to be lightly estimated or the less scrupulously and respectfully acknowledged because they are such as the working class, bent upon self-improvement, can ever command from Mr. Bright."

Mr. Bright's subsequent acknowledgment of the vote was in the following terms, in a letter addressed to Mr. William Cooper, Oldham Road, Rochdale:—

"Rochdale, January 19, 1863.

"Dear Sir,—I have to thank you and the Conference of Delegates for their resolution. It sets forth far greater services than I was able, but not more than I was wishful, to render you. I hope the Bill will do much good, which will be a satisfaction to all those who supported it."

Mr. Greenwood, the chairman, moved—

"That this Conference convey to the Rt. Hon. Sotheron Estcourt, M.P., the respectful thanks of all friends of Co-operation for the courtesy and liberality with which he undertook the charge of their 'Bill for the Amendment of the Industrial Societies Acts;' giving to it the advantages of his parliamentary position, which ensured it successfully passing the ordeal of the House of Commons."

Mr. Estcourt, who was then in Italy, replied in a letter to Mr. Abram Greenwood as follows :—

"Florence, 16th February, 1863.

"Sir,—I have just received the complimentary resolution passed at the delegates' meeting of the Co-operative Societies, held at Oldham on the 25th of December, in acknowledgment of the part which I took last session in regard to the 'Bill for the Amendment of the Industrial Societies Acts.'

"I request you to convey to the delegates the satisfaction which I feel in receiving this mark of their approval; and to assure them that it was a pleasure to me to undertake the work.

"I cannot forbear reminding you that in the preparation of the Bill and in carrying it through the House of Commons I received great assistance from the President of the Board of Trade and the Solicitor General; that the able lawyer employed by the Government in preparing their measures, was allowed to revise my scheme; and that Lord Portman took charge of the Bill in the House of Lords and greatly conduced to its success by his judicious management. I am, sir, your obedient servant,

"J. SOTHERON ESTCOURT."

Mr. Charles Howarth, the earliest organising co-operator of Rochdale, moved—

"That the chairman of this Conference be instructed to convey to Lord Portman, on the part of the co-operative representatives present, their sincere acknowledgments of the great service he has rendered to the industrial interests of the English workman by his kindness in undertaking the labour and responsibility of conducting the 'Bill for the Amendment of the Industrial Societies Acts' through the House of Lords, and to assure his lordship that the co-operators of England will know how to appreciate the consideration shown to the rights of labour by the passing of this measure."

Lord Portman's answer was made in the following terms to Mr. Cooper :—

"Bryanston, Blandford, Jan. 24, 1863.

"Sir,—I have the greatest confidence in the Co-operative industrial and friendly societies, and have laboured to aid them ever since I have been in Parliament, now 40 years; so I am not likely to fail in my exertions while I have strength to be useful. Your obedient servant,

PORTMAN."

Mr. Councillor Smithies, of Rochdale, moved—

"That this Conference would ill discharge its duty if it separated without expressing its high sense of the obligations the co-operators of England are under to Edward Vansittart Neale, Esq., for the munificent interest which he has ever taken in their welfare. Especially this Conference desires to record its heartiest thanks for his legal and professional services in drawing up this 'Bill for the Amendment of the Industrial Societies Acts'—services rendered with promptness and without stint; for advice, assistance, and influence, watchfully and unintermittently given through every stage of the Bill, for which the members of every co-operative society in the kingdom owe Mr. Neale personal thanks."

Mr. Neale's answer was of a nature to add to the obligations co-operators were under to him. It was expressed in the following letter:

"West Wickham.

"Dear Sir,—I trust that the Bill which I have been instrumental in obtaining for you will inaugurate an era of genuine co-operative effort among the working men of England, whence I am certain that an incalculable amount of good of every sort will arise. But we must be patient and persevering. The great thing to impress upon the minds of the workers is the importance of seeking to raise the position of their class, instead of limiting their efforts to raising their own position as individuals. This lies at the bottom of the dispute about giving workers, as such, a share in profits. A man who has saved up a little capital may say, 'I shall get more if I take all the profits to myself.' But will his children get more? *Is it not far more important to him, as a working man, to bring about a state of things whereby his children, or other relatives, will share in the profits of capital, whatever their occupation may be, rather than to get a few more shillings or pounds a year himself;* while he leaves the present state of things unchanged for every person connected with him who has not saved up capital, or has not been fortunate enough to place it advantageously?

Very sincerely yours,

"E. V. NEALE."

Mr. James Dyson, of the Working Tailors' Association, moved the following resolution, which was seconded by Mr. Edwards, of Manchester, and carried:—

"That this Conference, composed of the representatives of Co-operative Societies, desires to express its profound sympathy with the family of the late Hon. Robert A. Slaney, M.P., in their bereavement; and further desires to convey to them its high sense of, and cordial thanks for his many and valuable labours in the Commons House of Parliament to promote the passing of laws which have given permanence and security to these societies, thus enabling the people of Great Britain to organise for the improvement of their moral, social, physical, and pecuniary condition, and for which the industrial classes will ever hold his memory in grateful and sacred remembrance."

This resolution was replied to by Captain Kenyon Slaney, son-in-law of the late member for Shrewsbury.

"Walford Hall, Shrewsbury.

"I have the honour to acknowledge the receipt of your letter of the 13th January, enclosing a copy of a resolution passed at a conference of delegates from co-operative industrial societies, held at Oldham, on 25th December, expressing in most kindly terms their warm appreciation of the services rendered to their societies by the late Mr. Slaney, M.P. for Shrewsbury, and tendering their sympathy and condolence to his family under their bereavement.

"Such a record of Mr. Slaney's services, and of the estimation in which such services were held, is most gratifying to those to whom your communication is addressed. They know full well the importance Mr. Slaney ever attached to co-operative societies, and the zeal with which he applied himself, in Parliament and out of Parliament, to promote the success of such institutions, and in all ways to advance the interests and improve the condition of the industrial classes. But it is rarely that such deeds obtain a grateful recognition like that which it is now my duty to acknowledge. I am desired to convey to the delegates of the co-operative societies, whom you so ably represent, the warm and hearty thanks of every member of Mr. Slaney's family, for the good feeling which has prompted the resolution; for the generous tribute of gratitude and regard which has thereby been offered to his memory; and for the sympathy so kindly expressed for those who mourn his loss."

In passing these resolutions of thanks, the co-operative delegates spent gratefully and honourably their Christmas Day, 1863. The North of England Wholesale Agency mentioned in another chapter was founded the same day at the same meeting.

Oldham at that time was not the most encouraging place in the world to visit on a Christmas Day, and it would be late in the evening before many of the delegates would return by rail home. When all England, that can get it, devotes itself to roast turkey, festivity, and plum pudding, it is to the credit of these co-operators that they should have given the whole day to railway journeys and prosaic delegate business. Rochdale would be sure to do its share of this work, as anyone can testify who has had personal intercourse with the Pioneers. There has been on their part a consciousness of working for society as well as for Rochdale—they desired to show what could be done—that others might be incited to do the same. *They cared for others*, and this is why so many care for them. They wished to raise the class to which they belonged. They saw that the elevation of the working men as a class was the best security for the individual advancement of its members, and it is this sentiment, more than any success, which has given to Rochdale Co-operators an honoured name.

The leading co-operators of the Society took the trouble to get the resolutions of thanks recited, as well expressed as they could. I suppose they knew that most persons carry a stock of hate on hand, and that censure is always ready made. But praise is a very different thing. It only proceeds from generosity or gratitude, and those are deliberate sentiments. A man may rage without art, but he cannot applaud sensibly without it. This is why the quality of a man's mind is more easily seen in his praise than in his censure. Defamation shows his feeling, praise his understanding; and if he wishes to give an idea of his strong sense of a service rendered him, he can best do it by showing that he accurately estimates it, and this is the only praise anyone not vain, cares to receive, or which is an actual tribute to him. The Pioneers put themselves to some cost to get their resolutions into terms which they liked. They paid me 10s. to draft resolutions which should include the individual services and characteristics of each person, so that each vote should be different, and founded on personal knowledge.

Sixteen years ago, the Pioneers made a graceful acknowledgment to the present Vicar of Spotland (who was then incumbent of that church), for kindly services to them, and which services, it may now be said, have increased with the years which have since elapsed. One day they carried to Mr. Molesworth a beautiful bound copy of the "English Hexapla," which bore the following inscription:—

"Presented to the Rev. W. N. Molesworth (incumbent of Spotland), by the Educational Committee of the Rochdale Equitable Pioneers' Co-operative Society, as a testimonial in recognition of his valuable and disinterested services on behalf of the above Society and of Co-operation generally.

"December 20th, 1861. SAMUEL NEWTON, Secretary."

The Rev. Mr. Molesworth took a personal interest in the Society almost from the commencement, and visited Mr. William Cooper, and talked to him about it. It occurred to Mr. Molesworth that he would like to be a member of it in order that he might watch its progress more closely; but he could not overlook that if he joined it, and anything went wrong with it, he would, perhaps, be regarded as morally responsible in respect to it. A person of position belonging to a society, although he had no connection with its management, would be thought to lend a sort of guarantee of its financial and legal soundness, although all he might have in his mind would be to assist a useful society calculated to promote the social improvement of working people. Besides, if a society had no legal recognition or limited liability, a person of means might be made responsible in case of losses, for which members without means could not practically be made liable. More from regard to others than himself, it is within my knowledge that Mr. Molesworth asked Mr. Cooper "whether the liability was limited." Mr. Cooper said "it was," but he subsequently found he was mistaken. Mr. Molesworth then considerately pointed out to him what an objectionable thing it was that the members of the Society should each of them be liable to the full extent of his means if anything went wrong. Mr. Cooper becoming aware of the seriousness of this state of affairs, asked Mr. Molesworth, and one or two others of the leading men of the Society, to meet at his office and consider the matter. Mr. Molesworth complied with the request, and brought with him several suggestions, which were adopted by the meeting nearly, if not entirely, in the form in which he submitted them. They were sent to Mr. Vansittart Neale, who returned them and recommended them for adoption, and in that shape they were soon after published.

CHAPTER XVI.

QUERULOUS OUTSIDERS.

It is no mean part of the art of progress to know how to treat outsiders—that is supposing you have a good cause, clear principles, and earnest advocates. Therefore let us look with curiosity and intelligence on outsiders. If conversion is reasonably treated, they will be insiders one day. Here I deal with querulous outsiders—the discontented who are not ignorant—the critics who mean mischief, and know it. They swarmed about the Rochdale Society for years. Sometimes the shopkeeper is made an angry adversary by being needlessly alarmed. A co-operative speaker will say, "Look at the great profits made at the chief stores—£20,000, £30,000, or £40,000 a year. All this is rescued from the shopkeepers." Nothing of the kind. It is by buying wholesale by combination of capital; it is by purchasers buying largely at the stores by combination; it is by economy in distribution; it is by fewer shops, fewer servants, by avoiding advertisements and costly display, that the chief profits are made. The co-operator gains by avoiding the multiplied shops, the high rents, the heavy taxes, the useless servants, the cost of advertisements, glarish lights, and loss on unsold goods and bad debts. The co-operator grows rich by picking up what the shopkeeper drops, before he touches the tradesman's actual profits.

Co-operators are merely miners in the gold fields of commerce, who find what the shopkeeper has overlooked. Many a shopkeeper is made to grieve by the idea of the loss of profits he never had and never would have had, had co-operators never been born. The co-operator mainly gains by a superior mode of business and the natural economy of concert.

The Rochdale Co-operators publish an almanack which may be taken as their annual manifesto. It records their progress and current opinions. It is compiled by various hands, and now and then an article appears on the sheet which shows that the new writer is a recent convert who fails to comprehend the traditions of this great Society. In an almanack now and then there has been an attack on shopkeepers, which a sagacious co-operator avoids. For instance, in the year 1860 almanack there was a denial of the initiative principle which makes co-operation a wholesome power. Here is the questionable passage :—

"The present co-operative movement does not seek to level the various social inequalities which exists in society as regards wealth, excepting so far as enabling the labouring man to subscribe a portion of the capital necessary: first, for the purchase of articles of consumption from those, or as near to those as possible, who produce them, so as to appropriate to himself the profits which now flow into the pockets of the retail dealers; and next by enabling him also to assist in the contribution of such capital as is necessary for the carrying on of his own industrial occupation: by this means giving him a chance of participating in the profits of his own labour, and removing it farther out of the reach of men with a little capital to realise princely fortunes out of the energy and industry of the people, while the people themselves are barely, at the best, fed and clothed for the time. In a word, the present co-operative movement does not seek to enforce, or carry out, any particular doctrines of any particular individual. This acknowledgment, on the part of the co-operators of the present day, ought to set at rest the hitherto generally believed assertion that co-operation is only the Utopian idea of such enthusiasts as St. Simon, Robert Owen, Louis Blanc, and others, and that it is on that account impracticable."

Here is a needless tribute to public incompetence. This disavowal of all the antecedents of co-operation might have answered some purpose in the struggling days of the movement. In the day of its triumph it was gratuitous. Had it not been for St. Simon, Robert Owen, and Louis Blanc, and others, co-operation might not have lifted up its head for centuries. Save for the genius of St. Simon, the princely sacrifices of Owen, the brave risks of its eloquent advocates, like Louis Blanc, hundreds of thousands of workmen who have now competence, would have died the death of a blind *proletaire*, grateful for the permission to toil, breed, suffer, and perish.[1]

This language was calculated to give the querulous outsider good heart, who would renew his attempt to damage an adversary who

[1] The editor of the almanack has given this explanation of his views :—"We were charged with 'Socialism,' and 'Communism,' and these terms amongst most of the people we wanted to reach were only synonymous with 'atheism' and 'social anarchy.' We did not care for the shopkeepers ; we knew they would always be against us from former experience ; but there were the great mass of the working people to whom we wanted to bring the benefits only a few had tasted." Had the author of this passage confined himself to pointing out that the Rochdale Pioneers were walking in a distinct though coincident, path from that described by those eminent theorists,—had he pointed out that the Rochdale Co-operators were working in the same direction of social improvement, of self-created, self-directed, self-sustained, personal prosperity, which the great thinkers who inspired them meditated, he had better defended weavers from injurious misapprehension.

was defaming himself. There were, however, it must be owned, some few cantankerous shopkeepers in Rochdale in the early days of the Store. One instance, long forgotten, belonging to the pre-store days, deserves to be told. When the flannel weavers were out on strike in 1844, they were no doubt bad customers to the shopkeepers. It is very likely the shopkeepers had no reason to admire them. No doubt their necessities developed in them a strong desire for credit, attended by feeble capacity of payment, and when the men added to their sins of impecuniosity, the actual solicitation of assistance to sustain them on strike, a shopkeeper in Yorkshire Street, in the town, of the outlandish name of Pozzi, startled the weavers. He, like Mrs. Caudle, gave them "a bit of his mind." He told them they were "vagabonds, and should go to work." They were poor, but not idle men. They were starving, but they were starving on principle. They had a spirit above vagabondage, and they determined, as they said, "to punish the shopkeepers who insulted them." Thus resentment, as well as social philosophy, had to do in promoting the Store. This was thoroughly English. Seldom does a reform in this country originate because it is reasonable. It is an outrage or an insult which generally sets the reforming conviction in a blaze. Many an early co-operative weaver, who found difficulties causing the fire of principle to grow low within him, was blown into flame again by the resentful recollection of "that Pozzi." After seventeen years, as the Store Almanack of 1860 shows, his enraging memory was fresh in the co-operative mind. Naturally the weavers on strike were under the impression that, as their wages were principally spent at the shops, it was the interest of the shopkeepers to aid them in increasing their wages. They, however, obtained but "slender assistance." Many shopkeepers had no means of aiding largely, and more had no sympathy with them, and not a few were poor themselves by reason of the credit given by them to the weavers.

But if co-operators and trade unionists can be inconsiderate, shopkeepers can be fools when they give their minds to it, and many Rochdale tradesmen have shown desire and ability to distinguish themselves in this way. In 1859, two years after the issue of the first part of this history, and when they well knew that co-operation —like John Brown's soul—"was marching on," they took the field against Richard Cobden because he was known to be friendly to co-operative workmen. At a subsequent election, the shopkeepers supported Mr. Baliol Brett, a Tory lawyer, who had never done anything and was unknown for any human service to the people. The shopkeepers of Rochdale—not all of them, but a pretty substantial crowd of them—sought to give the seat of Richard Cobden to an adventuring Conservative barrister. So far as this was done not from political coincidence of opinion, but with a view to trade interest, it was not creditable.

To be without honest principle in commerce, is to be a thief—that is what it is called in criminal courts. To be without honest conviction and clear knowledge in public affairs and prefer your private interest or ambition to the public good—that is to be a thief in politics. Neither friendliness to co-operation nor opposition to it is a reason for voting for any candidate. His general fitness to serve the country is the only ground for preferring a member, as nations go in their daily and ordinary march.

In 1859, the shopkeepers of Rochdale started a Tory gentleman named Ramsay as the Anti-Store Candidate. He was selected on the respectable principle of local politics, namely, that he had never done anything. He was the author of no public reform; he had never laboured for any popular and unfriended interest, and therefore was to be electorally distinguished for his inability. This is the way the tradesmen put him forward. I quote from one of their bills, taken from the walls and preserved for me. It runs thus:—

"LOOK OUT!

"The shopkeepers of Rochdale will do well to 'look before they leap' in the approaching struggle. They will do well to ask this important question, 'Who are the men who are thus busying themselves in adopting means to secure the election of Richard Cobden?'

"Are the shopkeepers aware that the chief supporters of the Bright-and-Cobdenite faction are also the leading members of the Co-operative Stores?

"Is it not notorious that George Ashford (and family connections), Jacob Bright, John Petrie, Pagan (and their family connections), Livsey, Kemp and Kelsall (and their family connections), who are in the Radical front ranks, are all part and parcel of these Stores—are aiders and abetters of this iniquitous system?

"Will the shopkeepers of Rochdale never take a lesson from the past? Will they never be aroused to the real state of their affairs? Will they still go on aiding the men who are fostering the system which is destined at no distant period to snatch their daily bread from their very jaws?

"If the shopkeepers of Rochdale are fully aware of all these facts will they, I ask, give the vital stab to their future prospects by deliberately voting for the Bright-and-Cobden faction?

"There is but one sane course open to them, and that is to vote for Ramsay, liberty, and justice! and not for Cobden and Livsey's pet bastile!! A SHOPKEEPER."

This precious bill bore no personal name, but the shopkeepers did not disown it. It bore no printer's name, so that its parentage could not readily be traced. The answer to it bore a pretty broad, brief, abrupt and intelligible headline; it bore also a printer's address, and was signed by several distinguished and honoured names. Here it is. I have sent the printer one of the original placards to quote from:—

"TORY LIES.

"A handbill, anonymous, and without printer's name, has been industriously circulated among the shopkeepers of this borough, seeking by absolute and positive falsehoods to prejudice them against Richard Cobden.

"The statements referred to are to the effect that the leading supporters of Richard Cobden are connected with the Rochdale Co-operative Store.

"Without expressing any opinion concerning the 'Store,' we, the undersigned, being all the persons named in the handbill, give the most unqualified contradiction to the statement, and assert that we have no connection with that establishment directly or indirectly.

"Sir Alexander Ramsay's cause must, indeed, be considered hopeless by his friends when they are compelled to resort to such disgraceful means in the vain attempt to secure their ends.

"Shopkeepers of Rochdale! don't be blinded to your true interests by the silly attempts of the Tories to throw dust in your eyes. No man has done more for the trade of the country generally, nor for the shopkeepers especially, than has Richard Cobden. Give him your votes, and show the Tories that tricks and falsehood will never succeed with honest people.

"George Ashford.
"John Petrie.
"Jacob Bright.
"John Pagan.
"Kelsall & Kemp.
"Thomas Livsey.

"Rochdale, April 18th, 1859."

The placard sent me while the contest raged bore these words: "Richard Cobden will be member for Rochdale.—William Cooper." And so it proved. Tradesmen have, however, small cause to complain if the co-operator is sometimes antagonistic to them when they play these tricks. This is a sufficient example of the cantankerous tradesman on the stump.

The chief figures which used to come into prominence in the crowd of outsiders would be newspaper correspondents and pamphleteers under the name of "Merchant," "Looker on," or, of course, "Working man," who was a favourite character in which the outsiders appeared. There was some sense in the objections which the shopkeeper put under these disguises. The stores were inefficient, and these objectors did much to improve them. In cases in which I wrote pamphlets in reply,[1] I urged upon co-operators that the thing wanted in most districts is a good central, well-supplied depôt, on the co-operative plan, which can engage and maintain a good buyer-

[1] I wrote one for the Haddersfield Co-operators.

in.[1] The goods would then be carefully selected, the profits would be higher, and the smallest store would thus be on a level with the greatest wholesale shopkeeper. But it takes time to educate co-operative societies to see their own interests. Many prefer blundering along, making bad purchases for the sake of some immediate gain, while they lose in character, and injure themselves, the members, and the cause in the long run. This short-sightedness will cure itself in time. It can be cured by patience and reason. It cannot be cured by reproaches. Every society, of course, has a right to buy where it pleases. We must wait till good sense and enlightened interest gain the day. Men like our incendiary "Working Men" appear in every place; but they get fewer and fewer as the great principle travels on. There are errors and failures everywhere, but they are eclipsed by successes so unexpected and so important, that the great Social Reform advances, and co-operation is the now accepted principle of self-help for the people.

Every society has its "Working Men" objectors. They appear in every town, occasionally of a very bad type. They crawl out of the slime of competition. Sometimes they mean well, and sometimes they don't. I have seen them before, and know what they intend to say before they speak, and it would not be difficult to answer them in the dark. In the early years of a cause it is useful to notice them, and they like it. If they write like candid men, respect them; if they do not, answer them within certain limits. Error, misrepresentation, misapprehension, and prejudice are serpents, alive at both ends. If you cut them in two, they still live; while they can wriggle, they may sting. Since, however, they are damaged when divided, it is good policy to chop at them.

CHAPTER XVII.

FOUR DANGEROUS YEARS.

When the slave war, or rather the war instigated by the Southern American party in defence of slavery, came, it was known that the Cotton Famine would follow: the mills of Lancashire and Yorkshire would stop, hundreds of thousands of families would be without work—and that meant being without food—John Bull would be short of calico, and manufacturers short of profits. Then it was predicted that co-operation would stop spinning like a top, when the momentum of working-class prosperity was withdrawn.

The political economists shook their heavy heads in their wise

[1] There was no great "Wholesale" in those days. It had not even been debated at Jumbo Farm.

way. Not the better sort, like Mr. J. S. Mill or Professor Fawcett, who often vindicated co-operation. The professor, however, sent out in "Macmillan," a small professional moan—chiefly of kindly warning, but still distrustful of the new forces of concerted industry—to stand the shock of the dangerous years coming. He said :—

"Will a body of workmen, combined in a cotton manufactory, be able to keep together during two or three years, at low profits, and withstand the difficulties of a financial crisis? This is a problem which remains to be solved." [1]

When the dangerous years (from 1861 to 1864) set in, we had *Times* correspondents writing from Rochdale. What they had to tell will be remarkable reading for many years to come. In 1862 the relief committees had not dispensed very much among the unemployed families. On December 19th of that year, the *Times* commissioner wrote from Rochdale, saying :—"It is never very easy to ascertain with any degree of accuracy the extent to which the unemployed have taxed their own resources to meet the calamity which has fallen upon them. The investments most preferred by the working classes vary in different towns. In some the savings bank is the favoured depository; in others, building and benefit societies are the fashion; and of late there has been a very general run on the co-operative associations. On this account, comparison of savings bank accounts will not always be a correct indication of what is going on. In several towns where I have inquired into the point I have found that the withdrawals in this year of distress very little exceed those of last year, and the explanation given was that the operators had just begun to withdraw their deposits in order to invest them in this new movement. In Rochdale it may be said that the co-operative societies, which are on a very large scale, have absorbed pretty nearly the whole of the savings of the working classes. There are here three great concerns managed on this principle—the Store, the Corn Mill, and the Cotton Mill, representing among them a capital of close upon £140,000."

The "problem" was getting itself "solved" pretty well, and co-operative societies had no small share in enabling the people of the two great cotton spinning counties to resist the recognition of a slave dominion. But our commissioner relates unexpected facts of the Rochdale Store :—

"Last quarter," he said, "the profit to members on purchases amounted to 2s. 5d. in every pound—in other words, for every 17s. 7d. spent the member got a pound's worth of goods; so that instead of being perpetually in debt, as in the old times, the working man who deals here is absolutely earning for himself the profit which went into the shopkeeper's pocket,[2] and probably gets a better

[1] Professor Fawcett.—"Macmillan's Magazine," October, 1860.

[2] All these profits as we have said did not go into the shopkeepers' pockets. The co-operator gets the savings by cash payments, no bad debts, by occupying cheaper shops, making no display of gas, or of goods which perish by exposure; by numerous

article into the bargain. The more comfortably he lives, the larger is his share of the profits at the end of the year. One account taken at hazard, among others which I saw myself in the books of the Store, sets the advantages of the system to the working man in a very clear light. It was that of a member who in September, 1854, had £7 10s. standing to his credit. For all the eight years he had gone on clothing and feeding his family at the Store, he had never paid in a farthing in any way to increase his account; on the contrary, he had drawn out at various times £90 odd, and yet at the end of last quarter he had £50 placed against his name. The profits on his purchases during the last eight years, with interest, had actually produced him £132 10s., or rather more than £16 a year. In all probability, if he had gone on dealing all this time at an ordinary shop he might have spent 10 per cent. more, and would have been in debt at the end of the time some £5 at the least. It is only natural that the numbers of the members and the business done should have increased rapidly, and that the working classes in different parts of the country should have endeavoured to copy the very successful model thus set up. The capital increased so fast, in fact, spite of all the extensions, that it outgrew the necessities of the Society, and it became necessary to find other employment for it. First a Corn Mill was established, which has now been at work nine years, and in 1861 made a profit of £10,000. The original capital invested here was £2,000, and it has now risen to nearly £30,000, of which £9,000 has been contributed by the Store. It does a large trade in the surrounding district, and, like the Equitable Pioneers' Store, supplies other stores round about with goods wholesale. From this the co-operators took a still higher flight, and entered on an experiment which at first sight seemed not a little hazardous. They conceived the idea of combining labour and capital, of being their own employers, and sharing among themselves the fruits of their own labour."

No more impressive account of the practical economy of co-operation has ever been given. The good sense of concerted action pays when it yields £16 a year profit to a working man's family. It is worth listening to a writer whose words have gone all over the world. He says further:—"The Co-operative Manufacturing Society, which was formed in 1857, owns now one of the finest mills in the town, fitted with first-rate machinery, and another of equal dimensions, I am told, is in course of erection. Its capital is now £68,000, and in 1861, it divided profits to the amount of £5,599. It appears to have been skilfully managed from the first, and,

customers and few servants; by buying wholesale; advantages which small shopkeepers cannot command. Owing to his greater expenses the shopkeeper does not get half the profit the co-operator makes. It, therefore, creates needless ill-will to represent that co-operative profits formerly went into the shopkeeper's pocket. Co-operators often talk in this inaccurate way, and no wonder that a writer new to the subject fell into the same language.

though it suffers in common with other concerns, it is still able to run three days a week. I wish to point out how materially the existence here of the co-operative societies must have alleviated the pressure of the distress. In its early stages the movement had to encounter no little opposition from those who scented Communism, Socialism, and all sorts of bugbears in it; but its improving effects on the character and condition of the working classes are so unmistakable that none but the most selfish could refuse it their support. Manufacturers, as a rule, prefer co-operatives as workmen; the habits of self-reliance, prudence, and order which their connection with these societies engenders raise them considerably over the ordinary class, and their economy has certainly put them in a better position to bear the strain of the times."

Thus the "problem" of the political economist got "solved." Co-operation proved to be no hothouse plant, requiring hot-air apparatus and infinite watching, forcing, and coddling; but a hale, hearty, winter shrub, which will take root in any good soil, enjoys a blast, and grows strong by exposure.

The statements in the *Times* were written by a man of ability in putting facts, and not without sympathy with self-helping sense among working people. The profit to a family of well-managed, well-sustained co-operation, was never packed into smaller compass, or brought before the public eye in a more palpable way, than in the sentence in which he says "that a single family saved as much as £16 a year for eight years, while had they continued buying at the ordinary shops, they would have paid 10 per cent. more for their goods, and have been at least £5 in debt." Here is a distinct, solid, complete, picturesque thing said. This is one of those portable statements which the most casual reader can carry away in his mind. Art in statement is like cultivated taste in exhibiting treasures; the picture or statuette must be seen with the glory of space around it. All crowding is detraction. Multiplicity is not magnificence, as the uneducated think. All details have their place in statement, and out of place they are like meaner things which crowd about the nobler, hide the proportions of beauty, and distract, torment, and outrage the trained eye. The commissioner of the *Times* notices that communicativeness of the Rochdale Pioneers which has made theirs the great propagandist Store. He remarks—"Few are so communicative as to their actual position as the Equitable Pioneers, who are too firmly established to fear even this severe strain; but the restricted trade and diminished working capital must have told on the greater number. The trade of the Rochdale Store in the twelvemonth has fallen off by about one-third on the year, and £21,000 has been withdrawn from the funds, of which, probably, £16,000 at least has been withdrawn by unemployed members in order to meet the distress. All of it has come back to the Store in the purchase of provisions, and the profits on the purchasers of the year, together with the payment of share subscriptions, reduce the actual loss of capital to little more than £1,000. There is no transfer of stock, but the rule of the Society is that any member may withdraw as much of his capital invested as he pleases down to £5, and, with the special leave of the committee, down to £2. No deposits are allowed below that amount, and those whose necessities will not allow them to stop there must draw out the whole. About 300 members have been thus compelled to leave the Society, to rejoin it, it is to be hoped, when better times comes round."

They all came back, and, as an Irishman would say, many more came back who had never left. The above statement includes particulars of the rules and practices of the Rochdale Store, which will be informing and welcome to all readers. Narrative should, like leading articles in a newspaper, resemble a Scotch house, and be self-contained. The *Times* itself became the "leading journal" by this art. When its columns were crowded for five days with reports of Palmer's trial, the leading article upon it on the sixth day, when the case ended, gave a complete account of the fat, horse-racing, rascally, surgical poisoner's trial, which the busy man could understand though he had never read a line of the reports. The article was self-contained. It was lighted up with outside facts. The above-cited passages introduce into this story details which make it complete in itself, without irrelevant and formal repetition. It is of no use listening to a speaker, or reading an author, if you require first to hear or read someone else to understand him.

But the immediate point before the reader is to understand how Rochdale stood the slave and cotton storm. Co-operation stood like the Eddystone Lighthouse—as immovable as the north pole.

In December, 1861, when the cotton panic had commenced, the cash received at the Store over their counters for the sale of provisions and other articles of household and personal use amounted to £176,000. During the year of 1865, the cash received reached £196,000, showing an increase of £20,000. Their capital in 1861 was £42,000; in 1865 it was £78,000. Four years before their members were 3,900; four years later they were 5,300, showing an increase during the panic of 1,400 members. This looks as though co-operative crafts were places of safety in a storm.

In 1862 these Pioneers built a new shop at Blue Pits. There's a name!—an honest name, however, for the pits deserve it. This Blue Pit shop cost £700. Next year they built a slaughter-house and stables, at a cost of £1,000; and also a new shop at Pinfold, which cost £1,000. This was pretty well for 1863. In 1864 they put up a Store at Spotland Bridge, at a cost of £1,500; and another in the Oldham Road, at a cost of £1,700; and in 1863 they finished the Buersil branch, at a cost of £1,000. The Pioneers modestly said that these buildings do not disgrace the neighbourhood in which they stand. The fact is, there was little or nothing to disgrace—there being no lively or inspiring buildings anywhere about—and these stores are cheerful, wholesome, and not unpleasing buildings.

The Town Hall, Rochdale, which is a municipal glory now, was not then erected.

Nor is this all. The Pioneers commenced excavations in Toad Lane (which ought to be called the Pioneers' Highway, for it goes up a hill, and they have made the hill of difficulty easy) for the purpose of erecting a great Central Store, which they hoped would be an ornament to the town. There was reason for this hope; for Rochdale needed and deserved some architectural improvement. During the four years of "famine," the members drew out £83,000; the Society having been a savings bank on this great scale. Better than this, the Pioneers gave £750 for the relief of the distressed and to other charitable purposes. And quite as honourable to their intelligence as these gifts are to their humanity, they had appropriated £1,840 to the purposes of self-education. This is enough to show that the working men of Rochdale know how to dream dreams, and that the weavers' co-operative dream turned out a substantial and instructive reality.

If the reader has the courage to go through a paragraph having figures in it (p. 142), he may see how the Rochdale Store fared in the eventful years when the slave owners fought for the whip. The odd hundreds and fractions of pounds, shillings, and pence, usually included in any financial narrative, are omitted here. The writer recognises—what is not often done—that the general reader is not an auditor. He can only take figures in the bulk. The common rule is to fill into any narrative containing figures all the minor amounts and fractions, just as though the reader was going to send for the books and go over them to test the exact truth of the statement, in which case the writer would have to wait a fortnight before the reader would be able to attend to the continuation of the argument.

In the following statement the reader will find the grand figures in one round honest bulk, with all the fractional edges chipped off, so that they will not scratch the memory nor irritate the understanding.

Returns from Rochdale show the position of co-operation in that town for the four years preceding and subsequent to the civil war in America. From 1857 to 1860 the members increased from 1,800 to 4,600, the capital from £15,000 to £57,500, the business from £80,000 to £174,000, the profits from £5,000 yearly to £15,000.

From 1860 to 1864, the full period of the cotton crisis, the profits increased in uneven gradations from £15,000 to £22,000. In 1861, the Society felt the effects of the scarcity of cotton. In the March quarter of that year the receipts for sales were £47,000; in the December quarter they had fallen to £42,000. In 1862, the cotton famine was the most severe. Two-thirds of the operatives of Rochdale were almost entirely out of work. The greater part of the mills were entirely closed, and the people had to subsist to a great extent, on their previous savings. This year the number of members of the Store decreased 500. The capital of the Society decreased £4,500. The cash received for sales decreased £32,000; yet this year the profits made amounted to £17,000. Not only did co-operation stand its ground during a period which it was supposed would destroy it, but the Store, the Corn Mill, and Manufacturing Society of Rochdale gave together £1,500 for the relief of the unemployed, and the Store alone made £70,000 profit for its members. The Corn Mill Society made £10,000 a year profit in 1860 and 1861. In 1862, the profits fell to £8,000, but next year they returned to £10,000 again. The Manufacturing Society of Rochdale kept up its full payment of wages during the cotton famine, ran more time than any mill in the neighbourhood, and subscribed £3 weekly to the Distress Fund.

These societies of working men took their place by the side of manufacturers in the mill and market, and it does not appear that they shrunk from any responsibility which gentlemen in times of public distress undertake.

Productive manufactures fared no less hopefully as far as they went. We are in the habit of saying productive manufactures, in order to distinguish production from distribution. Of course all manufactures are productive—either of dividends or deficits—and of course always create articles of utility or desire. Manufacturing, however, had not then, nor has yet, got into complete co-operative ways. The mills reputedly co-operative of that date were mainly joint-stock enterprises with a dash of co-operation in the prospectus. In 1862, manufacturing societies of this nature in Rochdale worked three days a week, which was greatly above average of the time worked by the mills of the town. In Rochdale and its suburbs there were then 93 cotton mills, rather over three-fourths of which wholly ceased working. Taking the average of the whole, they worked less than one day per week. It was a creditable and unexpected thing that a semi-co-operative manufacturing mill which, it was said, would first fall in a cotton crisis, should find itself able to work more time than any of its competitive competitors.

The question, during the distress from which the working people suffered, was as to whether co-operators were to be entitled to relief. The Central Executive Relief Committee, of which the Lord Derby of that day was chairman, considered the question of disqualifying co-operators and other persons from participating in the national subscriptions then made. It was at this time that Lord Derby presented a scheme for the equitable administration of that fund, which was marked by a generous and unforeseen discrimination which has not been forgotten to this day. Lord Derby said:—

"The co-operative societies stand upon a peculiar footing. The societies known by this name comprise provision and clothing stores and flour mills, which are conducted to a great extent on co-operative principles; but cotton manufactories, called co-operative, are generally, if not universally, simply joint-stock companies of limited liability, the capital of which has been subscribed in small shares, chiefly by workmen in the cotton districts, and which are often built and conducted with the aid of loans. They have arisen out of motives which do the highest honour to the operative classes; and there is no question but they have induced habits of frugality, temperance, and self-restraint, which have operated greatly to the benefit of the working classes morally and physically. But it is indisputable that the shares in some of the co-operative societies are at the present moment greatly depreciated, and, in some cases, actually valueless. Is, then, the possession, say, of one or more shares in one of these societies to exclude the holder from a title to relief? On the principle applied to the savings banks, the answer should be in the affirmative; and the more so, as the investment hitherto has yielded a larger interest. But it is to be remembered, on the other hand, that whatever has been invested in the savings banks realises, on its withdrawal, the whole of its nominal amount; whereas the co-operative shares are, in many cases, not only depreciated, but, if compelled to be sold, would realise little or nothing to the possessors. The utmost, therefore, which can fairly be required is, that the holder shall have mortgaged his share, and that he is not at the present moment deriving any pecuniary benefit from it. In such a case, I think the holder might fairly be entitled to relief, as having, for the time, no other resources."

Dr. Watts, at the meeting when this was read, pointed out that shares in co-operative stores were not mortgageable; and mentioned instances of great hardship where sums had to be withdrawn, at a loss, before relief could be obtained.

Lord Derby, in reply, said: "I have not even stated that those conditions should be insisted upon in all cases. The whole intention of the paragraph is to moderate the application of the strict principle."

Lord Egerton, of Talton, quoted the previous statement of the committee, that these were cases for forbearance, and that it would not be wise to discourage habits of forethought, adding:—

"I can assure Dr. Watts that it is the general opinion of the Executive Committee that these cases should meet with the greatest forbearance, and be looked most carefully to, so that those who have profited by the opportunity of laying by some small store for themselves may not, in these days of adversity, be left entirely helpless."

The co-operators were not destined to find on local committees the same sense of industrial justice as animated the committee inspired by Lord Derby. In the face of these strong recommendations the local committee turned a deaf ear to the appeals of co-operative shareholders. Hence there arose the co-operative shareholders' Central Relief Committee, which in its public address remarked:—

"The mere refusal of money is only a part of the injustice. Thus, the girls of co-operative shareholders have been refused admission into the sewing classes. The articles of clothing so generously contributed have been refused to co-operators, though frequently in greater need of them than others who obtained them. Many have their clothes in the pawnshop, and yet at the release of goods therefrom, a few weeks ago, in Haslingden, not an article was returned that belonged to co-operative shareholders."

Lord Derby took a just and considerate view of the claims of co-operators ; but the shopkeepers on the committees took a shabby revenge upon their humble rivals. But that distressed them not. They got through with cheerful hearts.

CHAPTER XVIII.

HALTING ON THE WAY.

In 1844, the Equitable Pioneers, after a long period of controversy and distrust, founded their Store upon the principle of taking purchasers into partnership. From that time is dated the successful career of co-operative distribution, which before the adoption of that principle was in most towns vacillating, uncertain, and often ignominious in its operations. Many years later, when the value of partnership in consumption had been triumphantly tested, it was resolved to apply it to productive co-operation. In 1855, steps were taken to erect a spinning mill, which commenced business with 96 looms. In 1855, there was fitted up a second mill with new machinery. The two mills were calculated to run 50,000 spindles. The principle on which this mill was founded was that of taking the labourer into partnership, and giving him a reasonable share of the profits, which were the joint produce of capital, and the industry, good-will, good skill, and the carefulness of the workmen. It was strongly hoped that the sagacity of the Rochdale men would successfully set manufactures on the same ground of equity on which they had placed distribution. The determination of the promoters of the new mills was to carry into workshops the same social advantages they had created in homes. It was believed that success in Rochdale in creating a permanent industrial partnership would have great influence in other towns. Even on the Continent the success of the experiment was inquired after with great interest. It was known as a rule that workmen made bad masters. The subjection in which they have been kept, the dependence in which they have lived, the beggarly income which, as a rule, comes to them (the lowest for which poverty and competition compel them to sell their unwilling services), the parsimony of life imposed upon them—enter into their souls and narrow their judgment of their fellows. When they become masters themselves they are often jealous of the success of their late comrades. They regard good wages for good services, which make them profit, as so much money taken out of their own pockets. They aim at getting the utmost work out of those they employ, just as the worst master under which they have served did unto them. What they wished to be done to them when they were workmen, they commonly forget to do to others when they become employers themselves. Their masters kept all the profits in their own hands, and they determined to do the same thing. Therefore, friends of industrial progress were very anxious about the success of the co-operative mill, and great admiration was expressed of the Rochdale workmen that established it, when they showed the fine spirit of founding a real industrial partnership.

This excellent and long-looked-for vision of equity and industry loomed hopefully for a time in the immediate distance, and then went out of sight again. The "share list" being open to the whole town, shares were taken up by numerous persons who knew nothing of co-operation, and by others who cared little for it, and by many who actively disliked it; and the rule giving a participation of profit to workmen was rescinded.

The two noble engines erected in the mill of 60-horse power, one named "Co-operation," and the other "Perseverance,"[1] had to be rechristened by the more revelant names of "Joint-stock," and "Greed." As soon as the facts became noised abroad, the advocates of the artisan ceased to look to Rochdale for that organisation of industry which should terminate the increasing and unprofitable war between capital and labour. Thus co-operation halted on the way.

An article upon Co-operative Societies in the *London Spectator* (April 16, 1864), made this assertion :—" At Rochdale, the system of admitting journeymen to participation in profits was abandoned after trial."

" Abandoned after trial," suggests that it had been tried and did not answer. The truth is, it was frustrated during successful trial; it was not abandoned, it was put to death.

Professor Newman observed in a communication to the present writer (Jan. 23, 1863) :—

"Co-operative manufacturing 'hangs fire' in the matter that the members' interest as capitalists overpowers their sympathy with hirelings. If it be true that, as capitalists, they gain nothing by interesting the hireling in the prosperity of the concern, this means that co-operative capital can compete with private capital on equal terms; then the problem is really simplified. Each man who saves at all may be capitalist somewhere, though he be merely hireling elsewhere ; and, by co-operative stores, and abstinence from strong drink, all who have health and youth can save. But if co-operative capital cannot—or where it cannot—compete on equal terms with private capital, it becomes the interest of the co-operative capitalists to take the hire-

[1] They first went round August 11, 1860.

lings into quasi-partnership, by some bonus or other on the general success. But, by one or both methods, I think the way is open for prudent persons whenever moderate prosperity is general. But until the townsmen understand that the cause of the peasants is their own cause, and that depression of the country people weighs down the artisans, I do not expect any general and considerable elevation."

Professor Newman, though an author upon Political Economy, distinctly recognises the interest which workmen have when they become capitalists, of taking those in their employ into partnership with them. At that time, it was believed that the partnership system had been tried in Rochdale, and that the co-operators themselves had relinquished it. Whereas, they never did so; they never mistrusted the principle—they never gave it up; it was forced from their hands in the fourth year of its trial. The co-operators, like the Swedish monarch Charles, "were overmatched, overpowered, and outnumbered." The discredit was not upon the co-operators of that day. We shall describe the class of persons by whom the evil was accomplished.

The Almanac of 1860 said:—"The object of the Rochdale Co-operative Manufacturing Society is to provide arrangements by which *its members may have the profits arising from the employment of their own* capital and labour in the manufacturing of cotton and woollen fabrics, and so improve their social and domestic condition. The profits which arise from the business of the Society (first paying interest on capital after the rate of £5 per cent. per annum) *are divided amongst the members, giving an equal percentage to capital*[1] *subscribed and labour performed.* Each member has the same amount of votes and influence, whatever the amount of his investments." In 1861 the editor of the Almanac again repeated the same clear, sensible, semi-equitable and hopeful announcement.

In 1864 the co-operators hung their harps upon the willows of Mitchell Hey, and sang no more, At the same time they gave one good-natured but instructive and disowning shriek in the Almanac. They said:—"The principal object of the founders of this Society was the equitable division of the profits arising from the manufacturing of cotton and woollen fabrics. *They believed that all who contributed to the realisation of wealth, ought to participate in its distribution. To this principle the Society has proved recreant, to the great regret of its originators.*"

When, therefore, the anti-co-operators in Rochdale took the rule by the throat which gave only a share of profit to workmen, and strangled it, the gold-tinted eye of capitalism elsewhere grew bright on hearing of this proceeding, and there was rejoicing in countless counting-houses of manufactories where men had for generations worked like horses and died like dogs.

[1] This is not co-operation proper, because it treats capital as co-equal with labour, making it a partner, instead of an agent merely. But co-operation had got no further in that day.

Early in 1860, the enemy began to appear in the field, and a great meeting was held in September in the Public Hall, Baillie Street, to discuss the question of "*bounty or no bounty to labour.*" No doubt those hideous words "bonus and bounty" were the beginning of the mischief, and made the ignorant shareholders believe they were actually giving away their money in some foolish manner. Whereas, the profits divided on labour represent the profits created by labour, over and above that which, in the long run, would exist, if the participation is withheld. An unregarded workman gives more than merely dull, sullen, careless, uninterested service, during which he conspires — by trade unions or otherwise—to extort from his employer all he can, because he believes his employer conspires to withhold from him all he is able. This sort of industry is merely silent spite. At the great meeting, all the orators of greed appeared to argue that the workman was paid the market value of his labour, and that was the fair end of him. This sort of argument was for many years in great force in the distributive stores. It was argued that the purchaser obtained in goods the market value of his money, and what more did he want? Nearly two generations of men lived and lied and died, among whom this question was argued, before they could be taught to see that, by giving customers an interest in coming to the Store, these customers would themselves, by the certainty and magnitude of their purchases, create the very profits which were to be shared among them. It will probably take as long before it will be believed that the labourer in a manufactory can equally contribute the profits accorded to him. The conditions of production are more complicated than those of distribution, and it will take time and patience to discover all the methods whereby every person engaged in a manufactory shall be induced to do his best in consideration of his being a partner in the profits. At the great meeting of 1860, the old Pioneers stood up stoutly for the maintenance of the principle which recognised the workman as a partner. One of them said: "It was the duty of the Pioneers to base a manufactory on the same principle as a Pioneers' Store. It was their duty, as the pioneers of the country, to see that labour had its due." This was the public and generous propagandist principle upon which the question was argued by the co-operators at the first great meeting. When the votes were taken, 571 were given against the partnership of industry, and 270 for it. Nevertheless, the motion was lost, as the rules require a majority of three-fourths for the alteration of any law. Two years later, the enemy having consolidated their forces, gave battle again, won the day, and put back the dial of manufacturing industrial progress for their time, so far as the example of Rochdale was concerned. As soon as this was done, the cry went forth that the partnership of labour in Rochdale had failed, and if anyone denied it, he was sharply asked the question, "If it had not failed, why was the law of participation abrogated?" A rule may be cancelled by cupidity, but it does not therefore follow that it has failed. Greed of profit on the part of shareholders may have led to procuring the abolition of a law which they thought injurious to them; and who, having power to carry out their will, were not restrained by any feeling of equity to others. It was freely said "the Society was drifting to dissolution," as members were withdrawing their shares, and placing them in other companies where no participation law was in force. Several persons really did withdraw their shares, and others threatened to do so. But no greater number of withdrawals took place than is common in large societies, and this manufacturing company could well afford to spare these retreating members; and it would have been more honourable in them who did not agree with the law, to betake themselves to some other society more congenial to their views, than remain in one they had entered, for the purpose of abolishing the fundamental principle which distinguished it. There was never ground for the assertion that the Society was in danger of loosing its members or the needful supply of capital by continuing the participation law. Many months previous to the repeal of this law, the Society ceased taking new members, and, as a consequence, declined taking additional money, except from those already members, because members and money came in so rapidly that the Society did not see how it could use profitably at the time all the capital it possessed. It was well known that large numbers were ready to come into the Society when the new list should again be opened. It is a common experience of all societies that a certain class of shareholders who want some special change made will threaten to withdraw from the Society, and, of course, they spread the report that if they do that the Society will break up. The importance of their remaining, and of having their way, cannot in their opinion be too highly estimated. Experience, however, shows that a society does not always fail because a few persons think it will, or mean that it shall, or believe that it ought to fail when they leave it. At that day various writers appeared to defend the reactionary decision of the shareholders. One would sign his letters under the mask of "Old Pioneer." This writer strongly asserted that if the "anti-bountites," as they were called, had ceased to be members, the Manufacturing Society could no longer go on. This was quite an illusion; but it would have been fortunate for Rochdale if they had withdrawn, and formed another society on the mere joint-stock plan, which they had a right to do, and might have done without reproach. Then they would have left the original Society to test itself and to stand or fall on the principle on which it was founded. The charge against the "anti-bountites" is, that when they found themselves strong enough to seize this Society, which they had not founded, they did so, and prevented an honest public experiment being tried, and brought discredit on co-operation itself among those not acquainted with the facts of the case. It was alleged that "co-operators of old standing" voted for the destruction of the partnership of labour rule. If so they never owned to it. But the main body of the old co-operators strove by every means in their power, by their advocacy and their votes, to save it. Mr. William Cooper, who was a member of the first Rochdale Equitable Pioneer Society before and during the time the first rules were drawn up, which was some months before the Toad Lane Store was opened for business, knew all the persons who drew the black joint-stock line across the Manufacturing Society. He testified at the time that this defacement was the act of the "newer members." When the disastrous night arrived which was to cast conspicuous discredit on the partnership of industry in Rochdale, 162 votes were given for the retention of the labour profit rule, and 502 for its abolition.

When the white line of partnership of labour is for the first time drawn across a manufactory, it is not a matter of rejoicing to see a black line of the subjugation of labour supersede it.

Nothing can "pay" permanently, or ought to pay, which is not conducted on a principle of fairness to all concerned in creating its value. The pyramid of gain which is not based on equity is a mere rascally pile, which an honest man would rather not touch.

On the recalcitrant night when the anti-co-operative shareholders destroyed the hopeful law of industrial partnership, the Co-operative Manufacturing Society numbered over 1,500, of whom only 664 were present. There was, therefore, half the members who either did not attend the meeting, or who attended and did not vote, and who may be classed as indifferent, neutral, or satisfied with the Society in its then form. It is some satisfaction to record that only 502 out of 1,500 members actually lifted up their hands against the recognition of the workman. If all the consequences to the credit of Rochdale which has since followed upon that step had been foreseen, many of the 502 who brought the discredit about, would, from mere pride of townsmanship, apart from any care for the working class, have withheld their votes, and gone elsewhere and founded another society. The chief movers against the workers participating in the profits were at the time well-known to be of the class of managers, overlookers, small tradesmen, and such like. The mover of the motion to rescind the grand rule, and those who spoke on the side of its abrogation, were drawn from these classes. The committee of the Manufacturing Society were not all of them co-operators, or they would have held as sacred the great law, and would have given all their interest and influence against its repeal. But the majority of the committee were themselves continually agitating against the principle to the neglect of other important interests of the Society. One who was within "The Ring," and who knew all about it, put me in possession of the facts at the time. He admitted that some of the committee were dashing, fast-going men—not the sort of men who usually cared for principle. Their favourite argument against the labourer's claim of sharing in the profits of his labour, was that of calling it a "Socialist Theory."

Of course it was a "Socialist Theory." All co-operative stores are founded on the same "Socialist Theory," which gives profits to purchasers as well as to capitalists. Shopkeepers of common-sense often act now upon the same "Socialist Theory," and give their customers a share in the profits the customers help to create. The "Socialist (manufacturing) Theory" is that the capitalist may be made more secure, and even derive increased profits by making it the interest of the labourer to co-operate with him in the production of gain.

In the great discussion which finally disestablished and disendowed the workman as a sharer in the profits of his labour, James Smithies made one of his best speeches on the occasion. Mr. Abraham Greenwood and William Cooper were amongst the foremost champions of the claim of the workmen. Mr. Holden also spoke on the same side. I possess a full report of all the speeches published in the *Rochdale Spectator* of the time, annotated with the names of all the speakers, not given.

The under-placed tables show what this Society did down to 1866, when profit was taken from the workers.

Year—July.	Funds.	Business.	Profits.
	£	£	£
1854	...	...	...
1855	...	..	...
1856	...	...	...
1857	4,351	12,081	888
1858	8,790	13,381	679
1859	25,613	16,483	1,770
1860	56,857	23,634	3,643
1861	69,317	47,229	5,237
1862	67,513	65,368	3,325
1863	82,850	86,437	3,688

This company still retains its old style of "*Co-operative* Manufacturing Society"—fourteen years after it has relinquished the principle. In the meantime, co-operation has got to re-establish the workman as a participator in manufacturing profits. Masters may go back, as we have seen at the Whitwood Collieries; but co-operators should not. The trade unionists could carry the principle; and they will do it when they get advisers who can think above the level of strikes. I have seen Dutch workmen out in the Zuyder Zee accomplish what English trade unionists have never had the courage to attempt. As yet the main hope lies among unionists. In 1872 attempts were made to re-establish co-operative manufacturing in Rochdale by commencing card-making, but sufficient capital was not obtained to keep the Society "on the cards."

In this place and elsewhere I prefer to use the phrase *claim* of the workman instead of the term "right." A right of labour, like a right in politics, is what can be got to be ruled, or conceded. A claim is what ought morally to be conceded. A right is what is conceded. But the claim holds good, and is to be persisted in. If workmen were gentlemen in means no employed would dare to disallow it.

Comments on persons who, being directors or shareholders in a co-operative company, and knowing it to be so,. and joining it as co-operators, and then turning upon the principle and betraying it or destroying it—do not apply to persons who never were co-operators or accepted honour and trust as such. They are of the joint-stock species—a different kind of commercial creature altogether. But co-operation means more and higher. It means the recognition of the workmen, not indirectly—not in some infinitesimal, impalpable, hypothetical, and abstract way—but directly, plainly, personally, absolutely, permanently, as owner of an equitable share of the profits of labour.

A co-operative society is one which shares its profits equitably with all engaged in creating them, in labour and trade.

Mr. John Bright, meeting Mr. Abraham Greenwood, conversed on the subject of the decision of the members of the Society, expressed his disapproval, and asked if it could not be reversed, and the principle given another trial. Mr. Greenwood expressed the opinion that it would be best to try the principle again *de novo*, with members who have faith in that mode of working, and that they should be more careful as to who were admitted. Mr. Bright stated that a large number of members of Parliament had taken great interest in the experiment, and that he also knew manufacturers who would have been quite willing to allow workmen to share in a certain amount of the profits if it could have been carried out without themselves taking part in the business, and if the workpeople would rely on the amounts stated to have been realised, and jealousy not allowed to interfere. Mr. Greenwood assured Mr. Bright that good workmen believed in profit sharing, and that the principle had attracted a superior class of employés to Mitchell Hey. Mr. Bright replied that if the scheme had succeeded other manufacturers would have been compelled to offer to employés some inducement for vigilance and better work; that they ought not to be paid as a gift but for making the capital of the employer more remunerative, the machinery do more work, and to exercise greater economy in the material they had to manipulate.[1]

Mr. Bright's interest in this question is one of the most honourable things in his career. Experience shows that once a social experiment which has excited great hopes has been defeated, it is seldom that the same generation try it again. It is a pity Mr.

[1] Handbook of the Rochdale Congress, 1892, by William Robertson.

Bright's advice was not acted upon. Mr. Bright never gave his advice without giving his influence. Had an attempt been made to reverse the decision against the principle on which the mill was founded, the friendly minority would have been increased and probably inspired to recommence their vital experiment.

Mr. John T. W. Mitchell, whose name the reader has seen (p. 54), was one of the promoters and chairman—the Rochdale Congress Handbook records—of this manufacturing society. As such he must have believed in profit sharing. Had he remained faithful to that principle, the wholesale society had been the promoter instead of the organised discouragement of true co-operation.

Rochdale holds much of its old ground, and goes steadily forward in many excellent ways, but the ancient enthusiasm—which pushed forward into new paths, or fought its way back to the old principles, when driven out of them by adverse votes—has not been maintained with equal conspicuousness among the new generation of co-operators; else we should have seen the great principle of self-helping industry vindicated in Rochdale before this.

CHAPTER XIX

THE STORY OF THE CORN MILL.

The murder of the equitable industrial principle effected at Mitchell Hey by the seizure and perversion of the Co-operative Manufacturing Society was noised abroad, and spread discouragement throughout the earth. It was of the nature of a compliment to Rochdale, that what was done in that town should be thought much of elsewhere. Rochdale men had come to be considered as really pioneers of industrial progress. The abandonment of co-operative principle in the Manufacturing Society was treated as a "failure" of it. It was supposed that the principle had been tried by deliberate, sagacious, patient, earnest men, who had applied all their powers to it, exhausted all their resources upon it, made prolonged sacrifices to give it effect, had afforded ample time for the experiment to be fully tested, and that the failure of the principle was decisive. It has been shown now how mistaken all these impressions were. If the people of Oldham can build a new mill every week, the increasing and enterprising population of Rochdale might surely start other manufacturing societies, and try the experiment again and again and restore and increase the reputation of that historic town.

When I went to the Industrial Exhibition at Amsterdam, owing to the interest taken in it by Mr. Somerset Beaumont, M.P., the first question put to me by Baron Mackay on the Commission of Inquiry, at which he presided, was, "Had the Corn Mill failed?" The impression in Holland was that failure had set in in Rochdale, and that whatsoever was equitable, fair, and hopeful, and of good report, had been swallowed up by the impetuous dragon of unscrupulous dividend.

The Corn Mill Society was founded, as has been related (Part I.), in 1850. An account of its first years, dated now sixteen years ago, was written by Mr. W. Cooper. The Mill began in a dainty way. The co-operators had acquired some taste by dealing at the Store, and had learned to dislike as well as detect adulteration, and resolved to imitate the successful example of Leeds, and have a corn mill of their own. The rules were drawn up mainly by the same sagacious hands which drew up the Pioneers' rules six years before (Mr. Charles Howarth's), who was a factory worker, but was also a kind of "sea lawyer" to the Pioneers. He would give his nights to the humble work of codification. It took him a long time to see his way; but he was sure to find it. He was one of those ocular men who keep on looking until they see something.

The adventurous promoters of this Mill—though it is plain sailing now, it was quite an affair of unknown navigation then—held their first meetings, as we have said, at the Elephant and Castle Inn, Manchester Road, Rochdale. Afterwards they met at the Weavers' Arms, and, finally, at the meeting-room of the Pioneer Store, Toad Lane, that Society taking twenty shares of £5 each in the Corn Mill. John Butterworth carried the first treasury box, which, Mr. Cooper records, "was not very heavy, as it seldom had more than £6 at a time in it." When a capital of £1000 was provided, steps were taken to look out for a mill. At first an old one was taken about a mile and a half from Rochdale, called "Holme Mill," at a rental of £150. Members brought in all the money they could. Among the first committee were Laurence Melladay, Geo. Greenwood, John Turner, Edmund Hartley, and John Butterworth, of the "treasury box," all of whom subscribed to the extent of their means. Others put in only a portion of their money, investing at the same time elsewhere, lest the Corn Mill should grind up with the wheat what they had put in it. Others helped the Corn Mill with their good wishes, waiting to see how it succeeded before they helped it in any more expensive way. The Toad Lane Pioneers, however, made an investment of £100 more—a good deal for them to risk when their Society was only six years old. They appointed representatives in whose name the money should be invested, a plan afterwards followed by other societies—the plan being to give one representative to every £5. Before the end of 1850, the Equitable Pioneers had thirty representatives—quite a detachment—to look after their £200. About a mile and a half from Rochdale existed a Brickfield Equitable Pioneer Society. Though fewer in numbers than the Rochdale Society, it was never behind in support of the Mill. Its members were really what have since been called "bricks." They appointed representatives and paid their investments, and when the Mill got to work the Brickfield "bricks" bought all their flour from the Mill —good or bad, none else would they sell. The Rochdale Equitable Pioneers did the same.

Some persons who joined the Mill Society, conceived a clever little scheme of getting some profit out of it. They proposed to take at a rental a portion of the Holme Mill, with turning power for willows to break up cotton or other waste. As this scheme promised to lessen the risks of the Society by lessening its rental, all the timid members were likely to be influenced by it; while others wisely contended that the dust from the waste would get into the flour, and their customers might reasonably object to eat a mixture of cotton waste and wheat. After argument enough to turn a dozen corn mills, it was decided not to re-let.

The Pioneers' Almanac, in due course, set forth touching the Corn Mill: "The objects of this Society are to provide for its members and those who trade with it, pure, wholesome, and unadulterated flour at a price and quality equal to what can be done by any miller in the neighbourhood, and divide the profits arising from the trade amongst the members, in proportion to the amount of money expended, having first paid interest upon capital after the rate of five per cent. per annum."[1] The laws by which the Society is governed are the same in principle as those of the Equitable Pioneers, save in the exclusion of labour from profit.

In 1861, for the first time, the words "after the rate of five per cent. per annum" were changed into "after the rate of £5 per cent. per annum." The Toad Lane Store had been going sixteen years then, before it was discovered that an abstract statement of financial profits was not intelligible to the concrete minds of Rochdale. The increasing number of outsiders who were beginning to come into the stores and buy of the Mill did not quite understand what "five per cent." meant—they perfectly understood what "£5" meant. It takes a long time to acquire the art of making things plain.

Never was there a more obstinate corn mill than that of Holme. The flour would not be good—the mill would not pay—and the profits would not come. The first report of the Society was ashamed to show itself; the second, of June, 1851, showed a loss of £103; the third report, of September, showed a loss of £338 on the quarter's transactions. A total loss of £441 attracted an army of croakers. Mr. Darwin would have had no difficulty in tracing the

[1] This is so far the right form of productive co-operation; it hires capital and divides all profits among the purchasers who make it. But the Almanac is silent as to including the workmen.

descent of all of them in a town which had produced Toad Lane. But the croakers were not born round the mill. The Pioneers were said to be blundering. It was plain to everybody they did not understand corn milling. Their manager had mismanaged. The Society discharged him, and the directors and president, Mr. Abraham Greenwood, went to market themselves, taking a miller with them to judge the quality of the grain they bought, and they managed without a manager.

A revolutionary meeting was held at the Pioneers' meeting-rooms, when the prophets of evil were, as is their wont, eloquent in favour of running away. Some members argued that they had better give up supporting the Corn Mill; that the Store, by selling only the Corn Mill Society's flour, was losing its custom; that the Corn Mill Society was losing money, and could not be made to pay, and that the Mill would go down, and the Store had better shake the Mill off, buy their flour wherever they could buy it cheapest and best, else the Mill would drag the Store down along with it. Others maintained that private individuals could make it do, and get a fortune out of the business, and why not co-operators? The causes of the losses were shown to arise from shortness of money to work the business with, necessitating them to take grain from those factors who would give them credit, when sometimes that wheat was neither the best nor the cheapest; from neglect or want of skill, or both, in the head miller; and from want of better support from the members and stores. It was also said by others that if the Corn Mill Society was to fail, it would be a severe test for co-operation in Rochdale, for how would confidence in the Rochdale Equitable Pioneers' Society be maintained, when the members could be pointed to one Co-operative Society in the town that had already failed? We have related already how there came into play that vigorous sense and talismaniac faith of the Pioneer idea. Mr. James Smithies contended that duty, the honour of co-operation and pioneership, called upon them not to forsake the Mill. A majority voted in favour of continuing it. Some of the opposition shook their heads, and said the majority would not see their folly until they had brought ruin to the "Pioneers' Society." But though the Corn Mill Society had got one favourable vote in the Pioneers' Society, it was not yet safe; for an unfavourable one might be passed at some other meeting of the same Society. Parties went about enthusiastically crying the Mill up, while others were hysterically crying it down. As the same members belonged to the Corn Mill Committee and the Store Committee, they had to run from one room to another to divert an adverse vote. Mr. Cooper gives a picture of the social difficulty of doing this—one of those transcripts of the domestic sacrifices of reformers seldom brought into sight, though an important part of social history:—

"There were the monthly meetings of each of the societies, besides occasional special meetings, and two officers had to attend committee meetings one night, often more, in each week. Of course the men would be away from home while attending these meetings. The wife, who is mostly as good a supporter of the mill as her husband, generally putting up with the flour when it was not so good as it ought to be; and when she had a nice baking bread showing it to all neighbours and comers—that they might be convinced what good flour the Corn Mill Society was making. Certainly some husbands would find fault with the wife when the bread was not good, and say 'she had spoiled the flour,' to which some wives would reply, 'they could bake as well as other people if they had the same flour, and that they would not use the Corn Mill Society's flour if they were to be grumbled at because they could not make good bread out of bad flour.' The husband would be from home while attending meetings, the wife had to put the children to bed, and would be waiting with no one to speak a word to her, until the husband came from the meeting. All would be silent except the constant tick of the clock, the rain battering against the windows, and the wind whistling and howling as if it had risen in revolt against the restraints imposed upon it by nature. To the wife alone, minutes seem as long as hours, she thinks she is neglected, her husband attending meetings, or anything else rather than home. At another house little Elizabeth has been sickly some days, and father has been at work all day, and now, when his work is done, he has gone to the meeting. The mother cannot get the child to rest—she thinks it is getting worse, When the husband comes home, she tells him how sickly the child is, and that he ought not to have gone to the meeting—indeed, if he had any thought for the child he could not go. He tells her he has come home as soon as the meeting was over, but he cannot persuade her that he ought to have gone at all. He believes the child will be better in a few days, and promises to help her to nurse and take care of her till it is so. These, or many similar incidents, will have occurred to most persons engaged in promoting social or other reforms. But it must not be said that the women are opposed to co-operation; they are and ever have been as much interested and as zealous of its success as the men. There are many instances where the husband was lukewarm and the wife could not prevail on him to join the Co-operative Society, but she was not to be baffled, so she enters the Co-operative Society herself. After a while, the husband thinks he should like to have his name on the books. The wife will then withdraw so that he may take her number, or he will be proposed, and they will both become members."

By the end of 1851 fifteen co-operative stores traded with the Corn Mill. By the end of 1852 they had increased to fifty-two. Among the individual members of the Corn Mill, in its struggling days, were Mary Hawkes and Elizabeth Stott, James Smithies, Abraham Greenwood, William Cooper, and others familiar to the reader. In the first year Samuel Ashworth, Thomas Barlow, John

Grindrod, John Collier, John Pickles, Edmund Hartley, George Holt, Edmund Rhodes, John Clegg, and William Cooper had each £10 in the Mill, which meant a good deal in those days.

There was real difficulty about the flour. Besides its sale not making profit, it was not good—bad wheat being often bought; and when it was really good, numbers of the customers disliked it. It was not so white as that to which they had been accustomed. They called it "yellow flour." It had a cream-coloured look, instead of the nice alum colour with which they were familiar. They did not know good flour when they saw it, and did not like it when they tasted it. They had never known the taste of pure flour, and it took a long time to educate their taste. In taking the falling fortune of the Mill into his hands, Mr. A. Greenwood had to learn the art of buying wheat and the trade of milling, and the proper management of a flour mill. These difficult duties discharged, in addition to those in a mill of a very different kind where he was employed, made serious inroads both on his time and in his health. For some years the consequences were serious to him. He, however, succeeded in mastering the business, and pioneered the Mill out of its difficulties. Mr. Robert Hoyle, Richard Hoyle, William Ellis, William Taylor, and others, by enthusiasm and address aiding, it came to pass that the first quarter in which the Society had no manager it made a profit of £20.

We now arrive at the time, plain, tame, prosaic-looking 1855, when the Weir Street Mill first entered into the human mind—that is into that part of the human mind which understood co-operative enterprise in Rochdale. The fixed stock or fittings and machinery of the Holme Mill, where the Corn Mill first commenced business, cost £1,275. It really cost four shillings and a penny more (I mention the 4s. 1d. lest anyone should impugn the accuracy of this narrative). In the early part of the Society's operations nothing could be set aside for depreciation, owing to losses. When better days came, the losses were cleared off, which was done before any dividend was paid. At every subsequent report of the Society, £50 or £100, and sometimes as much as £300, were set aside for wear and tear, and by the end of 1855, everything had been paid for, excepting an amount of £27.

In 1856 a new mill and machinery was established at a cost of £6,827 16s. 10½d. (mark that "halfpenny!") The co-operators knew exactly what the Corn Mill cost them. It has since been known as the "Rochdale District Co-operative Corn Mill Society's New Mill, Weir Street, Rochdale." According to the engraving which represents it, and which I published at the Fleet Street House, sixteen years ago, it is the most melancholy mill that ever made a dividend. Dark, thick, murky clouds around it, and the sky line as grim as the ridges of a coffin. The white glass of the plain front meets the eye like the ghost of a disembodied factory. A dreary waggon, carrying bags of corn, guided by drivers that look like mutes, is making its way through a cold, Siberian defile. The builder might have made it pleasant to the eye, with as little expense as he made it ugly. But in those days nobody thought of comeliness, seemliness, or pleasantness in structure, in which men would work all their lives. The really pleasant part about the Corn Mill was in the minds of the gallant co-operators who set it going, and kept it going.

The Almanac repeated that, "The objects of this Society are to provide its members, and those who trade with it, with *pure, wholesome,* and *unadulterated flour.* The profits arising from the trade are divided amongst the members, in proportion to the amount of money expended, having first paid interest upon capital (nothing to the workmen) after the rate of £5 per cent. per annum. The laws by which the Society is governed are the same in principle [which was not the case] as those of the Equitable Pioneers."

The wise practice of reducing the cost of the mill by reserves made for depreciation was continued, so that in 1860, when the mill could be sold under the hammer for £6,000, it stood in the books as an asset at £3,862 only.

At the quarter ending June, 1860, the amount of business done at the melancholy mill amounted to £33,140. The Directors then announced that "it had then become obvious that their present mill and machinery could not be extended much farther with advantage." At that time the number of members was 550, the representatives of stores and sick and burial societies included. It was for the benefit of these societies that they should invest their accumulated funds in co-operative undertaking; for, at the bank, they only obtained two or three per cent. on their deposits, and they knew nothing further about their money, except that they had left it there. Being men of inquiring minds, they did not quite like this mystery about their money. At the co-operative societies they could get five per cent., and know where their money was, and what it was doing, and have votes in the management of the society, so as to make sure their money was doing well. Of course, it took some trouble to persuade the members of sick and burial societies that it was safe to invest their funds in the Corn Mill. It was necessary that they should be satisfied on this head, for if they had much anxiety about their money the Directors themselves might become sick, and, being sick, not get better, and then the Burial Society might have to inter the Directors. When the Corn Mill had been some four or five years at work, a lodge in the town took courage and voted to invest some of their money in the Mill, and appointed three representatives to take it. Mr. Cooper relates that, "when they got there and saw the committee of the Mill they durst not leave the money." Perturbed, confused, and not knowing how to explain their impressions, they retired shambling, suspicious, and speechless. They went back to their lodge, where they appeared like the Provost of Linlithgow, looking as though they had been "touched by a tor pedo, or seen of a wolf," and related that "they had beheld weavers sitting on the Corn Mill committee, and that none of the committee were rich men, so they had brought the money back to the lodge that it might be safer than in the hands of working men." They had been swindled by gentlemen before, as when the Savings Bank in the town failed, and brought dismay into thousands of poor families; but they had never been swindled by working men, and so they thought it a sort of duty to lose their money by respectable defaulters only. The lodge, however, took a more common-sense view of the matter. They held a consultation upon the subject, and came to the conclusion that weavers were as fit to be trusted as bankers. They appointed fresh representatives with a little more courage, and sent more money by them than they had entrusted to the first downcast set. It was all invested, and ever after it remained.

In later years the Almanac gave this pleasant report of its progress:—"This Society, although one of the most delicate in its infancy, has now grown to be one of the strongest and most healthy. About seven-eighths of the business done is with co-operative societies, there being about 50 who trade with it. It supplies its members, and others who trade with it, with pure, wholesome, unadulterated flour meal. Some people have objected to the flour from this mill, simply because, when supplied to them pure, it did not look so well to the eye when baked into bread; we know that when they have been most deceived they have been best pleased. Those who choose to adulterate for themselves can do so. The gradually increasing business has necessitated an increase in the productive power; consequently the Society added in 1862 (to its previous working plant) one 25-horse-power steam engine, and six pairs of French stones, which are now at work helping to supply the increased demand. It has also erected in the past year three cottage houses."

The difficulty about adulteration, which for a time was so serious, the Society had quite overcome, and was even vivacious about it. The members had become more intelligent; they had learned the nature of good flour when they had it; their tastes were better educated than that of many gentlemen of the middle class, and the Directors were able to tell the purchasers, in a reckless manner, "if they wanted to adulterate the flour they could do it themselves." The Society took upon themselves the responsibility of advising the formation of corn mills in different parts of the country where there were co-operative societies to support them. The propagandist sentiment has always been one of the honourable distinctions of Rochdale. For this purpose they consulted Mr. John Holmes, of Leeds, always a copious, fertile, quaint, and willing illustrator of co-operative principles. He had had great experience with the Leeds Corn Mill, of which he was a trustee. He explained that it may be taken as a general fact that 1,000 families would *not* support a corn mill, 2,000 will *probably* do it, and 3,000 families would be *certain* to do it. Of course this applied to demand alone. At Leeds the mill would not have paid with 1,000 members. At Garforth, near Leeds, where there were 1,500 members, the mill barely existed. At Rochdale, they fared better with 2,000 members, but then they sold to the public also. As to funds, the Leeds Society started with 21s. per member, and with this 1,000 could trade. Perhaps with a mill hired they might find machinery for 1,000 members for £2 each, or 2,000 for 30s. each; but for a freehold mill and works 2,000 people will require 50s. each, supposing all was done *well* and *cheaply*. A mill could not be built, including ground and machinery, for less than from five to seven thousand pounds, to grind for 2,000 people.

The conclusion to which the Rochdale people came was, that in any district where there are a group of co-operative stores not more than eight or ten miles distant, having altogether three thousand members, and these societies would furnish a capital of, say, 25s. per member, they would be safe in renting a mill and fitting the same up with their own machinery. The cost would be greater now.

The progress and fluctuations of the "Rochdale District Co-operative Corn Mill, Limited," is best told in its Almanac reports of 26 years.

Year.	Funds.	Business.	Profits.
	£	£	£
1850		None.	
1851	2,613	*	† None.
1852	2,898	7,636	336
1853	4,143	16,679	208
1854	3,971	22,047	557
1855	4,626	28,085	1,376
1856	8,784	38,070	773
1857	10,701	54,326	2,007
1858	14,181	59,188	3,135
1859	18,236	85,845	6,115
1860	26,618	133,125	10,164
1861	29,600	166,800	10,000
1862	30,254	155,696	8,227
1863	41,714	152,492	10,138
1864	46,739	141,309	7,806
1865	55,261	148,533	12,511
1866	72,020	224,122	18,163
1867	89,000	357,440	15,000
1868	86,400	349,439	4,824
1869	95,961	219,674	None.
1870	56,000	185,603	None.
1871	63,570	190,751	3,661

* Account mislaid. † Loss £441.

Year.	Funds.	Business.	Profits.
	£	£	£
1872	64,692	215,238	3,133
1873	67,898	241,399	5,145
1874	71,294	244,181	6,474
1875	79,615	204,242	2,532
1876	77,279	176,671	3,370
1877	78,234	252,045	5,333
1878	83,985	285,920	3,860
1879	88,857	270,037	5,822
1880	97,414	301,835	7,989
1881	96,609	299,670	6,933
1882	99,885	286,968	2,144
1883	101,323	259,397	3,295
1884	101,850	209,910	1,543
1885	99,980	192,632	None.
1886	95,319	167,654	330
1887	87,868	148,726	None.
1888	88,198	183,524	44
1889	85,340	196,067	Loss, 2,642
1890	86,899	235,274	4,510
1891	93,122	315,598	9,022
1892	103,358	254,061	2,384

CHAPTER XX.

THE ORIGIN OF THE "WHOLESALE."

ONE of the distinctions of Rochdale is that it gave practical form and force to the idea of a Federation of Purchasers, which ultimately took the style and title of "The North of England Co-operative Wholesale Society," otherwise known as the Great Manchester Wholesale Association.

Of course no one foresaw the great ascendancy which one day would be attained by this Society. It is very seldom that anyone does see the ascendancy of anything while it is upon the ground. When it is soaring over the mountain tops, the prophets of its failures declare that they predicted its rise, and now believe they made it float.

Of course somebody began everything, and we shall see in due course to whom the originating the wholesale ought to be mainly ascribed.

Mr. A. Greenwood's own history of attempts to promote a wholesale agency, given in his published "Plan," on which the Purchasing Federation of the north of England has been founded, relates that "an attempt in that direction was made (1850) by the Christian

Socialists, conspicuous amongst whom were Edward Vansittart Neale, Professor F. D. Maurice, the Rev. Canon Kingsley, J. M. Ludlow, Thomas Hughes, Q.C., J. F. Furnival, Joseph Woodin, and Lloyd Jones. They instituted the Central Co-operative Agency for the purpose of "counteracting the system of adulteration and fraud prevailing in trade, and for supplying to co-operative stores a quality of goods that could be relied upon, and in the highest state of purity." The agency did not succeed, and had to be given up, entailing great loss to its promoters. There was a remnant of the agency left, known as the firm of Woodin & Co., Sherborne Lane [now of Archer Street], London.

The main object here is to trace the part Rochdale took in giving effect to the idea. The records preserved in the long-buried pages of Toad Lane minute books were never very ample. Mr. Smithies, who was the secretary of the Store in its earlier days, had the Pioneer way of no more wasting words than money. Frugality in speech is certainly a virtue, though not usually counted in the list of meritorious economies. Mr. Bamford remarks that "Mr. Smithies evidently never contemplated any one looking up his records for information in after years." Writers of minutes in these days might check some tediousness by noticing to this effect Mr. Smithies' muscular brevity of style. The first entry concerning the wholesale was made in July, 1853, to this effect:—"That Joseph Clegg look after the wholesale department." There either was then a wholesale of some kind in existence, or one was there and then agreed upon; but only Dr. Darwin himself could trace the descent of the wholesale species from anterior records here. Mr. Bamford conjectures that the resolution refers only to the drapery department, as there are frequent references to the drapery business suggesting it. At a general members' meeting on September 18th of the same year, it was resolved "to accept the terms of the conference, and become the Central Depot." This conference is one supposed to have been held at Leeds. At a general meeting of members, held the following month, October 23rd, 1853, the first laws of the wholesale were adopted. The terms in which they were expressed have interest now. They were as follows:—

"1.—The business of the Society shall be divided into two departments, the wholesale and the retail.

"2.—The wholesale department shall be for the purpose of supplying those members who desire to have their goods in large quantities.

"3.—This department shall be managed by a committee of eight persons and the three trustees of the Society, who shall meet every Wednesday evening at half-past seven o'clock; they shall have the control of the buying and selling of such goods as are agreed upon by the Board of Directors to be kept in stock by that department. This committee shall be chosen at the quarterly meetings in April and October, four retiring alternately.

"4.—The said department shall be charged with interest after the rate of five per cent. per annum, for such capital as may be advanced by the Board of Directors.

"5.—The profits arising from this department, after paying for the cost of management and other expenses, including interest aforesaid, shall be divided quarterly into three parts, one of which shall be reserved to meet any loss that may arise in the course of trade, until it shall equal the fixed stock required, and the remaining two-thirds shall be divided amongst the members in proportion to the amount of their purchases in the said department [leaving out the workers]."[1]

(Signed) John Cockcroft,
Abraham Greenwood,
William Cooper,
James Smithies, *Secretary.*

Of course these rules had to be registered, and it is not until the first Board meeting in 1855 that any reference is made to them, which is done in these words :—"Resolved,—That we now go on under the new laws." A quarterly meeting in February following confirmed this resolution. The next clear reference to the wholesale of that day was in a minute of a quarterly meeting held April 2nd, 1855, appointing the following persons as a wholesale committee :—Thomas Hallows, Ed. Farrand, J. K. Clegg, Jonathan Crabtree, Jno. Aspden, James Meanock, Charles Clegg, and Ed. Holt. At the Board meeting held April 5th, 1855, the following minute was passed :—"That the Board meet the wholesale committee next Wednesday night, at half-past seven." The fluctuating fortunes of the earlier wholesale experiments were many. In the minutes of the Board meeting held November 8th, 1855, it was resolved, "That a special meeting be called to take into consideration the propriety of altering the law relating to the wholesale department." On December 17th, of the same year, the committee resolved: "That it is the opinion of the Board that the 15th, 16th, and 17th laws, relating to the wholesale department, ought to be repealed." At the ensuing quarterly meeting (January 7th, 1856), at which Mr. Abraham Greenwood was elected president, the seventh resolution is "That the wholesale department *be continued;*" and a committee of seven were appointed "to inquire into the grievances complained of in the present system of carrying on the wholesale department." The following persons constituted the committee :—Samuel Stott, John Morton, John Mitchell, Edward Farrand, John Nuttall, James Tweedale, and A. Howard. On March 3rd, 1856, the following were appointed delegates to attend a Wholesale Conference :—Abraham Hill, David Hill, Samuel Fielding, and William Ellis. No mention is made of the place where the conference was held, but the scheme of a new

[1] This plan bears resemblance to that Mr. L. Jones drew up, which probably the devisors had before them, as Mr. Smithies had once copied it out. Mr. Jones' plan divided profits into four parts, devoting one to the establishment of working men's association in connection with co-operative. The Rochdale plan drops this out and in other respects introduces local features and simplifications.

wholesale society appears to have been discussed there, for at the quarterly meeting held April 7th, 1856, the members passed the following resolution:—"That our delegates support the proposition of each member taking out four shares of £5 each for one representative, at the Wholesale Conference to be held on April 12th." At an adjourned meeting the report of the committee appointed to inquire into certain grievances was accepted with thanks. At a general meeting held May 5th, 1856, the following persons were appointed on the wholesale committee:—Thomas Lord, Edward Lord, William Huddlestone, and Jonathan Woolfenden. At the next Board meeting a committee appears to have been appointed to draw up rules for a wholesale society, but the names are not given. At the next quarterly meeting these rules appear to have been considered, as there is a resolution expunging the word "suggest" from rule 25. The following resolution was also passed:—"That our Society invest £1,500 in the North of England Wholesale Society." Mr. Jonathan Crabtree was appointed the representative. The earlier years in which the wholesale project was maturing will be of more interest hereafter than now.

On July 7th, 1856, there is a resolution of the quarterly meeting, empowering the delegates to the Wholesale Conference "to support the laws drawn up by the committee for a wholesale society, at the next delegate meeting to be held on July 12th, 1856." On September 4th, 1856, the Board gave Mr. Cooper authority "to collect the expenses incurred by the wholesale depot from the various stores." On December 7th, 1857, the following persons were appointed a committee "to inquire into the wholesale department":—William Diggle, Samuel Fielding, Matthew Ormerod, David Hill, and Edmund Hill. The report of this committee was presented to the quarterly meeting on January 4th, 1858, and it was decided that the report "be legibly written out and posted in some conspicuous place, to be read by the members, and reconsidered at next monthly meeting." The next resolution passed at the same meeting is, "That the laws relating to the wholesale department be suspended for an indefinite period." The Board, at its meeting three days afterwards, decided "That the resolution of the quarterly meeting respecting the wholesale department be carried out forthwith." One of the minutes at the adjourned quarterly meeting, held March 1st, 1858, is, "That the report of the committee appointed to inquire into the wholesale department be not received."

At the conclusion of the ordinary business of the quarterly meeting, held April 5th, 1858, the meeting was made special "for the purpose of rescinding the laws relating to the wholesale department, numbered 13, 14, 15, 16, and 17." The meeting does not appear to have done what it was called to do, however, for the decision it came to was "That the wholesale department be not altered." The interpretation of this, Mr Crabtree thinks, is that we will not kill the Rochdale wholesale department, but let it die quietly. No further reference is made to it till March 7th, 1859, when a general meeting passed the following resolution :—"That the question of re-opening the wholesale department be postponed to an indefinite period." This is the last reference the minutes contain to the wholesale in connection with the Equitable Pioneers' Society. In 1863, during the formation period of the North of England Society, delegates appear to have been regularly appointed at Rochdale to attend the meetings, and considerable interest was manifested.

These were the Aztec days of the wholesale idea. The giant we now know was not yet born. Failure of the idea which cost so much to carry forward, came in London, as the reader will see below. Fluctuation beset it in Rochdale. At length a new wholesale arose, whose statue was as that of Og, King of Bashan, nine cubits and a span (Was not that his measure ?).

The effort made by the Equitable Pioneers' Society in 1852, by initiating a wholesale department (as has already been related), originated for supplying goods to its members in large quantities, and also with a view to supplying the co-operative stores of Lancashire and Yorkshire, whose small capital did not enable them to purchase in the best market, nor command the services of what is indispensable to any store—*a good buyer*, who knew the markets, and *what*, *how*, and *where* to buy. The Pioneers' Society invited other stores to co-operate in carrying out practically the idea of a wholesale establishment, offering at the same time to find the necessary amount of capital for conducting the wholesale business. A few stores did join, but they never gave that hearty support necessary to make the scheme thoroughly successful. Notwithstanding this counteracting influence, the wholesale department, from the beginning, paid interest, not only on capital, but dividends, to the members trading in this department. However, after a time the demon of all working-class movements hitherto—jealousy—crept in here. The stores dealing with the wholesale department of the Pioneers' Society thought it had some advantage over them ; while on the other side, a large number of the members of the Pioneers' Society imagined they were giving privileges to the other stores which a due regard to their immediate interests did not warrant them in bestowing. Mr. Greenwood's opinion is that the Central Co-operative Agency and the Equitable Pioneers' Wholesale Department must inevitably have failed, from their efforts being too soon in the order of co-operative development.

The above is as brilliant a bit of genuine trade jealousy as the reader will meet with in ten years' reading. If a society purchasing from the Pioneers got an advantage thereby, what did it matter that the Pioneers got an advantage also ? If they did not they ought, as it would be a security that the arrangement could be maintained. Discontent may be founded on facts, and well founded thereon ; but jealousy, vigorous and virulent, is best sustained on entire ignorance, and generally begins by imagining its facts—a good plan, too, because then you get them to your mind. Thus it came to pass that the Pioneers' wholesale scheme, like that of the London Central Agency, disappeared. Mr. Greenwood, with clear discernment, saw that both the London and Rochdale wholesale projects must fail, being too early in the field. When the London Central began there were not sufficient stores in England to support it, nor when the Rochdalians renewed the attempt in 1852. Therefore Mr. Greenwood waited ten years, until 1863, when there were 300 co-operative stores in the United Kingdom, when he demonstrated the possibility of successfully commencing the great North of England Wholesale Society.

The argument by which Mr. Greenwood commended the new plan of 1864 was of the same texture as the addition table, usually considered a trustworthy material. There were in 1861 in the adjacent counties of Lancashire, Yorkshire, and Cheshire, 120 stores, and an aggregate of 40,000 members; 26 of the largest of these stores did business to the amount of £800,000. It was, therefore, calculated that if the weekly expenditure of 40,000 members averaged 10s. weekly (and it was known to exceed that), it would represent £20,000 weekly, or more than one million a year. There was plainly, then, an ample field for a wholesale agency to act in.

A calculation was made by Mr. Greenwood of the quantity of commodities of the grocery kind required to supply the 40,000 members of co-operative stores then associated in the northern districts. The calculations were made on the data of goods actually sold in one quarter at the Rochdale Pioneer Society, in 1863, when it had 3,500 members. This was it:—

Kinds of Articles.	One Week's Consumption.	Weekly Money Value.	Yearly Money Value.
	lbs.	£	£
Coffee	6,923	266	13,832
Tea	5,951	991	51,532
Tobacco	4,125	825	42,900
Snuff	108	22	1,144
Pepper	243	15	780
	Cwts:		
Sugar	1,400	3,500	182,000
Syrup, &c.	400	350	18,200
Currants	107	160	8,320
Butter	717	3,440	178,880
Soap	338	524	27,248
	Totals	£10,093	£524,836

There are mentioned in the tables several articles any one of which would of itself be sufficient to make an agency profitable. The agency would, at the beginning, supply those articles only upon which there was a sure profit. It will be seen from the statistics given that the state of the movement permitted, and, in fact, warranted, a further step being taken in wholesale progress.

That was Mr. Greenwood's argument. Within the knowledge of the new race of constructive co-operators, the wholesale house has been twice put up, and had come down again, because it had not sufficient solid ground to stand upon. So far as it was in my power to encourage those attempting to establish the co-operative wholesale, I did it by advising them ever to plead that they were simply re-establishing it. The best way of inclining the timid and unenterprising to attempt a new thing is by showing them that it has been done before, or how nearly it has been done already.

> "Men must be taught as though you taught them not,
> And things proposed as new as things forgot."

No doubt, in this way, we actually encouraged people to suppose that nothing original or distinctive was being accomplished. Since it required careful financial demonstration and much perseverance to prove and enforce it, it was practically quite a new adventure.

The Rochdale Pioneers' Society had then nine grocery branches, all supplied and managed from the Central Store in Toad Lane. The transactions between the branches and the Central Store are very simply managed. The head shopman at each branch makes out a list of all the things wanted on a form provided for the purpose, and forwards it to the Central Store. The manager upon receiving it gives directions to the railway or canal company, where the Store goods are lying, to send the parcels of articles required to each branch named on the delivery order. The Central Store in Rochdale stood in precisely the same relation to its branches as the proposed agency would do to the federated societies.

Mr. Greenwood pointed to this accomplished fact, and it was finally resolved to attempt for the third time the formation of a new wholesale agency. A company was formed under the title of the "North of England Co-operative Wholesale Industrial and Provident Society Limited." The Wholesale has now become like the historic and untraceable Nile—the Lord of Stores, as Mr. Stanley calls the great river the Lord of Floods. By the assistance of explorers, Mr. S. Bamford, Mr. James Crabtree, and Mr. A. Howard, as adventurous in their way as any who have preceded Mr. Stanley, we h .ve been able to trace the sources of the great commercial water which irrigates all the stores it touches, as the Nile itself irrigates the shores it laps.

There were in the Rochdale Society, in 1864, when the Manchester Wholesale took a tangible shape, many who had steadfastly opposed the development of the wholesale department. These belonged largely to the new members, who did not look with favour upon the establishment of a Wholesale Society at all, and, although not strong enough to prevent the Rochdale Society from taking up shares, were successful in hindering the development of a business connection such as the movement naturally expected from Rochdale. The influence of Rochdale in the wholesale appears in this, that it looked to Rochdale for officers. Mr. Samuel Ashworth, the manager of the Rochdale Store, was solicited to take charge of the Wholesale Society's business in Manchester. The wholesale department in connection with the Rochdale Society had ceased operations at that time. He was unwilling to go unless the committee of the Rochdale Society would undertake to reinstate him in his position provided the experiment did not succeed.[1] This guarantee not being consented to, he did not go. Some months later he had another opportunity of going to Manchester, which he accepted.[2]

We need not discuss here the Jumbo Farm theory[3] of the origin of the wholesale at certain meetings held there. That the subject was considered there, as at other places, there is no doubt. Mr. Marcroft, himself connected with the wholesale, supposes that it was devised at meetings held at that peculiar farm. But the road of our narrative lies through official facts. At the first meeting of the North of England Wholesale Society, held in Union Chambers, Manchester, December 10th, 1863, Mr. Thomas Cheetham was appointed Chairman, and Mr. Abram Greenwood, President; James Smithies, Treasurer; John C. Edwards, Secretary. Messrs. John Shelton, William Marcroft, Charles Howarth, and Thomas Cheetham were the Committee. Here are a cluster mostly of familiar and historic names in constructive co-operation. Four years later a resolution was come to that the prospectus of the Wholesale Agency should be publicly advertised. The following extract from the Society's minutes shows when and in what terms it was resolved upon :—

Copy of first minutes of adjourned committee meeting, March 2nd, 1867 :—

"Present: A. Greenwood, James Crabtree, John Hilton, James Smithies, Edward Hooson, Edward Thomason.

"Resolved: 1st—That the prospectus be published as an advertisement in the *Co-operator* until further notice."

The concluding part of this advertisement, which first appeared March 15th, 1867, contained the following words :—

"[Mr. Abraham Greenwood, of Rochdale, must be regarded as the principal originator of the Co-operative Wholesale Society, of which he has ever since been the President.] In the *Co-operator* for March, 1863 (vol. 3), Mr. Greenwood propounded his plan for a

[1] The following minute gives the official form of the circumstance :—"On November 7th, 1863, a deputation was appointed to invite Mr. Samuel Ashworth to become buyer for the wholesale, at a salary of £200 a year to commence with." At the next meeting, November 21st, it was reported that Mr. Ashworth had declined the offer, and that the Rochdale Board of Directors had increased his salary £30 per year in order to retain his services.

[2] Mr. A. Howard's statement.

[3] A theory started by Mr. Marcroft, who considers that the idea of the wholesale and most other things originated in discussions at Jumbo Farm.

wholesale agency, which, with some modifications, formed the basis of the present admirable organisation."

The first part, which is put here in brackets, was drawn by Mr. Smithies and Mr. Edwards, two of the most competent persons who could have written it, for their knowledge of its truth is undoubtable, and their concurrence in the statement is conclusive. The part following the brackets was written by Mr. Henry Pitman, as there were copies of the *Co-operator* mentioned on hand, which it was thought desirable should be further circulated. This conclusive and unchallenged testimony, repeated year after year, renders future doubt or denial absurd. When the notice was discontinued, it was done on the authority of the following minute:—

Copy of first minute of committee meeting, held October 16th, 1869:—

"Present: Messrs. Greenwood, Baxter, Fox, Hooson, Crabtree, Thomason, Sutcliffe, Swindels, and Marcroft.

"Resolved: 1st—That no co-operative or other agency be added to our advertisements in the *Co-operator*."

No objection was raised at this meeting, or had been at any meeting, as to the fact of the authorship of the wholesale. Neither Mr. Marcroft nor any other person raised a question as to its truth. It was discontinued, Mr. Crabtree explains, not because its truth was ever questioned, but because it was deemed no longer necessary. It was suggested that there was no further need for it to appear, "as it would *now* have served all that was intended."

No historic fact could well be more conclusively established, more continuously advertised by common consent, than this has been, that Mr. Greenwood was the "principal originator" of the wholesale.

All who had personal knowledge of the development of co-operation during the past thirty years were quite aware that the credit of originating the wholesale, and the working and organisation, belonged to Abraham Greenwood more than to anyone else. The conclusive and well-written letter of Mr. Edwards, in the *Co-operative News* of July 17th, 1875, is quite sufficient testimony to set that matter at rest. Only those—to use Mr. Edwards' expression—who had a strong weakness for believing, in spite of evidence to the contrary, could entertain a reasonable doubt thereupon. Next to Abraham Greenwood I should place James Smithies. Smithies, like most of the early co-operators, was a modest man; but though modest he was not weak, and he could always be depended upon to indicate justly what share each of his colleagues had borne in their common work. He had himself devised plans for federating purchasers. He had collected copies of the plans of others. He was for years secretary of committees for giving effect to the idea.

In a movement in which an important development is carried out mainly by the sagacity and persistent efforts of one person, it is in the interest of all that credit should be given where it has been earned. When Mr. Abram Greenwood first drew up the scheme of it, and put into coherent form the fragmentary conceptions of others, he set forth, for the first time, an intelligent scheme of working principles. He had, to use his phrase, "to stand the fire of the criticism, doubt, and distrust of the plan, of which no one else was willing to undertake the responsibility or defence of." Since it became successful, sponsors for it and originators of it have sprung up from Jumbo Farm to Cronkey Shaw, and generally elsewhere.

Mr. Howard has an ingenious theory that the nature of the residences of the co-operators can be determined from the books of the stores, which record the amount of their savings. Those members who have the highest balances are found to be persons who live upon the hills which abound in the town. If a member has a low balance, he is found to live in the low lands. If his balance is high, so is the altitude of the place where he resides. If a member has no balance, it ought to follow that he lives underground. I am told the figures in some societies do favour this theory, and that high balances and elevated dwellings do go together. If this be true, it is probably owing to the greater clearness of the climate on the hill, better enabling members to see their way to save. I remember now that Mr. Greenwood always lived in some elevated part of the town, which, no doubt, enabled him to take comprehensive views of the wholesale before the cogitators of Jumbo Farm (which, if I remember rightly, is a low-lying place) got sight of it.

The sense in which it appears to me Mr. Greenwood is to be regarded as the main founder of the wholesale is that of his having been the advocate of it, and known to be distinctively the advocate of it, during more years than any other person laying claim to its origination. He kept it in mind himself from the time (1850) when the project was first formally discussed in Rochdale and London, and during all subsequent years of its trial, which preceded its final establishment in 1864. He not only kept the idea in his own mind, but kept it in the minds of others, when otherwise it would have lain in abeyance. His calculations mainly proved it to be a feasible undertaking. His statement of the possible mode of working it was the first which seemed complete and practicable. James Smithies, William Cooper, Lloyd Jones, George Booth, W. Marcroft, Mr. Ashworth, Charles Howarth, Thomas Cheetham, Mr. Edwards, Mr. Stott, William Nuttall, and of later years, James Crabtree, A. Howard, J. T. W. Mitchell, and others, should all in fairness be included; whose sagacity and energy have contributed to its origination and development. All the leading thinkers of the Rochdale Store were undoubtedly concerned in furthering the great project by plans, suggestions, and advocacy.

If I could collect a list of all the names of persons who have promoted the prosperity of the wholesale, I should insert them. Mr. Field, of Mossley, was on the committee three or four years, and was deemed a good member. Mr. John Hilton also served four or five years. Mr. Marcroft, as we have seen, was upon it. Mr. Charles Howarth, who was also upon the committee, ceased after a time to be so, because he was a dealer in soda, which was sometimes purchased by the agency. Mr. Edwards shared in the heat and burden of the service of the wholesale four or five years. Several names occur incidentally in committees which have been quoted, which the co-operative reader will recognise as those of distinguished promoters of the wholesale. Mr. Mitchell, of Rochdale, and Mr. James Crabtree, of Heckmondwike (who has both faith and pride in co-operative principle), have both been chairmen of the wholesale.

CHAPTER XXI.

CO-OPERATIVE ADMINISTRATION.

THE Almanacs of the Pioneers' Store—quite worthy of being preserved and bound for reference—give a curious picture of its progress, vicissitudes, and the manner of the Pioneer mind from time to time. The 1854 Almanac gives a complete statement of the "objects and rules" of the Society, as they stood in force exactly in the tenth year of its existence. They are expressed with clearness and conciseness. All clearness is not concise, and some conciseness is not clear; but these Almanac expositions possess both, as the reader has seen on p. 11.

By the rules of the Society a person proposed and his character and qualifications duly discussed, and not accepted, had his entrance shilling returned. The good-natured Society debated his merits and demerits gratuitously. One would imagine that a person whose virtues were not generally admitted, or not very obvious, would gladly pay a shilling for having them inquired into by this willing association, so that he might know how he stood among his class. Each member has to take five one-pound shares. How many stores have languished for years, flabby in pocket and lean in limb, because its shabby-minded members starved it by hardly subscribing one pound each. Many societies are pale in the face for want of the nourishment of capital which a wise five-pound rule would have brought it.[1] These are the Rochdale rules:—

"2. Any person desirous of becoming a member of this Society shall be proposed and seconded by two members, and if approved of at the next general meeting by a majority then present, shall be admitted to membership. A person proposed and not making his appearance within two months shall forfeit his proposition money,

[1] The amount of capital which each member ought to supply in order that the Store may do well for him is £8. Members who do not furnish this amount each do not understand their own interest and expect to reap where they do not sow

and shall not be admitted to membership unless again proposed. Each person, on the night of his admission, shall appear personally in the meeting-room, and state his willingness to take out five shares of one pound each, and conform to the laws of the Society, and pay a deposit of not less than one shilling.

"3. That each member shall have five shares in the capital of the Society, and not more than fifty shares.

"4. That the capital be raised in shares of one pound each.

"5. That each member pay not less than threepence per week, or three shillings and threepence quarterly, until he have five shares in the capital of the Society.. Any member neglecting to pay as above, except through sickness, distress, or want of employment, shall be fined threepence.

"6. That two pounds of each member's investment be permanent or fixed capital.

"7. That three pounds may be withdrawn at the discretion of the Board.

"8. That members may withdraw any sum due to them above five pounds according to the following scale of notice:—One pound five shillings on application to the Board; one pound five shillings to two pounds ten shillings, two weeks. And larger sums on giving longer notice; from forty to forty-five pounds being to be had on twelve months' notice.

"16. That meetings on the first Monday in January, April, July, and October be the quarterly meetings of the Society, at which meetings the officers shall make their quarterly report, in which shall be specified the amount of funds and value of stock possessed by the Society.

"23. [1] The officers of this Society shall not in any case, nor any pretence, either sell or purchase any article except for ready money. Any officer acting contrary to this law shall be fined 10s., and be disqualified from performing the duties of such office.

"32. That the profits realised by the Society be divided thus:—Interest at the rate of 5 per cent. per annum shall be paid on all shares paid up previous to the quarter commencing. The remainder shall be divided amongst the members in proportion to the amount of their purchases at the Store during the quarter."

The last is the rule which introduced into England and into all store practices the new policy of dividing profits on purchases.

The 1854 Almanac also contained the economical announcement, of which the like had never appeared in Great Britain (and would be difficult to find elsewhere in 1877), namely, that the news-room, a bounteously filled room in those days, abounding in dailies, weeklies, and quarterlies, was open from nine in the morning until nine at night, at a charge of twopence per month. As this room was, and still is, open on Sundays as well as week days, this gave an

[1] The Almanac omits 17, 18, 19, 20, and others, quoting those of main interest to the outside reader.

average of 2,520 hours' reading for twopence; or 600 hours, with fire and light, for one halfpenny. Co-operative information is the cheapest the working class ever found, if regard be had to convenience of hour and day; and the quality of it is higher, because two-sided, than gentlemen can usually command. More wanting in intellectual boldness than workmen, gentlemen's news-rooms and libraries are subjected to clerical censorship, who, with the best intentions, impose the impotence of half-knowledge upon the members who do not think it "good taste" to object to it or demand "forbidden books." In all Scotland there is not a single public library or news-room, in city, or club, or college, where periodicals and books on both sides of theology and politics can be seen. Nor would co-operators be in the freer and manlier state they are, did not their own money buy their books, and build their news-rooms and libraries, and their own members administer their affairs themselves. Owing nothing to anyone, they fear nobody, nor suffer intellectual control by any.

The honourable feature of the Pioneers is that they did not go back, they went forward. The Almanac, the yearly manifesto of the Society, said:—"The objects of this Society are the *social* and *intellectual* advancement of its members. It provides its members with groceries, butchers' meat, drapery goods, clothing, shoes, clogs. They have competent workmen on the premises to do the work of the members and execute all repairs. The profits are divided quarterly: 1st, interest, five per cent. per annum on all paid-up shares; 2nd, 2½ *per cent. off net profits for educational purposes;* remaining profits divided amongst the members in proportion to money expended. For the intellectual improvement of the members a library has been formed, consisting (1877) of more than 3,000 volumes. The library is free to all the members."

Mark, the objects are "the social and intellectual improvement of members," as well as their secular betterance. "Social and intellectual" improvement was a wholesale phrase put there or kept there by Mr. Abram Howard.

Their library soon grew to 3,000 volumes. The newspapers and periodicals increased in number; and they have discovered how to make reading cheaper than 2,000 hours of it for twopence. Reading is now "free," and the library thrown into that. The Almanac of 1861 announces that globes, maps, microscopes, and telescopes are now added, so that the co-operator can look into things small and great, far and near. The gentlemen of Rochdale had no such institution for their use.

It is that golden rule for the division of profits which includes 2½ per cent. off net gains for educational purposes, which has exalted the Rochdale Society above all others, made its wise example so valuable, brought it so many friends, so much fame, and kept it from being overrun by fools or uninformed members, who else would long ere this have destroyed it, on the ground that intelligence does not pay. Not having any themselves, and not knowing what it means, they naturally take this view. They think dividends sufficient without knowledge, not knowing that without knowledge there would be no dividends, either in co-operative stores or elsewhere.

When the cotton famine began to gnash its lean jaws in 1862, the forecasting and confident co-operators came out—in that penurious year above all others—with their golden Almanac. Mr. Smithies and Mr. Cooper both sent me copies with pride. It was printed in gold on a blue ground. It mentioned a "Wholesale warehouse at 8 Toad Lane, and, for the first time, gave a central compartment to the educational department." It recounted that the library had grown to 5,000 volumes, that a reference library of most valuable works had been added, that the news-room contained fourteen daily papers, thirty-two weeklies, and monthlies and quarterlies of all kinds, representing all opinions in politics and religion. The co-operators wisely set themselves against being made into half-minded men. They would not imitate those timid creatures who are afraid to know the other side of the question, and go squinting at truth all their days, never looking it square in the face, so that when they meet it right plain in their way they do not know it. Opera glasses, atlases, and stereoscopes are now provided for the use of members, and for a small fee they can take them away, as well as microscopes and telescopes. The slave war was then waging, and if a slave-owner's agent came their way, as many of them did, the co-operators had telescopes to discern his approach, and microscopic instruments ready to examine him when he arrived.

Things generally had a vagabond appearance in Lancashire. The outlook for an operative was bad, and destined to be worse. The golden Almanac said so, and gave this excellent advice to co-operators :—

"1. Let your earnings be spent only on strict necessaries. Cut off everything else.

"2. Withdraw sparingly of your accumulated savings.

"3. Make the best use of the time thrown on your hands for your intellectual improvement, means for which are provided in our library and news-rooms.

"4. Add to the honour of our movement, by waiting patiently for the better time which will one day come."

And they did wait. No venal or other agitators ever won co-operators to join in any clamour that the Government should intervene on behalf of the south, in order to bring cotton to Lancashire and Yorkshire. A week's clamour would have turned the scale against the slave. It made the nation proud of English working men to see the stout and generous silence they kept. The advice I have quoted was addressed "to the co-operators of Rochdale and the nation." It is the only time they acted on their well-earned authority to speak in this manner to the outside world.

A Sick and Burial Society was commenced before 1860. Provision for relief during sickness and also for decent interment at the death of any of its members are the cares of the co-operators. None but members of the Rochdale Equitable Pioneers, or their families, can enter this Society; but a member may withdraw from the Pioneers' Society without losing his or her membership in this. Contributions, of course, vary according to age; and the tables are based upon authorised calculations. The Pioneers have always had among them a creditable taste for temperance, and had the Society's meetings held at the board-room to prevent pay nights turning into tippling nights at a beerhouse, which soon brings members on the "box" of the sick club. The founders of the Society were too shrewd to think that anything would be saved by insuring saturated subscribers. Dry members pay best. The Almanac of 1862 stated that "meeting at public-houses was neither suitable nor consistent with the objects of a sick and burial society—an appetite for drink and company bring on disease and premature death." The Pioneers meant their arrangements to be "suitable and consistent with a society whose interest rather is the prevention of sickness and burials. Tippling is alone suitable and consistent with a society whose objects are promoting sickness and burial. Temperance in drink is sensible; it is fuddling which is foolishness."

A House Society is another feature of Pioneer organisation. Improvement in England grows fast out of grievance. Reason seldom or never creates it. If, indeed, pure intellect discovers a new course, it generally remains barren until some irritation drives men into it. The Land and House Society began this way. One of its founders relates that a certain gentleman who was a shopkeeper, was also an owner of cottages, some of which were occupied by members of "co-operative societies," who were in the habit of receiving store profits. He, in an unwise hour, declared that "they should not have all the dividends to themselves; he would have a part of them by advancing their rents 3d. per week." If it be weak to wait for an outrage before you do a sensible thing, it is undoubtedly a proof of some spirit to take steps to make the repetition of the outrage, when it does occur, impossible in the future. This is what the Pioneers soon did. They formed a society, and began to buy land and put up houses for themselves. Their rules give power to build, buy, and sell houses, workshops, mills, factories, or to purchase, lease, or rent land upon which to erect such property. Their proposed capital was £25,000, in shares of £1. Thirty-six cottages were put up before 1867, covering the whole of the land they then held. Their erections were an improvement on the generality of cottages then built. Subsequently they have built a co-operative town.

The *Irish Times* of 1868 remarked in a leader by the editor,— "We have before us an Almanac for 1868, published for the use and information of its members by the Rochdale Equitable Pioneers' Society, Limited. It is a sheet Almanac, illustrated with a view of 'The new Central Store,' a cut-stone building 70 feet high, and bearing some resemblance to the stately edifice belonging to the Hibernian Bank, in College Green. This building cost the Rochdale Pioneers £17,000. Some idea of the wonderful effects of the co-operative system, duly and honourably carried out, may be formed from some facts stated by the Directors, who are all working men, in an address published in the Almanac."

After recounting what the business and profits of the Society then were, the editor adds:—

"The capital is so large and so rapidly increases that the Directors are now spending £10,000 as a beginning in the erection of a good class of cottage houses for artisans, and they have purchased a small estate within the borough of Rochdale, which is to be laid out for building immediately. The quality and construction of the houses are greatly superior to any erected for the working class in Rochdale before the Pioneer time," excepting, perhaps, a pleasant, wide-windowed and healthy range erected by Mr. Bright for his workpeople.

The early co-operators in Rochdale took with regard to their buildings what used to be called "the bare-bone utilitarian view," like that which Abram Combe took at Orbiston. They were content that their store should be of the plainest kind, indeed, they had an early resolution on their minutes, "not to spend a farthing on finery." This was a wise resolution then, because they had not the farthing by them. Besides, the instinct of art hardly existed among the working class in those days. They thought refinement of taste belonged alone to the rich; they did not know that the rich were often vulgar, and that refinement was a property of the mind, and that the poor might have it as well as the wealthy. They did not know that plainness, grimness, and ugliness were more expensive than modest comeliness and modest taste. Their central stores and their branch stores are well and substantially built now; but had it occurred to their architects, they might have made them brighter, and still more graceful, at less expense. It would be a benefit to society if a few architects were publicly hanged in half-a-dozen places, as Voltaire said of Admiral Byng, "for the encouragement of others."

The observations by the Irish editor quoted, are all founded upon one Almanac, that of 1868. Much that has been written upon Rochdale has been suggested in like manner by a stray copy of this annual calendar of the year falling under the notice of persons who became interested by its unexpected contents. The Almanac has been the annual manifesto of the Store. It has been the sole historical publication of the Store.

In Part I. of this history, the part published twenty years ago, at p. 58, it is represented that the loan asked of Mr. Coningham, then M. P. for Brighton, fell through because their securities were naturally required to be submitted to the examination of Mr. Coningham's solicitor, and the "Board refused to have anything to do with a lawyer." No doubt this distrust of lawyers existed. But this was not the exact reason why the solicited loan came to an end. It is not of moment now;

but I am unwilling to leave on record unrevised any statement which subsequent information has shown me to be incorrect. Mr. Coningham has sent to me the following letter which he received at the time, and which puts the fact accurately :—

13, George Street, Rochdale,
14th October, 1851.

Sir,—I am directed by the members of the "Rochdale District Corn Mill Society" to return their thanks for your offer and anxious desire to meet their wishes relative to the loan of £500.

You will find by the enclosed letter we received from your solicitor, Edward Tyler, Esq., however willing we may be we *cannot* give the property of the Society in security. This the members regret, for it precludes them from getting that help which they at *this* time greatly require. But yet the members would esteem it a great favour if you, on the good faith of the Society, advance to it £200, to be repaid by quarterly instalments of £50, which would repay the loan in 12 months.—Respectfully yours,

W. Coningham, Esq. ABRAHAM GREENWOOD.

When Abraham Lincoln became President of America, his familiar-tongued countrymen dropped out the "ha," and reduced him to the more manageable name of "Abram." Since Mr. Greenwood has oft been president of the various wholesale and other co-operative projects, he also has been called "Abram," and it has been the above letter, bearing Mr. Coningham's endorsement (I send the original to the printer), written twenty-six years ago, that enables me to furnish historical proof that Mr. Greenwood's rightful name is the good old resonant, Hebraic, patriarchal, three-syllabled name of Abraham, the most honoured name in Lancashire next to "Mesopotamia."

In the first part of this history, mention was made of the Christian Socialists, the professors, lawyers, clergymen, and other members of that party. It is a duty to acknowledge now how much the movement has been indebted to the generous zeal and devotion which, during the twenty succeeding years, they have continued to promote, which in various places, in this narrative and elsewhere, has been ungrudgingly acknowledged.

On Mr. Ashworth's appointment at the Wholesale, Manchester, Mr. Brierley, of the Brickfield Equitable Society, became manager. He began his duties when the progress of the Society was in full course. The local policy was changed. New notions of making dividend by seeking cheaper markets, with risk of worse quality, were permitted.

The rules were altered to the effect that interest on invested capital of five per cent. should only be paid in certain fixed proportion to the amount of the member's quarterly purchases of provisions or goods at the Store. Thus, if a member had invested £60 in the capital of the Store, and his purchases amounted to only £1 a week during the quarter, he only received interest on £8 of his capital invested, and the other £47 paid him nothing. One reason for this singular rule was a distrust or jealousy of capitalists. It is a curious feature in the working class that at one time their great grievance is that they have no capital (which is always a grievance to any persons in that state), and, next, they use all their ingenuity to devise rules for getting rid of capital, which we wanted for establishing co-operative workshops. They grow afraid of their friend. The rules herein questioned had the merit of answering the purpose intended. The members who could not eat up to the required amount, and could not otherwise augment their purchases sufficiently, began to draw out their capital which yielded no return. The result was that, in 1869-70, £100,000 were withdrawn, and £30,000 more was under notice. It will surprise the un-co-operative reader to find that the members of the Store had so large an amount of money. In due time good sense got uppermost, as it often has done in Rochdale. The members had the disturbing rule rescinded.[1] From June, 1870, business and prosperity returned to its usual standard of growth; the capital has more than doubled again. Mr. Joseph Booth, of the Hyde Store, son of Mr. George Booth, of Middleton, has succeeded as manager. Mr. Brierley set up a rival society in the town, of which he is manager. But the Rochdale Society continues to prosper in its own enduring way.

About the years 1859 and 1860, Mr John Bright took, as he had often done before, considerable interest in the progress of the Pioneers' Society. He knew several of the workpeople of his firm with whom, as old servants, he was on friendly and conversational terms; and sometimes the affairs of the Store were the topic of his remarks. He said some of his friends in the Metropolis and other parts of the country expressed doubts as to the financial soundness of the Society, and based their doubts upon the fact that the accounts were only

---

1 This curious rule is worth preserving. Each member shall receive out of the surplus receipts of the Society, after providing for the expenses thereof, in each year, such interest not exceeding five per cent. per annum upon the capital standing to his account in the books of the Society, as is declared at the quarterly meetings of the Society, providing his purchases are according to the following scale, namely: If a member purchase

£1	per quarter,	shall only	be allowed interest	up to £8
2	"	"	"	16
3	"	"	"	24
4	"	"	"	32
5	"	"	"	40
6	"	"	"	48
7	"	"	"	56
8	"	"	"	64
9	"	"	"	72
10	"	"	"	80
11	"	"	"	88
12		"	"	100

audited by members. He himself had no misgiving concerning them; but he thought it might give confidence to other persons who were both willing and able to speak well of the movement, but who desired to be certain that the statements made were verified by some acknowledged public auditor. This was talked about among the leading members, and ultimately, on the appointment of the auditors in January, 1861, the matter was mentioned, and the appointment of a public accountant was moved and carried, mainly through the influence of the reported remarks of Mr. Bright.

Mr. Frank Hunter, of Bacup, was appointed. The books were not entered up in a systematic manner, and Mr. Hunter had to bring out the whole of the strength of his office. The great number of the entries in the share accounts were more than he was prepared to find, and the number of the entries in the share accounts were such as he had had no former experience of. He wanted to take all the books away, but could not be permitted. When Mr. Hunter's report was produced it showed a sum of £200 unaccounted for. Mr. Cooper said it could not be correct, but the error could only be discovered by a fresh audit. Mr. Ashworth and the President went to see Mr. Hunter to ask him to show them how he had arrived at the result. He could give no particulars. He had corrected a number of members' share books without keeping account of the corrections, nor could he give any clue to the mystery. After much trouble and research it was discovered that *Mr. Hunter had made a mistake* by inserting on the credit side of the trade account an item of £70 odd as *sales*, which ought to have been entered on the debit side of *purchases*. It is not difficult to understand that if an auditor puts down £70 as received which the cashier had actually paid, that would make an error against him of £140. But all the cash was there. Mr. Hunter acknowledged in a letter his mistake, and the Society was satisfied. Since that time the Society has been satisfied with the audits made by those appointed; besides, auditors have subsequently been better paid.[1]

It will be clear to the reader that Mr. Bright did great service to the Society by the discerning practical suggestion which he made. At that time doubts were often expressed as to whether co-operators, being working men, understood enough of book-keeping to render a sound financial statement of their affairs. This short story, the financial verification of the Rochdale Society, is a necessary part of its history.

The following table shows at a glance the progress which the Society has made from 1844 onwards :—

[1] The facts of this chapter were furnished by Mr. Abram Howard.

Year.	Members.	Funds.	Business.	Profits, including interest
1844	28	£28	......	......
1845	74	181	£710	£22
1846	80	252	1,146	80
1847	110	286	1,924	72
1848	149	397	2,276	117
1849	390	1,193	6,611	561
1850	600	2,289	13,179	880
1851	630	2,785	17,633	990
1852	680	3,471	16,352	1,206
1853	720	5,848	22,700	1,674
1854	900	7,172	33,374	1,763
1855	1,400	11,032	44,902	3,109
1856	1,600	12,920	63,197	3,921
1857	1,850	15,142	79,789	5,470
1858	1,950	18,160	74,680	6,284
1859	2,703	27,060	104,012	10,739
1860	3,450	37,710	152,063	15,906
1861	3,900	42,925	176,206	18,020
1862	3,501	38,465	141,074	17,564
1863	4,013	49,961	158,632	19,671
1864	4,747	62,105	174,937	22,717
1865	5,326	78,778	196,234	25,156
1866	6,246	99,989	249,122	31,931
1867	6,823	128,435	284,912	41,619
1868	6,731	123,233	390,900	37,459
1869	5,809	93,423	236,438	28,642
1870	5,560	80,291	223,021	25,209
1871	6,021	107,500	246,522	29,026
1872	6,444	132,912	267,577	33,640
1873	7,021	160,886	287,212	38,749
1874	7,639	192,814	298,888	40,679
1875	8,415	225,682	305,657	48,212
1876	8,892	254,000	305,190	50,668
1877	9,722	280,275	311,754	51,648
1878	10,187	292,344	298,679	52,694
1879	10,427	288,035	270,072	49,751
1880	10,613	292,570	283,665	48,545
1881	10,697	302,151	272,142	46,242
1882	10,894	315,243	274,627	47,608
1883	11,050	326,875	276,456	51,599
1884	11,161	329,470	262,270	50,268
1885	11,084	324,645	252,072	45,254
1886	10,984	321,678	246,031	44,111
1887	11,152	338,100	256,736	46,047
1888	11,278	344,669	267,726	47,119
1889	11,342	353,470	270,685	47,263
1890	11,352	362,358	270,583	47,764
1891	11,647	370,792	296,025	52,198

The progress of the Store shown in columns was first done on my suggestion, and Mr. T. S. Mill put in his "Principles of Political Economy" this table down to 1860.

CHAPTER XXII.

THE BRANCH STORE AGITATION.

THE Society soon came to possess fourteen or more Branch Stores and nearly as many news-rooms. But how came these Branches into being? Did they come by spontaneous generation or evolution, or development of species process, silently and naturally; or were they the offspring of discussion, with agitation for accoucheur? The following facts will enable the reader to judge:—

It was in the year 1856, when the receipts at the two Central Stores had amounted to £1,000 per week, that the members began to talk of having shops opened in other parts of the town, more convenient to their residences.

Many of the members lived at great distances, and the labour of carrying their weekly purchases from the stores in Toad Lane had been freely undertaken while there was no economy in having more than one shop. But now the shop was crowded every night, and the day was scarcely long enough for the shopmen to make the necessary preparations for the night's work.

Discussions arose on which part of the town the first Branch should be opened; it was soon decided. A numerously signed memorial from the members on the Castleton side of the town was presented to the quarterly meeting, held in June, 1856. The prayer of the memorialists was granted, themselves being at the meeting in great strength to promote it and support it by their votes. Indeed, this has been the case in the opening of nearly all the Branches, and is a notable feature in the democratic character of our institution.

A shop in Oldham Road was procured, and was opened No. 1 Branch for the sale of grocery goods on the 7th day of October of the same year. The business at this new Branch soon outgrew the premises which the committee had rented, and it was soon seen that further steps would have to be taken in the same direction.

There was on the Castleton side of the town a society which had been formed in the earlier years of the Pioneers' Society. It was called "The Castleton Co-operative Society." It was doing but a small business. I believe it was in the year 1855 it was irregularly assessed by the Income Tax Commissioners on a profit of £45, and compelled to pay at that time.

The greater popularity of the larger society threatened to swallow up this small society, and now when the Branch movement had begun, an agitation was set on foot for amalgamation. The result was that the business and premises of the Castleton Society were taken up by the Pioneers, and the Store was opened on March 7th, 1857, as the No. 2 School Lane Branch. It still retains the name, although a new store has been built in another street a considerable distance away.

The new idea of Branches gained ground so fast that two more were opened within the next few weeks, No. 3, in Whitworth Road, within ten minutes' walk of the Toad Lane Stores, and the first on the same side of the town; and No. 4, Pinfold Branch, being in another part of the township of Castleton.

The latter Branch was opened on the 2nd June, 1857, but no further steps were taken in this direction till the beginning of the year 1859. Although great relief had been given to the Central Stores by the opening of the four Branches, yet the increase of members and business continued at such a rate that further relief was now found to be necessary.

The Castleton side of the town was well served! Only one Branch had been established on the same side as the Central was situated, and it was now argued that they might extend in the Spotland direction. After some opposition, and great difficulty in finding a suitable shop, the Spotland Bridge Branch, No. 5, commenced business on the 17th February, 1859.

The agitation for another Branch at Bamford was immediately commenced. This was, indeed, an agitation, inasmuch as it involved a new principle—that of the Pioneers opening shops in the neighbourhood of other societies.

At a small village, situate but a short distance from Bamford, there was one of those small societies formed very early in the new history of the movement, and must have been in existence a considerable number of years at the time when the memorial for a Branch at Bamford was being signed. The memorial was signed by a great many of the members of the Hooley Bridge Society, and a great many more opposed it. It was seen at once that if the Pioneers opened a shop here it would be the death-blow to their small Society. The principle of self-government was set against the principle of economy on the side of the memorialists. While on the side of their opponents in the town it was urged that it would not be fair to charge the Society's funds with the cost of carrying the goods to such an outlying Branch, when members who lived at great distances in other directions had to carry their own, but more especially would it be wrong to open such a Branch so near a neighbouring society at which the memorialists could not only make their purchases, but where they could take a more active share in the management than was possible for them to do in the Rochdale Society.

The memorialists, however, succeeded, and at the April Quarterly Meeting, in 1859, it was decided to open a shop at Bamford. The announcement of the voting was received with an outburst of applause from the supporters of the memorial.

No one seems to have thought of the danger of this example of overlapping which has wrought much mischief since. A Store is better than a Branch since the Store developes local energy and business education. A federation of Stores around a wholesale centre is better than Branches.

I have dwelt longer on the circumstances attending the opening of the No. 6 Bamford Branch (which took place on May 26th, 1859), because it settled the principle that the Society might safely carry its Branches to such places beyond the boundaries of the town where the members residing in the neighbourhood could guarantee a certain weekly business, such as would give fair employment to a shopman.

The sixteen Society's Branches were opened as follows :—

Oldham Road,	No.	1	in	1856
School Lane Branch,	,,	2	,,	1857
Whitworth Road	,,	3	,,	1857
Pinfold,	,,	4	,,	1857
Spotland Bridge Branch,	,,	5	,,	1859
Bamford Branch,	,,	6	,,	1859
Wardleworth Brow,	,,	7	,,	1860
Bluepits,	,,	8	,,	1860
Buersil,	,,	9	,,	1864 (?)
Shawclough,	,,	10	,,	1866
Sudden,	,,	11	,,	1869
Newbold,	,,	12	,,	1872
Milkstone,	,,	13	,,	1872
Slattocks,	,,	14	,,	1873
Gravel Hole,	,,	15	,,	1874
Norden,	,,	16	,,	1875

At ten out of the sixteen there are commodious shops, which the Society has built from its own funds, and two more where the premises are its own by purchase. At the remaining four the business is conducted in rented shops. There are news-rooms at twelve of them, and preparation is being made at another.[1] Four or five of the branches do a business under £2,000 per quarter, but the rest vary from that sum to £5,500 per quarter.

The Branch system has been of great service to the members, and there is no doubt but it has been a principal means of the rapid and ultimately secure development of the Society's progress.

The Central Store from which the Branches radiate is a very interesting building. There is a meeting-room at the top, covering the whole area of the building. It is capable of seating at least

[1] There are now 19 news-rooms and 35,493 books in the libraries (1892).

1,400 persons, and has often held meetings of 2,000 and upwards. This meeting-room affords a commanding view of the town which is seen from 15 lofty windows. The library contains 12,000 volumes.

The building was commenced in the beginning of 1866, and opened in September, 1867. The whole cost including site was £13,360 ; all or the greater part of the cost has long since been defrayed. The premises at ten of the Branches belonging to the Society were erected at a cost of upwards of £14,000, including fixtures. Close to the river, and in a central part of the town, are the Society's manufacturing departments, newly arranged and rebuilt, comprising tobacco manufacturing; bread, biscuit, and cake baking; the business of pork butchering, currant cleaning, coffee roasting, coffee and pepper grinding ; and in the same yard are the stables and slaughter houses; the whole being so arranged that the produce of each department can be delivered at the shops when wanted with the precision of a machine.

The business of the Society was £311,754, and the members numbered 9,722 at the end of 1877; profits, £51,648. The Society constitutes an important part of the town, which numbers 65,000 inhabitants.

It was a festive day when the Central Stores were opened. I invited Colonel R. J. Hinton, of Washington, to be present, who had drilled and taken part in training coloured regiments in the Slave War for freedom, in America. He was witness of the proceedings, and spoke in the theatre.[1] The Central Store stands at the junction of St. Mary's Gate and Toad Lane, presenting a copious frontage to both roads, and raising its head higher than any building in the town. Standing on the site of the old theatre and the Temperance Hall, all know the place, and if they did not they can see it. It has been proposed to erect an observatory upon it, and furnish it with powerful telescopes. The immense range of view from the top will make it the finest observatory in Lancashire. Speeches were delivered at the Theatre Royal, the Mayor, Mr. J. Robinson, presiding. Mr. John Bright, M.P., sent a cordial letter, being unable to be in Rochdale that day. Earl Russel, Lord Stanley, Mr. Goldwin Smith, Mr. T. B. Potter, M.P. for the borough, Mr. Jacob Bright, and others, sent words of acknowledgment or congratulation. Mr. Thomas Hughes, M.P., Mr. Walter Morrison, M.P., Mr. E. V. Neale, Mr. E. O. Greening, the Rev. W. N. Molesworth, the Rev. J. Freeston, and the present writer, were among the speakers. Twenty-three years before the co-operators had commenced their humble and doubtful career in Toad Lane, and that day, September 28th, 1867, they obtained acknowledged ascendency in the town. They had become the greatest trading body in it; their Central Store tower, like Saul, head and shoulders above every other establishment about it.

[1] In a volume, the "Radical Leaders of England" (Putnam and Sons), this gentleman has given recollections of this visit.

The Rev. Mr. Molesworth said he regarded that celebration as of European importance. Throughout the Continent co-operation had spread rapidly since they had adopted the principles of the Rochdale Pioneers. All true believers in co-operation turn their eyes to Rochdale as the Mecca and Medina of the system.

Mr. Morrison, M.P., said that nothing could be done by the Pioneers in a corner. It was, therefore, important that they should maintain their reputation. If other societies saw that Rochdale departed from its first faith, they would plead their eminent example for departing also.

At this meeting Mr. John Brierley, the Secretary, read an elaborate report. It ended with this passage:—"In 1855 a Manufacturing Society was established in this town chiefly by the members of the Store. Its principle was to apportion the profits made—in part to capital and in part to labour. This Society made great success in its earlier years, but the capitalist shareholder began to think the worker had too much profit, so the bounty to labour was abolished. (Loud cries of "shame."[1]) But we hope ere long to see it re-adopted (hear, hear, and cheers), and the principles of co-operation fully developed, believing that it is fraught with incalculable blessings to the people."

Mr. Hughes accepted this as a promise that efforts would be made to restore the character of the Manufacturing Society.

Mr. William Cooper spoke, and in alluding to Mr. Neale described him as "their own lawyer," for whose services they were all grateful.

Mr. Councillor Smithies said that the Pioneers, who were registered under the Friendly Societies Act of 1845, had applied for an amendment of the law which would enable them to devote a tenth of their net profits to educational purposes; but, notwithstanding the services of Mr. Hughes and Mr. Neale, the proposed rule was vetoed by Mr. Tidd Pratt, the registrar.

The co-operators had never been hosts before on so large a scale, and had never before been able to invite such distinguished guests as those to whom they sent invitations. The chief guests had the choice of two dinners. One was provided for them at the Central Stores, and another by the Mayor, with whom, as the intention of his worship was to show courtesy to the Pioneers by making their visitors his guests, they dined. After the speech, multitudes of people went to the soiree at the Stores, and the ball at the Public Hall.

1 Report in *Rochdale Observer*.

CHAPTER XXIII.

OTHER CHARACTERISTICS OF THE ROCHDALE PIONEERS.

There is no doubt that the persistence of leading Rochdale Co-operators in maturing the "Wholesale" entitles their Store to be regarded as the practical founder of it. They furnished those who conceived the idea in its working form, put it in motion, and kept it in motion.

Long before, Rochdale had the merit to demonstrate the value of the principle of dividing profits upon purchases instead of upon shares. Mr. Alexander Campbell, of Glasgow, was an advocate of this principle. It was first stated by Mr. Campbell in 1822, and afterwards put by him in the rules of the Cambuslang Society of 1829. The principle was in the rules of the Melthan Mills Society of 1827, as Mr. Nuttall has shown: yet it would never have been in Rochdale save for Mr. Howarth. He re-discovered it, and was certainly the first to appreciate its importance, and to urge its adoption there. Double discovery is very common in literature, mechanics, and commerce. Poets and authors often hit upon ideas which have occurred to others before they were born, and of whose writings they had no knowledge. Bell, in Scotland, and Fulton, in America, both discovered the steamship at the same time. No doubt Mr. Howarth himself originated the very idea in Rochdale which Mr. Campbell had long before thought of. But they made nothing of it in Scotland. Indeed, they did not know they had it among them, until Rochdale successes with it made it of the nature of a famous discovery. Many discoveries of great pith and moment are made over and over again, and die over and over again. At last the old idea, being re-born, falls into the hands of knowing nurses, who bring the doubtful "bairn" up until it grows strong, tall, and rich. It is wonderful then what a number of parents the young man finds he had! This plan of sharing profits with the consumer, without whom no profits could be made, ensured a following for a store. It gave the customer an interest in the concern. Other societies soon adopted the same rule, but none made so much of it as Rochdale has done. The use other stores of that day put it to would never have given it distinction. Indeed, the division of profit idea would never have made the noise it has, but for the Rochdale way of carrying it out. It has been the ever-growing amounts of profit that attracted the pecuniary eye of the country to it there. The early co-operators there, having a world-amending scheme in view, foresaw that money would be required for that purpose, and this led them to adopt a plan of saving all they gained. After paying capitalists five per cent. it was open to the co-operators to sell their goods without further profit, which would have given to each purchaser his articles at almost cost prices. The consumer would thus have had, in another form, his full share of advantage by buying at the Store. The other plan open to them to adopt was to charge the current prices for all goods sold, and save for the customer the difference of profit accruing. This plan they adopted; though it was theoretical and somewhat Utopian, and not likely to be so popular with members generally, who like cheap articles, who prefer to know what they save, and to have it at once. Uneducated people do not believe in saving; they have no confidence in it; they do not believe in an unknown, untried committee saving money for them; they want it the moment it is available. With them a penny in hand is worth twenty in the bush.

In one of his lectures on capital and labour, Mr. Holmes, of Leeds, relates a before-told but still instructive story:—"During one of the Irish famines, Mr. Forster (the father of the then M.P. for Bradford) went out there, as the agent of the Society of Friends, to give special relief, and found the people at one place famished down to chewing seaweed. He asked them if there was no fish in the sea; they replied 'Yes,' but said 'they could not get them, as they had neither boats nor nets.' Mr. Forster provided them with boats and nets, upon which they eagerly inquired, 'Who's to pay us our day's wages?' Mr. Forster told them 'the fish they got would pay them their wages,' but they declined to go out on these problematical conditions, and it was not until Mr. Forster guaranteed them their wages that they set off. The consequence was that a good trade was carried on, and Mr. Forster soon found that the boats and nets were cleared—all paid for—and that plenty of money might be made. He offered the men the boats and nets free of expense; but they would not take them in their own hands, and nothing would satisfy them but '*their day's wages!*'"

The ignorant trust in nothing. Near gain of ten times the amount seems to them a cheat. The pecuniary eye of the mind is like the natural eye of the body—sometimes shortsighted, and cannot carry far enough to see profit even a little way off. An economic telescope is wanted to lengthen the sight. Co-operation proved to be the very telescope which did the thing for thousands. I know co-operators now who can see a profit a mile off; but, singularly, this long range of eye does not apply to a principle. The principle sometimes lies much nearer, and they never see it. I suppose they overlook it.

The poor are a fastidious and demonstrative class—they require to see the results of their conduct day by day and hour by hour. Yet, the old plan of selling goods cheaper than ordinary tradesmen—turning all profits into reduction of price—was not one that promised permanence. When errors in purchasing, or spoilt stock, caused the price at the Store to rise, the supporters of the Store fell. Even when the Store was successful as to maintaining lowness of price, the amount of advantage was often infinitesimal on some articles, and when the advantage could scarcely be seen, its influence waned. The old plan of taking all profits made, and paying them in the shape of dividends to the shareholders, had yet greater disadvantages. These dividends were drawn out and spent. When high, enthusiasm was high. When the dividends came down, popular support sunk to zero, and sometimes below, and then the Store broke up.

However, the rule of forced saving and deferred spending was calculated to delay the progress of the Society—to repel members—to breed discontent. It required enthusiasts to carry it out, and that rare combination of enthusiasts, zealots with patience, who could wait long years for results—in fact, to wait for their own success, which could not arrive until they had educated their neighbours, and brought up the town about them to their level. Luckily, the early Rochdale co-operators were enthusiasts, men who had the courage to dream dreams in flannel jackets, and with a very poor outlook in the streets—there being reductions of wages very near them, and the poorhouse not "looming" in the remote distance—but near and palpable; and yet they adopted the plan which forced members to save. Thus was born in Lancashire the idea of accumulating profits. Mr. William Chambers, in his paper on co-operation, says, with true insight, "Without the principle of accumulating profits, co-operation remains a very insignificant affair." The long years of store experience which preceded the commencement of the Rochdale Store of 1844, were the "insignificant" days of co-operation. There was no alluring accumulations then. Rochdale proved that an average population can be educated in foresight and thrift—quite a new fact in human working-class nature then. Happily, the Pioneers may come to be outstripped in material successes and in numbers; but they can never be surpassed in the credit which belongs to faith when believers are few, and to courage when all others despaired.

If the Rochdale plan of dividing profits on purchases was a Scotch discovery, it was unknown to the Messrs. Chambers. Clearly it had never attracted any attention in Scotch hands, else we had never seen, from such an observant economist as William Chambers, the following singular comment:—

"The Rochdale plan of paying not only dividends on capital, but a share of profits along with wages, is, on the first view of it, new and revolutionary. It seems to overturn all our ordinary ideas as to the relationship between those who find the money and those who give the hands in trading operations."

When Lord Westbury brought in his County Courts Bill for the abolition of the power of imprisonment for debt, he explained, in a note to Mr. Pitman, then editor of the *Co-operator*, "that he should be glad to see the Bill supported by the petitions of co-operative societies, feeling as he did that the taking away of such power would, by loosening the facility of obtaining credit, conduce to render more general habits of providence—habits which the system of co-operation had shown to exist among some of the members of the working class." Mr. John Whittaker, pleasantly known as "A Lancashire lad," endeavoured to elicit the opinions of leading co-operators upon the Lord Chancellor's Bill, and put the reason for it in these conclusive words :—

"As the Lord Chancellor's new Bill strikes directly at this credit system, it deserves the support of all who are interested in social improvement, and especially of those who are concerned about the success of co-operative associations. So soon as it becomes difficult for working men to obtain credit, they will learn the value of societies which will enable them to keep for their wn use the profits which they would otherwise have to pay to the ordinary retail dealer."

This was in 1864. Mr. William Cooper endeavoured in vain to induce the Rochdale Society to petition in favour of the Bill. The reason for this needs explaining, which can best be done in Mr. Cooper's own words :—

"I believe the system of credit does the working man a great deal more harm than good; for when a man 'goes behind,' as we say, or gets in debt, his hope and his spirit somewhat desert him, and he is liable to get more and more tied to his crediting shopkeeper. I have heard it said that some shopkeepers like to have their customers a little in debt, as then they know they are not able to go elsewhere for goods. If the Lord Chancellor's Bill becomes law, the tradesmen would still have one side of the bargain—that is, they could please themselves who they credited; and perhaps they would be more cautious about leading people into debt. But if the co-operative societies were to agitate for the passing of the Bill, the shopkeepers would be apt to attribute their interference to a desire on the part of co-operators to injure their interests. At least such a construction would be put on their motives in this town, as the Tories want a pretext to raise the hostility of the shopkeepers against the stores, so that in the excitement they may use the shopkeepers as instruments to unseat our representative, Richard Cobden."

But it must be owned that this solicitude concerning the action and interest of shopkeepers was sacrificing the larger interests of the working class and the stores. Lord Westbury's Bill would have saved tens of thousands from debt and have given an impetus to ready-money purchasing at stores.

The Working Men's Industrial Associations of Italy, which were originated by Mazzini, and of which he was president, were animated by a strong spirit of citizenship. With them public life and social life went together. It was in the belief that co-operation was not divorced from citizenship in Rochdale that at a meeting held there in December, 1861, I made a communication, on the authority of the president of the chief societies in Italy, with a view to establishing a personal intercourse between them and the trade societies of England. The Italian societies act upon the principle some time before urged upon the trade societies of England by Mr. Bright, and seek the unity of their country as the first condition of their industrial independence. At the conclusion of the communication Mr. Abraham Greenwood moved the following resolution, which was carried unanimously, Mr. Isaac Hoyle presiding:—"This meeting learns with pleasure that Italian workmen are following the advice long ago given to the workmen of England by Sir Robert Peel, and 'are taking their own affairs into their own hands.'" In England at that time the trade societies had it under their consideration to use their organisation for securing their political enfranchisement; for it is impossible that any men can protect the interests of their order, or their labour, who have no political existence themselves. The Rochdale meeting, therefore, was glad to see that the workmen of Italy included the unity of their country as a supreme and essential object with them.

The announcements in the Rochdale Almanacs of the number and magnitude of the news-rooms and libraries are noble notices. Just as when the English colonise any country they carry representative institutions with them, so whenever the Rochdale Society opens a new branch they open a new news-room, and it is "always" open. Every member is wiser in mind for it, and no poorer in pocket. Knowledge is economy as well as foresight and good sense.

Mr. John Ormerod wrote to me in 1864 an account of the origin of the Co-operative Loan Fund of Rochdale. In 1862, some gentlemen in Wiltshire, fearing that the cotton famine would seriously affect the stability of co-operative stores in Lancashire, generously proposed to render assistance which might help to avert this evil. "Considering," says Mr. Ormerod, "that Rochdale had been (so to speak) the cradle of co-operation, these gentlemen made offer of help in Rochdale, lest co-operation in general should suffer through a shock received there." To this end they sent a sum of £500 through Mr. Sotheron Estcourt, M.P., to the Rev. W. N. Molesworth, the Vicar of Spotland, for the use of the co-operators, free of interest, on the condition that it was lent free of interest to co-operative families suffering from the cotton famine. Six trustees were appointed—two from the Pioneer Society, two from the Corn Mill, and two from the Manufacturing Society. The trustees undertook to do their best to collect the money when prosperity returned, and to hand it over to the Rev. Mr. Molesworth. The money was lent in sums from £1 to £5 to persons depositing their "law books," containing a record of their deposits in the Store. By this means, a member having a few pounds in the Store could borrow money to that amount without withdrawing his capital from the Store. By continuing to deal with the Store, the profit upon his purchases and interest upon his capital invested, continued to accumulate, enabling him eventually to pay back the loan. Only £361 required to be lent up to the end of 1864. During the first half-year of 1863 £13 were repaid. In the second half-year £37 were repaid. In the third quarter of 1864 £26 were repaid, and the fourth quarter of 1864 £32. Ultimately, it was all repaid, and £100 of interest was accumulated. The gentlemen who lent the money, at the same time, gave it to the co-operators, should it be refunded, provided they put it to some useful purpose, which met the approval of the donors. It was permitted to be devoted to the instruction of members under the title of a Special Education Fund. Mr. Ormerod related that the expenses of distributing the fund up to the end of 1864 scarcely exceeded £2. But though they advertised the existence of the fund, and explained the advantages it offered to those members who needed help, it went out so slowly that some began to think that co-operators were too independent to borrow, or that they were really better off than their fellow-workers who had never been co-operators.

The interest arising from the Special Educational Fund enables instructional classes to be assisted for the advantage of the families of members. Some years lectures have been given to the members by persons likely to add to their instruction. When they were specially engaged the expenses were paid out of the proceeds of this fund. Recent Almanacs of the Store now contain this announcement:—"Science, Art, and French Classes.—These classes were inaugurated by the Educational Committee in 1873, and have since continued to be carried on successfully. The following subjects are now taught by able teachers, *viz.*, :—Mathematics, geometrical and mechanical drawing, theoretical mechanics, physiology, botany, magnetism and electricity, inorganic chemistry, freehand and model drawing, geometry and perspective, accoustics, light and heat, and the French language. All sons and daughters of members should avail themselves of these classes."

Seeing the generous interest in the fortunes of the Pioneers shown by Mr. Sotheron Estcourt, Estcourt Square, or Terrace, or Street, would be a pleasant name to give to one of the lines of buildings (when a new name is wanted) on the Pioneers' estate. It concerns us all who care for the honour and progress of co-operation to bear in grateful regard the memory of everyone who has signally aided it in the past, when it was unfriended and struggling.

The following table shows the number of students in each division since the commencement of the classes :—

Year.	In Science Classes.	Examined in Science.	In Art Classes.	Examined in Art	In the Technology Classes.	Examined in Technology.
1873	31	16	...	...	...	...
1874	51	30	49	40	...	...
1875	83	68	88	59	...	...
1876	103	68	94	63	...	...
1877	88	73	68	60	...	...
1878	131	86	86	43	...	...
1879	174	134	84	48	...	...
1880	162	121	76	51	...	...
1881	143	110	77	55	...	...
1882	188	134	58	39	6	4
1883	222	164	78	51	92	57
1884	222	151	85	66	87	47
1885	232	170	75	43	42	27
1886	261	192	73	50	141	75
1887	201	163	54	36	74	50
1888	207	155	37	30	50	26
1889	207	167	54	34	49	30
1890	199	160	39	22	36	26
1891	157	124	46	27	33	28

The decrease in the number of students during the past few years is accounted for by the starting of other classes, and especially by the art and technological work which the Technical School Committee have undertaken since 1887 and 1888. But the Pioneers at the Whitworth Road Store have by far the best chemical laboratory in the town, and they alone offer prizes in all their classes. The income for the prizes is derived from the Sotheron-Estcourt Fund (of which mention has been made) which realises about £26 per year. With this money prizes of 10s. and 5s. are given to the most successful students in each stage of each subject.

It ought to be put on record that for fifteen or sixteen years they provided the larger part of the science and art teaching in Rochdale ; and this at but trifling expense to themselves, for the Government grant has practically sufficed to meet the cost of tuition.

The following return, issued by Mr. Barnish, the librarian, shows the number of volumes in the library, and the extent to which they were used in 1890-91 :—

	No. of Vols.	No. Issued.
Theology, Morals, Metaphysics.	702	722
Arts and Sciences	905	1,904
History and Biography	2,798	1,235
Natural History	482	502
Social and Political Philosophy, &c.	780	391
Poetry, Fine Arts, and the Drama	766	1,092
Geography, Voyages, and Travels	987	1,883
Works of Fiction, Tales, &c.	4,103	25,039
Miscellaneous Literature	3,268	2,730
	14,791	35,498

REFERENCE LIBRARY.

			Vols.
Central Library,		Toad Lane	547
Branch	,,	Castleton	95
,,	,,	Buersil	74
,,	,,	Bamford	75
,,	,,	Oldham Road	81
,,	,,	Pinfold	83
,,	,,	Whitworth Road	84
,,	,,	Shawclough	78
,,	,,	Spotland Bridge	87
,,	,,	School Lane	78
,,	,,	Wardleworth Brow	79
,,	,,	Sudden Brow	70
,,	,,	Milkstone	71
,,	,,	Norden	71
,,	,,	Newbold	66
,,	,,	Gravel Hole	65
,,	,,	Slattocks	69
,,	,,	Greenbooth	64
Branch Lending Library, Greenbooth			316
The Branch Libraries contain			2,153

In addition there are 374 "select books and local pamphlets." These libraries are a noble achievement for a society of working men.

While there have been a few grumblers, almost from the first, the bulk of the members gave no sign of dissatisfaction at part of the profits being used for educational purposes.

THE PRESIDENTS OF THE SOCIETY.

The office of president has been filled each year as follows :—

1844 Miles Ashworth
1845 Charles Howarth
1846 James Smithies
1847 John Kershaw
1848 James Tweedale
1849 John Cockcroft
1850 John Cockcroft
1851 John Kershaw
1852 J. J. Hill
1853 John Cockcroft
1854 John Cockcroft
1855 John Cockcroft
1856 Abraham Greenwood
1857 John Cockcroft
1858 John Cockcroft
1859 John Cockcroft
1860 John Cockcroft
1861 Abraham Howard
1862 Thomas Cheetham
1863 Samuel Newton
1864 Robert Briggs
1865 Robert Briggs
1866 Robert Briggs
1867 John Ormerod
1868 John Ormerod
1869 J. R. Shepherd
1870 J. R. Shepherd
1871 J. R. Shepherd
1872 J. R. Shepherd
1873 J. R. Shepherd
1874 J. R. Shepherd
1875 Abraham Howard
1876 Abraham Howard
1877 Abraham Howard
1878 Benjamin Horbury
1879 Benjamin Horbury
1880 Benjamin Horbury
1881 Benjamin Horbury
1882 Benjamin Horbury
1883 Benjamin Horbury
1884 James Whitworth
1885 James Whitworth
1886 Thomas Cheetham
1887 Thomas Cheetham
1888 Thomas Cheetham
1889 Thomas Cheetham
1890 Thomas Cheetham
1891 Thomas Cheetham
1892 Thomas Cheetham

The following are the fourteen principal features of the "Rochdale System" :—

1. The Pioneers set the example of beginning a Store with funds of their own providing mainly.

2. Supplying the purest provisions they could get.

3. Giving full weight and measure.

4. Charging market prices, and not underselling or competing with shopkeepers.

5. Taking no credit, nor giving any; thus discouraging debt among working-people.

6. Giving the profits made to members in proportion to their purchases; acknowledging that they who make the profit should share it.

7. Inducing members to leave their profits in the Profit Bank of the Store to accumulate, thus teaching them thrift.

8. Fixing interest at 5 per cent. that Labour and Trade (which alone make capital fruitful) may have a fair chance of gain.

9. Dividing in the workshop the profits among those who have earned them, in proportion to their wages.

10. Devoting $2\frac{1}{2}$ per cent. of all profits to education, to promote the improvement and efficiency of the members.

11. According to all members the democratic right of voting (one person one vote) upon all appointments and propositions, and according to women the like right to vote and to receive their saving whether they were single or married, and this long before the Married Woman's Property Act existed.

12. The intention of extending co-operative commerce and manufacture by the establishment of an Industrial City, in which crime and competition should cease.

13. In originating the Wholesale Buying Society, they created means of fulfilling their own professions, of supplying provisions of ascertained genuineness, which otherwise would have been impossible to them.

14. The conception of the Store as an Institution as the germ of a new social life, which should by well directed self-help ensure morality and competence to all the industrious.[1]

CHAPTER XXIV.

CONTESTS FOR PRINCIPLE.

SEVERAL exclusive characteristics of the Rochdale Society have been, happily, introduced into other societies, and therefore are now common features of co-operative associations. The determination to deal in pure provisions only, as far as they could get them, which all co-operative societies do now, required quite a propagandism to establish at first. Many members were willing to give up the endeavour to sell only pure articles, from the impossibility of getting them. To persist in trying to do what could not be done did seem absurd. It was because it ought to be done that the better class of members persisted in attempting it. It was this feeling that the pure provisions ought to be obtained that led to the working of the wholesale idea, which has since made it possible for every society to do the same thing. It was up-hill work, hardly conceivable now, to keep up an agitation for pure food. Everybody had an idea that pure food was the best; but, unfortunately, many did not like it when they got it. They did not, as we have said, know the taste of it, and their taste had to be educated; and many people no more like having their taste educated than having their minds educated. When it is done they are very glad, but they take very ill to the process.

It was the honourable boast of the Pioneers' Almanac of 1861

[1] Quoted from the "Co-operative Movement To-day," published by Methuen & Co.

that it was "a principle of the Rochdale Society to have no creditors." That meant that they did not trust anybody—not even their own members. Everybody had to pay cash down. There was no going into debt. Working people had never been accustomed to this, and did not at all like it. Most of them had no ready money at all, and therefore found it difficult to pay when they bought. They were all in debt to some local grocer, and the more honourable of them did not like taking ready money to the Store when they had not paid off their score at their next door neighbour's shop. When the middle class of people and the families of gentlemen are in debt, which every tradesman unfortunately knows, it is a very difficult thing to learn the poor a lesson which their betters could not be taught. But this is what the Co-operators of Rochdale did, and a very great merit it was to do it. When Lord Westbury's wise Bill for rendering credit illegal was brought in, the Co-operators of Rochdale were restrained from supporting it, as we have told, by reluctance to embroil themselves with the shopkeepers who were their neighbours. It is a stronger argument against shopkeeping than any co-operator ever invented—that it should be the interest of tradesmen to keep up a state of the law which affords facilities for poor people getting into debt. It was, however, by the voluntary and peremptory abolition of credit by themselves that the Rochdale Co-operators attained their great commercial success.

At the great Co-operative Festival in the Free Trade Hall, Manchester, in 1864, Mr. Thomas Bayley Potter, M.P. for Rochdale, presided, and gave important testimony to the character of co-operation. He said:—"From my experience, at the head of what is, I believe, the oldest home-trade house in Manchester, I can say that we have no accounts that are more satisfactory than those with the co-operative societies. We observe that they buy good and genuine articles only. And this does not apply merely to the drapery trade, such as I am connected with, but I have reason to know, from friends in Liverpool, dealers in sugars and dried fruits, that the buyers from the co-operative stores invariably purchase sterling articles, such as will give satisfaction to their customers. They devote £500 a year to education and recreation. I can bear testimony to the excellence of the Rochdale flour. I have not tasted better bread than that made from the Rochdale flour. During the distress these two societies have distributed £1,529 in relief, and subscribed liberally towards local charitable institutions."

By abolishing credit, co-operative societies taught saving, and saving made many rich. To this, however, there is another side. In many cases these societies, by imparting to men who never had anything, nor expected to have anything, the sweet taste of saving and possessing property, have demoralised some useful persons. Many people under the influence of these societies have forsaken patriotism for profits. And I know both co-operators and Chartists who were loud-mouthed for social and political reform, who now care no more for it than a Conservative Government; and decline to attend a public meeting on a fine night, while they would crawl, like a serpent in Eden, through a gutter in a storm after a good security. They have tasted land, and the gravel has got into their souls.

Yet to many others these societies have taught a healthy frugality they never else would have known; and enabled many an industrious son to take to his home his poor old father, who expected and dreaded to die in the workhouse, and set him down to smoke his pipe in the sunshine in the garden, of which the land and the house belong to his child.

These fine instances of benefit are not to be obscured by cases of selfishness which always occur in the transitious state of men from bad to better. As Tacitus says: "There are more willing slaves who make tyrants than there are tyrants who make forced slaves!" There are always people who are born mean, and who like to crawl and to be kicked. When such men get money they mostly turn out fools. But this class of people are a good deal generated by the greed—which never knows when to stop—which they see in the classes above them. And it is a great credit to any class of men who set a better example than they find around them.

In the last letter I received from Mr. Cooper, he criticised a remark in the "History of Co-operation in Halifax," to the effect that in the Brighouse Society they had not an average of the intelligent working men join as members. "If this be true, I conclude," wrote Mr. Cooper, "that the Brighouse—like some other societies—has made a mistake, for the very opposite of this ought to take place, and does in the best societies. Where there are no news-rooms, libraries, or educational objects connected with a store, the intelligent workman may be expected to go elsewhere, if his needs are not met at the Co-operative Society, but stores wise enough to provide news-rooms, are sure to attract those who seek food for the understanding. The libraries and reading-rooms of the Rochdale, Oldham, Bury, and some other societies draw a class of members which would not come for the money dividend alone."

In the same letter, Mr. Cooper refers to a letter I had published for him in favour of continuing open the Rochdale news-room on the Sunday. A member has made a motion that "I (William Cooper) be instructed to apologise to some half-dozen members of the Society who six months ago made a motion to close the Society's news-rooms on Sunday. However, the meeting did not pass the motion that I make an apology. As our members are not anxious to be gagged themselves, so they agreed that I also might be allowed to speak or write. I think those are misguided and misguiding members who wish to establish a censorship in co-operative societies to interdict freedom of speech or pen to servants and members thereof."

Mr. Bamford, in answer to inquiries addressed to him by me,

says :—"You ask me to write you, as if you were an ignorant outsider, understanding nothing, and wanting to know everything and see everything, as people on the spot see it. I will endeavour to do so. On the part of what has now become a large section in the Society there is a natural fear lest too much credit be given to a few individuals for having brought the co-operative system to what it is in Rochdale. Those who come into a movement after the rough work has been got through, and who by their numbers give magnitude to it, are apt to claim more credit for its successes than is their due.

"The early minute books are certainly an interesting study, and give to the student an idea of the type of men who carried this movement through its early struggles. There was a spirit of earnest reality about them that found unequivocal expression in curt records. The following minute, passed by the committee in June, 1854, is an apt illustration of this. It is as follows :—'That Cooper, the cashier, be exempt from coffee grinding.' What a curious combination of duties that would be thought to-day. Fancy the smart cashier at one of our large stores taking his turn at the coffee mill. Yet it appears these men had to fulfil the functions of clerks, committee-men, coffee-grinders, and shopmen. I wonder, if circumstances required it, whether the present generation of co-operators would be found equal to that."

About this period, twenty years after the formation of the Store, a new set of men appear to be brought upon the stage. And there is about the records a different class of entries from those the Society has recorded before. The storm is over, the battle has ceased, the ground won is being steadily occupied, and the new generation have chiefly to cultivate their inheritance and bury the old Pioneers. Before we quit the field let us take a last look at the watercourses which brought it fertility.

One of the skilful explorers for materials who have aided me in this final narrative has been, like Mr. Stanley, to the Ujiji of early stores—namely, to Rochdale, and investigated the archives there. The minutes there kept may be likened to the tributary streams which fed from the first the great Nile of co-operation. He first comes upon a curious little rivulet. On April 4, 1861, a resolution of the Board decides that "William Cooper have a month's notice to leave."

But at the next meeting he was re-engaged. What follows no doubt sufficiently explains this.

At a quarterly meeting, October 7th, 1861, the following resolution was passed :—"That the president of this Society be instructed to entirely repudiate the statement appearing in the *Counsellor*, September, 1861, which statement is said to have been furnished by Mr. Cooper, the secretary of the Society." This repudiation prepared by the president (Mr. Howard), approved by the Board, read at the monthly meeting, and at the subsequent quarterly meeting, by a special resolution, was entered in the minute book. It was as follows :—

"Dear Sir,—You will excuse me while I draw your attention to an article which appeared in the *Counsellor* for September, headed 'The Sects among the Co-operators,' containing statements (said to be facts) leading your readers to believe that some sectarian influence has been brought to bear upon the discussion of a certain question [the Labour Question] which was a short time ago under consideration in this town, and warning new co-operative bodies from accepting members who are connected with certain religious denominations [no such warning was given] which are there named. The article has been much condemned and deplored, so much so that, on its being submitted to the consideration of our quarterly meeting on Monday night, the 7th inst., a resolution was moved and carried—'That our president be instructed to entirely repudiate a statement said to be furnished by our financial clerk, Mr. Wm. Cooper, and which appeared in a publication denominated the *Counsellor*, for September, 1861, such statement being considered detrimental to the interests of this Society ; also that the people of this country in forming new co-operative societies, be recommended to seek their members from all classes and conditions of men.' I beg to inform your readers that the principles of the Rochdale Co-operators are—1st, not to inquire into the political or religious opinions of those who apply for membership into ours or any of the various co-operative societies in our town ; 2nd, that the consideration of the various political and religious differences of the members who compose our societies should prevent us from allowing into our councils or practices anything which might be construed into an advantage to any single one of each sect or opinion. The result of these principles has been that in the discussion and determination of all the great questions which have divided us, there might be seen ranged on both sides men of various creeds and opinions. That our policy has been such I need only quote from an article which appeared in the Equitable Pioneers' Society's Almanac, for 1860, where the writer is, for the time being, the mouthpiece of the Society. He says—'The present co-operative movement does not intend to meddle with the various religious or political differences which now exist in society, but by a common bond, namely, that of self-interest, to join together the means, the energies, and talents of all for the common benefit of each.' The co-operator does not seek to inforce or carry out any particular doctrines of any particular individual.' We think that all such statements and recommendations [Mr. Cooper made none] in your article of September can only be followed by mischievous effects, and ought not to have been made by those professing themselves the dearest friends of our hitherto successful principles. I recommend, in the name of the Pioneers and Co-operators of Rochdale, all new societies never to inquire what politics or what religion the persons applying for membership are, but take all those who are willing to subscribe to the rules.—I am, dear sir, on behalf of the Society, yours most respectfully, ABRAHAM HOWARD, *President.*"

This letter was published by me for Mr. Howard, I being editor of the *Counsellor*, a quiet quarto journal, in which secular, co-operative, political, and religious writers endeavoured to give counsel to working men on public affairs, without dictation, assumption, arbitrary authority, or invective. Those who gave advice or suggestions in it were understood to examine both sides of the question on which they presumed to offer an opinion. At that time Mr. William Cooper, on my solicitation, wrote a paper on the Manufacturing Society in Rochdale, which was then a co-operative company, and which had for three years been regarded with satisfaction and pride as such. But there had sprung up a set of Aaron-rod shareholders, who thought work should have bare wages, and capital swallow all the profits, just as that hungry rod of Aaron swallowed up all the other rods. Mr. Cooper divided the capitalists into two classes—monopolising capitalists and participating capitalists. He was afraid the monopolists would out-vote the participators, which they eventually did. I asked him to give me an account of the sects among the co-operators in Rochdale. Mr. Cooper did not volunteer the information, I asked him for it. There was no concealment of the source, for I mentioned his name in the *Counsellor*. None of us were underground agitators, we always worked above board. I wanted to know how far different classes of Christians in the Rochdale Society were in favour of industrial partnerships, so that when you knew the religious composition of a society you might know what the prospects of the recognition of labour in manufacturing might be. Mr. Cooper gave me this information, particularising the sects who supported the principle, and those who were against it.

This was the little playful communication against which Mr. Howard levelled his grave official letter. In a note upon it, I said, "It concluded with some sentiments I very cordially agreed with, and had never transgressed against." There was not a word of criticism or inculcation of any sectarian principle in anything I published. All I sought was an estimate of the tendencies of sects in regard to industrial partnerships, just as the chemist would estimate the specific gravity of the different liquids with the view to determine their value in different experiments.[1] I always counselled co-operators to be tolerant of each other's opinions, and to remember, with Paul, that charity was greater than faith or hope.

The other day a new café was opened near St. Mary's Church, in

[1] What Mr. Cooper reported was that for the Recognition of Labour to participate in Profit "Secularists voted as one man, next the Unitarians, after them Churchmen. Against the principle were a united party from the Milton Church (Independents), after them the Methodists, and a number from other sects ranked on the same side."—*Counsellor*, Sept., 1861. What I added was that new societies seeking members who would vote for Labour, knew what sects to visit.

the Strand, by two clever Swiss gentlemen. Probably a thousand pounds have been spent in fitting up the place, and no handsomer or completer café has been opened in London. The interior is quite that of another country than this, yet it has only one penny ink pot, and a halfpenny pen in it, and if a visitor requires it he has to wait while the proprietor finishes his letter to his grandmother. It is quite right the old lady should be written to, but it is a loss of time to have to wait every day while it is done. I thought how often a splendid conception is marred by a small omission. So it is with co-operative stores which have no propagandist department. Rochdale would not be famous as it now is, nor would co-operation be what it is, had not the early Pioneers wisely provided for the propagation of their principles.

In an open space on the left bank of the river Roche, and in the most public thoroughfare in the town, is a drinking fountain erected by the Society and made over to the town authorities on April 19th, 1855, in the following terms:—"To the mayor, aldermen, and burgesses of Rochdale: On behalf of the members of the Rochdale Equitable Pioneers' Society we beg to present to you, for the use of the inhabitants of and strangers visiting the town of Rochdale, the bronze drinking fountain and lamp erected at the bottom of Drake Street, opposite the Wellington Hotel. Hoping that you will accept the same in the spirit in which it is given, and that it may long be a use and an ornament to the town, is the sincere desire of yours, very respectfully, on behalf of the Rochdale Equitable Pioneers' Society,

"JOHN COCKCROFT, *President.*
"ROBT. BRIGGS, *Secretary.*"

This gift was accepted. The utilitarian monument stands on the spot proposed for it. As the parched Oriental traveller from Egypt or India, visiting the earliest shrine of co-operation, enters the town of Rochdale, he passes by the Pioneers' fountain, and can quench his thirst before exploring the wonders of the great Store.

CHAPTER XXV.

DEAD PIONEERS.

IT may seem to contemporary co-operators, who know how largely the present development and prosperity of the movement is owing to the new generation of advocates, that too much credit is given to the former generation, who set it going and laid down the lines upon which it has proceeded, and that these pages are of the nature of a partisan history. But the reader will find that this is not so. The Apostles never made Christianity what it is. George Stephenson had no idea of the railway system as we now know it. But had there been no intrepid and enthusiastic Apostles to travel and preach and suffer martyrdom, in evil days, there had been no Christianity; and had not George Stephenson thought and toiled and plotted for railways, amid ignorant capitalists and an unfriendly public, railways might now be regarded as a mere mechanical craze. Not to give honour to these originators would be injustice; not to recognise the intrinsic merit of their successors would be blindness. It happens to be a matter of historic fact that co-operation grew out of the famous social theories promulgated in the early part of this century, and the gallant and practical co-operators who first put their industrial scheme in operation planned its method of procedure and worked for it, stood by it and defended it against a world of unfriendly adversaries, until it was accepted and adopted by others—were themselves inspired and animated by the ideas of eminent theorists who went before them. I did not invent them; I found them. I did not derive their names from hearsay; I knew them. They were of all religions and all opinions—political, social, and speculative; but all stood on the side of that socialism which sought social improvement by creating new arrangements of production and distribution, by honesty in trade, and equity in the distribution of profits.

Mr. Charles Howarth died on the last day in June, 1868, and was buried in the Heywood Cemetery. He had died at 28 Wilton Street, Heywood. He went down in the mid-year time.

There were present a concourse of his friends, mostly co-operators. The Rochdale Equitable Pioneers' Society was represented by the president and two of the committee, beside some twenty other co-operators from Rochdale, who, with those from other places, formed a numerous procession. The Rev. Mr. Fox (of Heywood) read the burial service, after which Mr. Councillor Smithies (of Rochdale) said that before the relatives and friends of the deceased separated, a few remarks would be made by Mr. William Cooper, at the particular desire of Mr. Howarth. Mr. Cooper then spoke as follows:—

"Our friend who is now interred here was known and respected by all of us, and we regret that he has not lived many years longer amongst us, who have held him in high estimation. Our companion who now rests here has been distinguished by sound judgment, and for holding advanced opinions, and has laboured with steady earnestness in many causes for the freedom and benefit of himself and his fellow-man. I have known him for upwards of thirty years. He formerly was connected with the Radical movement, which aimed at obtaining political rights for the people of Great Britain and Ireland; and he just lived long enough to see the opinions which he long advocated when they were opposed by both Whig and Tory statesmen, become the law of the land. At least, every householder is a citizen; but the ballot, which he also claimed, is not yet conceded. Some of us may live to see this measure granted, to be freed from coercion and oppression by the capitalist and employer classes. Let us look at what he did as a socialist reformer. Having common sense and a strong desire to promote the welfare of the working class, he always laboured to reduce his plans and principles to practice for their benefit. He became a disciple of the late Robert Owen, and an active member of the Socialist body, and assisted in the establishment of communities of united interest, or a New *Moral* World where each should work for the good of all, and knowledge and plenty reign, and ignorance and want be unknown. But these noble objects being in advance of the people generally—could not then succeed. Yet they remind those amongst us who are here, and who then made common cause with him in these objects, of the calm, temperate, and sound judgment which he brought to bear, and the dignified and steady perseverance which he applied to make the faith which was within him a living practice. He was a warper by trade, in a cotton mill, and saw the hardships and injury to health which the long hours' system in tainted atmosphere produced. He took a prominent part in the agitation for the Ten Hours Factory Act, making speeches at public meetings in its favour, and collecting subscriptions to defray the expenses of the short time movement. He laboured mostly amongst his Rochdale townsmen. He was sent as a delegate to London to confer with members of Parliament and watch the Ten Hours Bill while before the House of Commons. In those days employers of labour were not in favour of legislation as between themselves and their workpeople. On one occasion he was called into the office by his employers, and they made the proposal that he should remain in the office, and they would send for the hands one by one out of the mill and put the question to each whether he wanted the Ten Hours Bill with a reduction in wages corresponding with the shorter time. By this means, said they, it could be ascertained whether a majority of their workpeople were in favour or against the proposed Ten Hours Factory Act. Mr. Howarth agreed so to do, provided his employers would first consent for him to have a meeting with the workpeople in one of the rooms of the mill to explain to them the subject. The employers did not assent to this, so there was no meeting of the workpeople or calling them into the office. Our friend saw many evils in society, and like a skilful reformer, sought remedies for them.

"The people's earnings were in part absorbed by middlemen; they were also in debt with the shopkeepers, and adulterations of food detrimental to their health were being imposed upon them. To rectify these evils, Mr. Howarth propounded that the working classes should become their own purveyors and shopkeepers. The Pioneers' Society's rules were mostly drawn up by him, and the principle of dividing profits on purchases in proportion to each member's trade was his proposal. The rules further provide that the government of the Society should be in the hands of the members, the management being vested in a committee elected by and from amongst themselves. Mr. Howarth also assisted in drawing up the constitution of the Rochdale District Corn Mill Society. Later still he assisted in forming the North of England Co-operative Wholesale Society, Limited, of 58 Dantzie St., Manchester, and was one of its first directors; and up to the time of his death was a director of the Co-operative Insurance Company. In life he was a useful citizen; a free-thinker in religion; in political and social questions an advanced and consistent reformer; a good husband and father; a true, constant, and faithful friend."

Mr. Cooper, not long after, needed a friend to speak at his own grave.

William Cooper was one of the "twenty-eight." The Rochdale papers gave a long report of the proceedings at his grave. The most complete narrative appeared in the *Social Economist* of London, then edited by myself and Mr. E. O. Greening (a journal which was discontinued by arrangement, that the *Co-operative News* might become the official and chief organ of Co-operation).

It was in the October following the death of Mr. Howarth that Mr. Cooper died. He was the first cashier of the Toad Lane Store. He carried the gold to the bank when it was so light a quantity that a rabbit might have drawn it; and he carried it when it was so heavy a load that it produced a rupture, from which the carrier suffered ever after. The classic athlete trained himself by carrying a calf daily as it grew, and his strength gradually increasing with the weight of his load, he was eventually able to carry the cow. But Mr. Cooper was not so fortunate. His death, however, came by typhus. He had lost a child by it; its nurse (a relative) then suffered; the mother was seized, but happily recovered; then Mr. Cooper was stricken. He got about again, when a relapse, thought to be occasioned by too early exposure, killed him on the 31st of October, 1868. He died at his residence in the Oldham Road, Rochdale. The Store salary did not do much for the cashier in its earlier days, and it always bore small proportion to his services. "His death," the *Rochdale Observer* said, "took the town by surprise," which meant that all the town knew him, which was true.

He was interred in the Rochdale Cemetery, when a public funeral was arranged by the Society. The day was most unfavourable. Besides mourning coaches, almost every coach in the town was engaged to protect his friends from the pitiless rain; and the procession, as it passed from his residence through the town, was watched by crowds of people at the corners of the various streets. The co-operative establishments were partially closed from the time of his death, and a flag, half-mast high, floated from the roof of the centre Store in Toad Lane.

The funeral procession was as follows:—Mr. G. J. Holyoake, Mr. Lloyd Jones, Mr. James Smithies, Mr. Abraham Greenwood, Mrs. Cooper and family; the Clerks; the President and Committee of the Equitable Pioneers' Society; of the Library; of Mitchell Hey

Mills; of the Corn Mill Society; Mr. Wm. Nuttall of Oldham and others; Committees, Managers of the various departments; and the co-operative workpeople.

Mrs. Cooper wished me, as a near friend of her husband, to speak at his grave. Owing to the heavy rain the address was delivered in the chapel of the cemetery. Standing at the reading-desk, I said:—

"We depart from the ceremonies usual on these occasions, from a preference for others which, to us of the school of thought to which Mr. Cooper belonged, are simpler and more sincere. I have not for many years come to the interment of any one, not of my own blood, for whose death I have felt a sharper or deeper regret than for that of Mr. Cooper. In this assembly there are many who will have honoured names in the history of co-operation, but I think I may say safely that there will be no one who will earn it by more patience, by more self-sacrifice, by more ceaseless toil, than Cooper has done. I have been accustomed to regard him as the drudge of co-operation. When visitors arriving in London from abroad have applied to me for information, or for a letter of introduction to him, I was always sure that Cooper would be at their service. It was one of the satisfactions, it was part of the pride I had in Rochdale, that there were persons in this town, beyond those in any other town, who not only cared for the principles they had chosen to promote, but who would take trouble to diffuse them. Cooper was not only the drudge, he was the newsman of co-operation. He was always ready for service in any way. I have wondered at the unwearied way in which he wrote letters. That was his self-imposed mission. It was his distinction that he had a passion for writing letters. Whoever wanted information could obtain it from Cooper. He spared himself no trouble; he gave the leisure of his mornings, of his mid-day, of his evenings, and of his Sabbaths, freely and ungrudgingly to sending replies to the most distant or unknown person in any part of the country, or in any part of the world, who asked him for co-operative news. Now, that unnoticed work—that trouble which so few people think of, which so few perform, and fewer still regard—that sort of service it was Cooper's pride and pleasure and credit to render. Knowledge of the equity of co-operation he cared to diffuse abroad. He saw that equity was the soul of co-operation, and was anxious for it to prevail. He thought much higher of the benefits co-operative principles would render morally, than of the mere pecuniary benefits they would confer. Who now will do what he did so long and did so well? His letters were of necessity often reiterative, but they were always direct, relevant, and instructive, written with a purpose; and they might always be relied upon. He had also another claim upon our regard for services which must have been to him in his latter days a source of great personal satisfaction. When the question of the freedom of the slave hung in the balance, and rested upon what was done by the working classes of this part of England, he had a zeal which an American abolitionist would have been proud of, to preserve a right public opinion on that question. He had never seen those dusky millions of men who were held in slavery, and who might have been again precipitated into it but for the tone and feeling taken in this country ; yet he cared for them with almost the vehemence and sympathies of a woman. His zeal was personal and persistent. Having chosen his own principles, he advanced them with singleness of purpose. That must have been a satisfaction to him in the presence of death. I do not know that better credentials could be presented by anyone hereafter than those of a life of earnest and sincere work intended for the benefit of others. What we witnessed in this town as we came here—despite the dreariness of the day, and its inclement unfitness for any persons to be abroad—the number of people who assembled to witness his remains pass by, testify to the esteem in which he was held by his fellow-townsmen. In other towns in Great Britain, in Germany, in France, in America—in all rising centres of co-operation—his death will be deplored by co-operative inquirers. Those who were nearest and dearest to him may take some consolation in the consciousness that the services which he so generously rendered have been so widely useful, so widely known and regarded."

The editor of the *Co-operator*, in a notice of the death of Mr. Cooper, quoted these apposite lines :—

"There is no death : what seems so is transition ;
This life of mortal breath
Is but the suburb to the life Elysian,
Whose portal we call death."

Let us hope all this is true. So hard-working and zealous a co-operator as Cooper had as good claims as anyone to be in Elysium. And if there be a post-office on his side, and anyone in want of information about the movement on this planet, he will be very happy in furnishing it.

Next, news came to me of the death of Samuel Ashworth in a letter from Mr. Nuttall. Being characteristic of the writer, and containing facts honourable to Mr. Ashworth not otherwise mentioned, I quote it here :—

"Samuel Ashworth is dead. The youngest, I believe, of the Rochdale 'twenty-eight.' He was only 46 years of age. He was the buyer and manager for the Rochdale Pioneers for about twenty years, and gave up that position to take another still higher in the co-operative world, *viz.*, the North of England Co-operative Wholesale, which he retained to his death. In both positions he made many friends, and I question whether any enemies. When he left Rochdale Society (in 1866) its figures stood thus :—members, 6,246 ; capital, £99,989 ; annual trade, £249,122 ; and profit, £31,931 ;

while for 1870, four years later, the following decreases appear—members, 5,560; funds, £80,291; annual trade, £223,021; and profit, £25,209. Ashworth's loss will be felt at the Wholesale many days. He had the confidence of both buyers, masters, and servants. His word of advice to the former was always relied on and respected, and rarely indeed was he mistaken. When he undertook the buying at the Wholesale Society its annual trade was at the rate of £180,000; at his death it was £800,000. Although he took no part in its formation, yet when placed in a position where his business tact, sterling honesty, sound judgment and firmness, without rudeness, enabled him to serve the movement, he did it thoroughly. Reared in the 'market world,' he was no theorist, but some trouble to theorists until their plans were matured, when, being convinced, he was a good and useful supporter. He hated changes and changers, had strong convictions, and long ones, which frequently troubled his best friends. A more faithful servant never lived. He died yesterday morning, and leaves nine of the active workers of the 'old twenty-eight' who are known to have made the world move. Within three years there have now passed from amongst us—

"CHARLES HOWARTH, aged 50.
"WILLIAM COOPER, aged 46.
"JAMES SMITHIES, aged 50.
"MILES ASHWORTH (Father), aged 76
"SAMUEL ASHWORTH (Son), aged 46."

Mr. Nuttall has the genius of figures. He marks Mr. Ashworth's merit by an exhibition of financial facts, showing declensions occurring in the Society which he left, and the growth of that which he next joined. Had Mr. Nuttall been an apostle, he had estimated Christianity by the *number* of its miracles. But he marks, in well chosen terms that we all well know, that Mr. Ashworth's death made another gap in the ranks of the famous Rochdale Co-operators. Many men die and it does not matter; when a man like Ashworth dies it does matter. Men miss him, and to be missed is distinction and praise.

James Smithies, the chief, one may say, of the Fighting Pioneers, is also gone. During the years 1855-6 there appears to have been a continuous struggle against the imposition of the Income-tax. Mr. Smithies was always chosen to fight the battle in the courts and before the Commissioners. The committee seem to have become tired of the fruitless representations made by them, and they passed the following resolution:—"That we do not pay the Income-tax until we are made." The week following they entered a not less decisive minute, namely, "That the Income-tax Commissioner take his own course." The said Commissioner did so, and desisted from his bewildered work. To receive 6,000 letters demanding the return of the tax, to inquire into them and return the amount illegally gathered was a discomforting prospect.[1]

James Smithies was the only one of the Pioneers belonging to the "twenty-eight" who obtained municipal honour. He was one of the Town Council in his later years. In some important respects he was the greatest of the Pioneers. Without him, Mr. Howarth had devised principles in vain. Without him, Mr. Cooper had had a limited sphere of propagandism. Without him, Mr. Greenwood had had to labour much longer before he had got the Wholesale to go. It was Mr. Smithies' measureless merriment which kept co-operation in good countenance in the evil days. He laughed the Society into existence, gave the timid courage, and made the grim-faced members genial. His happy nature, his wise tolerance, his boundless patience with dulness, ignorance, and discontent, made him to exercise the great influence which kept the Society together. He was my first friend among the Pioneers. In his house, among the wool, I had my home in all the earlier years when I was a wandering lecturer in Rochdale. It was he also who caused me to maintain the theory that human nature was different in Rochdale to what it was elsewhere in England. It was Smithies who made the difference. What merriment we have had by his pleasant fireside! Ah, how sad I was when I looked last in his bright face on his dying bed—which not even death could darken, nor dim the hope and generous ardour which inspired his last injunction to a friend, "Stick to Toad Lane." What watchfulness, what fervour, what resources, what incessant toil, what ceaseless service, what radiant enthusiasm he displayed! How generous, how self-denying, how self-regardless he was! If portrait be painted or bust carved of the old Pioneers, Smithies should first be taken. I hope that to Mrs. Smithies it may long be consolation to know that her husband's devotion to co-operation, which in earlier years cost her many attentions, and her pleasant hospitality to her husband's friends are not unregarded or forgotten.

This narrative ought to include some notice of Mr. Alderman Livsey, one of the earliest public friends of the Pioneers. In their service he was ready all the days of his life in counsel and defence. As the speech made in the Public Hall after his burial took place mainly at the desire of the Pioneers as a public expression of their regard for him, I venture to include in this story some record of it, more especially as it affords glimpses of the local life of the town, which has notable features besides that of co-operation.[2]

---

[1] What would be the effect, in the case of Rochdale, where there were then about 6,000 co-operators, of levying that tax upon the transactions of the Societies? The managers would advise the members, the vast majority of whom were, by the smallness of their income, not liable to the tax, to apply for its return, as paid upon their proportion of the profits. The collectors found that to levy this tax would give them infinitely more trouble than it was worth, and they wisely thought it better to take it from the people where they were liable to pay it, individually.—*Speech of E. O. Greening*, Society of Arts, London.

[2] An interesting record of the Life and Times of the late Alderman Livsey has been published by Miss M. R. Lahee. Abel Heywood and Son, Manchester, 1866.

Mr. Alderman Livsey, born June 17th, 1815, the year of the Peace, died in January 25th, 1864. For some time before his death there was a strong desire in the town to see him elected mayor. Had it not been for his failing health the honour would have been accorded him. A public meeting was held, at which the burgesses expressed their wish that the civic chair should be offered him by the Town Council. The Tories, uniting against it, turned the balance against the proposal. Livsey was not a favourite in that quarter. On November 18th, 1863, at a great meeting at the Public Hall, an address was presented to him by his townsmen in acknowledgment of his public and political services, Mr. Bright bearing testimony to thirty years' knowledge of his exertions on behalf of the town and un-enfranchised classes. His death two months later was really a matter of town sorrow. Even the party politically opposed to him regretted the loss of the quaint, vigorous, original character, which had often won attention and respect for Rochdale, of which his qualities were taken to be representative.

The Mayor, Mr. Samuel Stott, wrote a public letter to Mrs. Livsey and her daughter, expressing condolence and regret at Mr. Livsey's death. Mr. Bright—who would have attended the funeral had he not been detained by political duties at Birmingham—wrote to say that "he would like to join in raising a sum of money to erect a modest memorial over the grave of a man who had been useful both to the town and country," and added, "Tom Livsey was a diamond, though not highly polished." Mr. Cobden wrote from Midhurst valued words of tribute. He said:—"It is not too much to say that during the last quarter of a century there were no working men in Rochdale who, if they believed themselves aggrieved by those in authority, did not turn their footsteps instinctively towards the door of Mr. Livsey for advice and assistance; and if their grievance was a just one, not otherwise, they found in him a self-sacrificing friend and protector."

Mr. Cobden was a representative who took interest in every class of his constituents. Mr. Alderman G. L. Ashworth, who spoke at the opening of the Central Stores, related that when he took Mr. Cobden to see the library and news-rooms of the Pioneers he said, "These co-operators have advantages which could hardly be surpassed by any club in London."

In a letter I some time ago addressed to Co-operative Societies, I have mentioned that at one time I had views of obtaining a settlement in the parish of Rochdale. The following passage in the life of Livsey in part explains this choice. Mr. Livsey had the strongest aversion to the Poor Law, as subjecting honest indigence to penal treatment, and he resisted any attempt to erect a "Bastile," as a poorhouse was then called, in Rochdale. The Poor Law Inspector of that day, Mr. Mayne Waring, insisted upon this being done. Mr. Livsey was equal to half-a-dozen inspectors, but impatient of wasting weeks of correspondence with red tapists he decided at once to appeal to Cæsar himself. In the winter of 1858 he went to London, and by Mr. Bright, M.P., and Sir A. Ramsay, M.P., was introduced to Mr. Sotheron-Estcourt, the then president of the Poor Law Board. It was to this interview that Mr. Alderman Livsey referred with so much just pride and gratification at the Public Hall, when presented with the address of the burgesses. The *Rochdale Observer* said :—"We cannot do better than give the conversation in Mr. Livsey's own words—'Mr. Sotheron-Estcourt said to us, "Oh, but yours are not workhouses, you know; they are almshouses." "Yes," I replied, "that is exactly the word; they are almshouses, and they are not intended to be workhouses in your sense of the word. They are intended as homes for the homeless poor." That was one of the most pleasurable moments I ever remember, to hear Mr. Estcourt acknowledge that our workhouses so-called were almshouses.'"

When his burial day came all the town was literally in the streets, showing regard to his memory. A large assembly afterwards met in the Public Hall, when Mr. Alderman George Healey, a valued colleague of Mr. Livsey, presided, and I spoke upon Mr. Livsey's public character and services to social as well as political reform. The following is the substance of what appeared in the forgotten or inaccessible newspaper reports of the time :—

"Our common friend, the late Mr. Alderman Livsey, loved public life. Next to his home he was happiest on the platform. Here the people were accustomed to meet him. It is, therefore, fitting that we should here, in this hall, where we so lately greeted him in life, prove that the words then addressed to his own ear were not the mere political compliments of the hour, but the echo of feelings having that stamp of sincerity which exists beyond the grave. We owe it to ourselves to show this; hearing no longer that hearty voice—missing evermore that co-operation, that untiring devotion, given to the good of others which we all knew so well in him.

"Never, except in London when some royal head was laid low, has there been witnessed such thronged streets as filled this town at his burial. 'Tom Livsey,' to use the affectionate term of Mr. Bright, 'was carried to his last home with honour. He lived among the people like a man, he fought for them like a hero, and they buried him like a king.'

"We all felt the earnestness and appropriateness of the addresses at the cemetery by the Rev. Mr. Lewis and the Rev. Mr. Burchell. Nor do we pass unnoticed the pleasant Christian feeling with which the reverend vicar, Dr. Molesworth, cancelling the ancient Church Rate feud with our lost friend, Mr. Livsey, made calls of kindness upon him in his illness, and caused the muffled bells of the church to peal at his death; acts which carried with them the influence of many sermons.

"The characteristic of Mr. Livsey was that he not only meant to do good—he did it. He had not only the will, he had the power, to be useful. He was a strong man in his place. He was no fireside reformer. He sacrificed his ease—he gave his time—he spent his means to accomplish what he thought beneficial to his townsmen and his countrymen. He gave himself trouble to serve the people. Many think they do a great deal if they take in a paper which tells them of public affairs. Mr. Livsey helped to make the affairs. He did rough work, without which no public affairs, worthy of the name, are made. Having a manly and generous heart, he could never rest while he knew that any man was suffering from an injustice which he thought he could redress or abridge.

"I think much of municipal service. I wish to increase the respect in which municipal distinctions are held. The Corporation is the wholesome part of our town life—it carries the soul over the counter and causes private men to take interest in public affairs—it converts the artisan, the tradesman, the merchant, into the citizen. It is, therefore, in my mind praise to say that Mr. Livsey was, as an alderman, worth caring for, and was one who kept his principles with his elevation. He always stood by the honest 'Old Charter.' He loved men who meant something. I know that when illustrious exiles—when Mazzini, or Kossuth, or Garibaldi, or Louis Blanc wanted the aid of English public opinion to raise an oppressed nation, Livsey was to be counted upon to aid, as were others here. He was foremost among those who helped to connect the public men of England with the public life of the world—by the living bond of political sympathy. The working men of this town have made Rochdale a place of mark. I have myself given letters of introduction here to professors and political economists from France, Spain, Germany, Italy, Russia, and India. When, however, the idea of co-operation was in its infancy in this place, Thomas Livsey was the first man of the master-class who gave it his encouragement and serviceable support; and he, until the last, fitly represented its sagacity, its perseverance, and cordiality, as he did, in his society and station, represent the best qualities of the intelligence and sturdy honesty of his native town.

"Of the achievements of his active life two deserve special remembrance—his efforts to procure the Ten Hours Bill and to fix at a democratic amount the municipal franchise in this town. The Ten Hours Bill has proved to be a signal act of domestic humanity. For such a purpose as limiting the hours of labour of children no Act of Parliament ought ever to have been needed. No parent of common sense and spirit ought to have ever permitted a child to be excessively worked. But, since it was permitted, it was the right thing to put it down by force. Mr. Livsey gave years of labour to aid in this. The result has increased the health and the stature of this generation.

"None but a democrat who knew what his principles meant would ever have fought the 'Three Wards' battle in this town, which ended in reducing the municipal franchise lower than in any other town in the kingdom. By this measure Mr. Livsey extended the boundary of freedom in this country. Democracy signifies respect for the equal liberty of others—its spirit is that of confidence in the good sense, the self-respect, and instinct of order in your own countrymen. The more there are brought within the pale of the constitution the better. He who is not recognised by the State is not responsible to it. It is a crime in all who withhold the vote; it is a crime in all who do not wish for it. The one party imposes slavery, and the other consents to it. Who says the workmen of England are not to be trusted with the franchise? The Government takes one or another of the common people from the streets. In the dark day of Inkerman he turns up in the bloody defiles of that fatal field, and leaderless and alone he protects the honour of England with his solitary sword. On the burning plains of Hindostan, in the swamps of China, at any lonely or distant post, the English plebeian pours out his blood with as much promptness and bravery as any nobleman—his courage is as high, his faithfulness as inviolable—neglect does not move him, death does not deter him. Are not men of this order, whose swords carve our renown, who make our history, who save our empire, worthy of a vote in the choice or rejection of the titled charlatan who shall sit in the House of Commons to levy or dispose of our taxes, or plunge us into new wars? It was against this discreditable exclusion that the late Alderman Livsey set his face with indignation. He had 'that greatness which belongs to a life spent in struggling against powerful wrong.'[1] He had an insurgent nature. He regarded injustice as infamous, and as an imputation on all who submitted to it, and he conspired against it resolutely. Prayer is well meant, and consolation is kind, yet holier are those acts which bring deliverance and make sorrow unnecessary. To trample down some haughty wrong—to build up some generous improvement—bring good thoughts in death. A thousand prayers are condensed in one material improvement for the good of humanity.

"Let us not forget that there is one tribute which it is in the power of all to pay in some degree, and which, if neglected, would render all works of praise very poor, and that tribute is the continuance of the work upon which he set his heart. The best applause to give to a man of worth is to imitate him.

"We live in the main under a government of reason—not in a very brilliant form yet, but that is what it comes to. Denunciation of persons we do not want, but denunciation of wrong we do want. Honest agitators are not demagogues, they are advocates; and advocates are very much wanted. Revolution is no longer necessary in English politics. We had some wise forefathers in old times, of whom modern Radicals in many towns know too little,

[1] George Eliot.

who laid broad foundations of freedom in our midst. It only needs that we build upon these resolutely, and the English educated classes, who always move in the grooves of precedent, will acquiesce with a reasonable readiness. Mr. Livsey had this knowledge. With all his abruptness of speech at times, he had deference to the opinions of others, with the instinct of a gentleman. I never witnessed a more conspicuous instance than when he last stood in this hall. The manly, uncomplaining grace with which he alluded to and accepted his defeat of the mayoralty; his refusal to allow it to be a cause of difference in the Liberal party, which needs always to be united, struck me at the time as a sign of superior nature—jealous not to put himself or his personal claims in the place of his cause.

"What could indicate higher practical quality in a reformer than his successful exertions in transferring the gas company from private hands to those of the Corporation? This step, accomplished by three years of costly advocacy to himself, saved, as Mr. Alderman Healey computed on a late occasion, £30,000 to this town; and enabled valuable improvements to be effected without the imposition of taxes for the purpose. In no town in England has the same thing been done to the same extent. This example has a higher value than the saving even of so large a sum of money—it proves that Radicalism, in wise hands, is not declamatory, but practical; it proved that the most democratic corporation of England is the best capable of self-government—strengthening the argument in favour of trusting the people. I am glad that Rochdale has wise honour to give to the memory of such a townsman as she has lost. If good feeling did not prompt it, it would be good policy, in these days, not to let public and personal worth like his pass to the grave unrecognised. Those do well who try to preclude degeneracy among reformers. As I go over the towns of the empire, I find in many places that the sons are not equal to their fathers. Families of whom the last generation honourably heard have no representatives in this. The race continues, but the spirit is extinct. It is necessary to give attention to the public education of young men. Otherwise, Mr. Livsey caused Rochdale to be respected wherever he has acted in its name. His townsmen, low and high, have profited alike by his exertions and his example. His work will live after him, and his name become part of the best wealth of his native town.

"I do not speak of him so because he shared opinions which I sometimes express. We never spoke together upon religious topics. We always met on those happier platforms where the common purpose of the common good, so far as we could promote it, was the sole creed exacted. I always regarded him as an honest Christian gentleman, who saw in Christ the servant of the poor, and in Christianity the consecration of practical sympathy for the oppressed, whether near or afar of, of whatever colour or clime. I knew him as one whose trust was in doing right—whose worship was work—whose grace and privilege were charity. I have lived long enough to know that bigotry or intolerance is merely the outward sign of inward narrowness and self-distrust—warning you that there are men whom it is no moral good to know. Mr. Livsey, like all men who have an intelligent honesty of their own, respected that of others.

"'They nothing know to fear,
And nothing fear to know.'

"Those of us who come from afar knew him as one of the forces of opinion in these parts. Like your own great townsman, whose eloquence has given a new splendour to the English tongue, Mr. Livsey had 'firm words to put in slippery places that the country might be helped across into purpose and a definite policy of freedom.' When the public occasion required men of purpose you looked around and you always saw Livsey well up in the front. If all who meant work could count on his co-operation, all who meant public mischief had to count upon his opposition. There are many men who have a conscience, but it totters in its steps; there are many who have a just will, but it is feeble. The world is full of people who are not exactly ill-meaning; their fault is that they have no meaning, and when they act at all they act for themselves. If a fellow creature is in the water they will help him out—if they can do so without much trouble. They do not see why they should put themselves into his situation to assist him. They are sorry for him, but they will run no risk to save him. They see people struggling in poverty which will never end—in ignorance which will never be dispelled—in unhealthy circumstances which should be at once improved, suffering under pressure of unequal laws which bore upon their fathers and will depress their children, but these persons give no care, or money, or time, or trouble to alter all this. Themselves comfortable or content, they leave things to alter as they may, and leave those to suffer who must, and those to help who will. With the laborious meetings, the anxious agitations, the costly, unrequited exertions by which men are instructed and their social condition improved, these do-nothings will have nothing to do. If you want to know how numerous these people are, think of any good cause and count up those who do *not* help it. Go to any public meeting for a noble object and count up those you know who are *absent*, and then you will learn amid what a crowd of people without heart we live. To such no man owes honour—for them we feel no love. When they die we do not miss them. We do not mourn them, and when they are buried none care where they lie. Their unhonoured graves awaken no emotion that we wish to know.

"Yet, in this Egyptian darkness of self and sordidness, no sooner does a man of nobler impulse appear than men discern him by the moral light which he diffuses. The very path is, in a sense, luminous on which he treads. His unselfish aims—his care for the good of others—make gladsome all places which know him. His spontaneous words of sympathy for distress, which has no personal claims upon him, check crime in the ignorant and prevent despair in the educated. His daily efforts of service to others, notwithstanding the weariness and thanklessness, loss and pain, are worship, song, and prayer. The very grave is sacred where we lay him. The visitor to it treads on the ashes of honest men. The very spot is an inspiration in future time. In the unforeseen disappointments and sadness which beset our lives, we remember such men with relief, and turn from courts and conventionalities, and all the pomp and circumstance of fashion and greed, and give our best homage to the memory of the generous dead."[1]

If I may speak of myself for once in this narrative it is to relate a circumstance I remember with pride. When I next met Mr. Cobden in the House of Commons he spoke of Livsey with much regard, and mentioned having read this address in terms which gave me much pleasure, and he showed me frequent marks of friendship until the end of his life. The last note I received from him was from the platform in the great mill in Rochdale where he spoke for the last time before his death. I recall that on the night referred to at the House of Commons he said, "Come with me and allow me to introduce you to a young man from whom I think great usefulness is to be expected." It was Mr. Henry Fawcett, whom the public have since known as Professor Fawcett, M.P.

CHAPTER XXVI.

THE ROCHDALE CONGRESS OF 1892.

Being one of the speakers at the forty-fourth anniversary of the Rochdale Society, the large meeting then assembled passed unanimously on the motion of Thomas Cheetham, president, and Abram Greenwood, the following message of sympathy to Mr. Bright :—

"That this assembly, celebrating the forty-fourth anniversary of the Rochdale Equitable Pioneers' Society, desires to send to Mr. Bright a message of regard for acts of neighbourly friendship and counsel to the early Pioneers, and for his aid in Parliament in procuring legal protection for societies of self-help in their unfriended days. The Rochdale members send him their grateful wishes. They know he is sustained by a simple and noble faith, and by a

[1] Weiss—written of Theodore Parker.

conscience rich in a thousand memories of services to those who dwell in cottages or labour in our towns. The days of one who gave his strength for the benefit of the people ought to be 'long in the land,' and they who send him this message are glad to believe that his days will be yet long extended."

This was the only message to Mr. Bright in his last illness which had no dash of the undertaker in it. The usual resolutions of condolence sent him all had a foreboding implication in them. It gave him pleasure to receive the Pioneers' message.

On a visit to Rochdale shortly before I spent a few hours at One Ash. It was the last time I saw Mr. Bright. He showed me his presents from America—spoke of Wendell Phillips and others whom I had visited in America, and pointed out the portraits on his walls of members of his family whom I had known. On the day of our message I went up to his home, arresting the cab outside the grounds, as I knew he would hear the sound of wheels at his door, ask questions and send a message when repose was better for him. I wished that he should learn only incidentally of my call of inquiry.

In 1892, forty-eight years after the formation of the famous Store in 1844, the Co-operative Congress, which had been since 1869 wandering over the United Kingdom, for the first time found its tardy way to Rochdale.

VISIT TO THE GRAVE OF MR. BRIGHT.

The *Rochdale Observer* related that, after the opening of the Congress Exhibition, on Saturday, June 4th, a party of about thirty earnest co-operators and Radicals, headed by Mr. and Mrs. Holyoake and Miss E. A. Holyoake, proceeded on a pilgrimage to the grave of the late John Bright, in the quiet unpretentious and secluded burial-ground of the "Friends," adjoining the meeting-house in George Street. Standing at the foot of Mr. Bright's grave, Mr. Holyoake said:

"There is the grave of the great Tribune. I was once with him at the grave of his sister. I found him, as we all knew him, simple and unassuming. The reason why co-operators should pay a visit to this grave is that Mr. Bright was the ready and effective defender of co-operation in Parliament, and was the first who raised his voice there on behalf of that system. He believed in the principle of competition, and thought that justice would come thereby, but if it came by other means which were honest he was content. What he most cared for was the comfort and competence of the working class, as you may read on his monument in the Square we have just left.

The people for whom he spoke were not the rich, but the poor, who could make him no requital for his efforts on their behalf. As Carlyle observes: 'A man cannot be a saint in his sleep.' Serving his country as Bright served it could only be done by a saint awake. What we want in co-operation is that good speeches shall be followed by consistent acts. Mr. Bright was one of the few persons in Parliament of whom it could be said they had a conscience. He, Gladstone, Cobden, Stansfeld, Trevelyan, were of this class. I do not say that none others had consciences, but if they had it has been so little apparent in public affairs that we never knew it. Mr. Bright was trusted because he had a conscience in public affairs. In contests for principle, whoever wants inspiration let him come to this grave. In the stormy battles against slavery and for the English franchise Mr. Bright was the chief person assailed. For the last two years of the contest, I witnessed in the House of Commons that Tories and Liberals with Tory tendencies attacked him until it appeared to be a calamity to any public question that Mr. Bright favoured it. Yet all the while his adversaries were convinced, and screamed their opprobrium to conceal their conversion. How few are they who will be at trouble to obtain advantages they do not need for themselves. Mr. Bright would do that. What could be nobler than that he, a manufacturer, should seek to restore to workmen the participation in profit of which they had been deprived at Mitchell Hey Mill? Had the principle been established in practice there we might have seen it introduced into his own mills at Conkey Shaw, as the son of his great friend Thomasson did at Bolton. On personal as well as on public ground we do well to come to this grave to testify our regard. His noble taste was to dwell among his own people, and it was by his wish that he was buried here among them. He endowed Rochdale with his reputation and his country by his services."

THE GRAVES OF THE OLD PIONEERS.

The next day, at the sermon in the parish church, the Rev. Vicar, the Venerable Archdeacon Wilson, courteously announced that at the close of the service Mr. Holyoake intended visiting the graves of the Old Pioneers, and invited the company of those like-minded to meet him at the church gates.

The procession, on arriving at the cemetery, proceeded to the tomb of William Cooper, the first cashier of the Society.

Mr. Holyoake said that yesterday he invited such delegates to the Congress as had honour in their hearts for Mr. Bright, to accompany him to the grave of the great Tribune, who put conscience into politics. Coóper—and Smithies, whose grave they would next go to—put

Conscience into Co-operation in their sphere.

They put principle *first*, of which we heard little now in Rochdale. They cared not merely for the wages of workmen, they cared for the emancipation of labour. Cooper ran more risks than others in those days. He cared for the public more than he cared for friendship or himself. He was always willing to go on to platforms, and speak or write, in defence of Liberalism of Co-operation and of Labour. Twenty or more years ago a great number of people came to that place at his death to do honour to his memory. They cared for him because he was entirely honest; because his principle of co-operation meant equity, not merely in the store but in the workshop.

"Cooper! if thou canst hear our voices over thy tomb, we come to tell thee that thy protests for justice to the unrequited worker are not dead, that the memory of thy generous zeal still lives in our hearts. Like the fire of Montezuma kept burning for three centuries in the temple of his followers, the light of thy example is still kept burning in the grim and unadorned, but not less sacred, Temples of Labour.

"The great Lord of this Vale said to the Greeks:

> "'You have the Pyric dance as yet;
> Where is the Pyric phalanx gone?

"The battles of labour though less classic are not less noble than those of war, and we over thy grave, Cooper, demand of thy townsmen who now profit by self-regardless efforts—

> "'You have the Toad Lane Store as yet,
> Where is the Toad Lane workshop gone?
> Of two such lessons why forget
> The nobler and the manlier one?'

"Let us hope that the co-operators of Rochdale who set the people a nobler lesson in the past will not forget the 'manlier one' in the future. Now let us go to Smithies, whose grave I have not yet seen."

Near the entrance to the chapel mortuary, said the *Observer*, is the grave of James Smithies—that containing the remains of Cooper is just at the back—and here the crowd went in response to Mr. Holyoake's last sentence. Arrived there he proceeded:

"Someone said the other day that Smithies threw himself into the movement, but he did more than that; he made the movement. There was no movement for any man to throw himself into, in the days of Smithies and Cooper. Smithies was the leader of the fighting Pioneers. Whether on the platform or at our discussions, or in the meeting rooms of the Mitchell Hey Mills—wherever principle was to be upheld, or the enemy to be confronted, there

Smithies was. He often said that Smithies—such was his shadowless vivacity—laughed co-operation into existence. A disciple of Robert Owen, he had learned that the errors and apathy of men proceeded less from malice of mind than from want of knowing more. He understood that mankind are moulded by a destiny that went before them, and a wise man will look on his fellow-men with unexpectant eyes wondering what manifestation of taste, ideas and conduct they will make. Thus to him a hateful manner was a misfortune to him who had it, to be met not with anger but compassion. Error he confronted with instruction, not disdain; therefore he was always light-hearted and trusting. When shareholders from the town came into the Mitchell Hey Mill, allured by interest being paid them twice over, they, aided by a few false co-operators, seized all the profits of the workers. Smithies was the leader of those who withstood them, not alone in meetings, but in the town. He, like Cooper, shortened his days by his zeal for the rights of industry. Look down from this hill at quarters of the town where the smoke of factories ascend like the smoke of the bottomless pit. Think of the infernal din, the dust, the grease, the poisonous air in which the workmen's days are spent. Traverse the cheerless, hideous, hopeless streets and alleys in which the workman's family is reared. It was for them Smithies cared. It was to endow them with the right of profit of their labour that he devoted his unwearying energies. It was to raise them as a class that he came to his grave before his days were spent. Therefore we honour his memory—therefore we come here to tell him that the names 'Co-operation' and 'Perseverance,' which he gave to the engines of Mitchell Hey Mills, before they were perverted into a Joint-Stock Society—express principles in our hearts which we will vindicate as our best tribute to the honour of the dead. Smithies would ask, Why should men spend their cheerless lives in making profit for others and have none for themselves? We answer, They shall yet have it. Now, in all Rochdale there is not a single profit-sharing workshop. But we came here to tell Smithies that the principle is not dead. If he can hear us it will rejoice him that the sounds of equity and justice to labour are spoken over his grave. Let none here believe that a principle will live because it is true—unless it is sustained. Do not believe that justice always comes uppermost. It never does until it is made to come. The Old Pioneers knew this. I told Smithies that if they stood their ground their story should be known to the world so far as I had power. Now it is published in the six European languages. Their heroism, unregarded in their day, has made Rochdale known to the workmen of the world, and though long years have elapsed since their death, we come to their graves to do them honour."

On the assemblage leaving the cemetery, it stood before the monument to Thomas Livsey, which stands near the entrance; here the last speech was made.

Mr. Holyoake said: "Here lies 'Poor Tom Livsey,' as Mr. Bright affectionately called him. 'He was,' said Cobden, 'an unpolished gem.' Livsey was entirely that. He had fire and light in him which, though no lapidary magnified, no circumstances could obscure. He came up to London when meetings of resistance to Lord Palmerston's Conspiracy Bill were being held. Everybody said, no speeches so English, so bold, so inspiring were made by any one. Did you not all know him as the friend of the Chartists in this town when they had no friend else of official position? He was the friend of the Socialists who preceded the co-operators, and he was the personal friend of the Pioneers. He was one of those friends of the people who stood up for their interest, and forgot his own. Like your great townsman, Bright, and your illustrious member, Cobden, Livsey had a private affection for public affairs. Therefore we offer grateful homage to his memory. Now we leave the dead Pioneers and their honoured friend.

'They are gone,—the holy ones
Who trod with me this lovely vale;
The strong, star-bright companions
Are silent, low, and pale.'"

SPEECH AT THE STORE HALL.

On the last speaking night of the Congress it fell to me to deliver the last speech at the Conversazione in the great meeting hall of the Central Stores, when I said: "It has long been my wish to live until our Congress met in Rochdale, where co-operation as we know it began. The devices of the Pioneers gave to this movement commercial vitality which it had never known before. They did more than that, they put conscience into co-operation—conscience which, though of slower growth than profit, is far more honourable and enduring. In their day it was easy to get conscience into co-operation; our difficulty is to keep it there. (Applause.) It was the merit of the Equitable Pioneers that they sought not merely the better remuneration of labour, but its emancipation. They did their best to establish co-operative industry in Rochdale, and though they were defeated their principle was not killed. It is represented now at Hebden Bridge. Thanks to Mr. Ruskin and Mr. George Thomson, it is established in Huddersfield. It is seen in Coventry, in the hosiery and 'Eagle Brand' works of Leicester, in Kettering, and in many other places. In Scotland it has notable official recognition. Leaders of co-operation there discern principles where in England some see only an 'impracticable sentiment.' But the sentiment of the emancipation of labour is real, and is part of co-operation itself. Our stores give the principle not only of recognition, but sympathy, the sympathy of preferential purchases. The inspiration of profit-sharing by labour belongs to this movement, to this town; and by this movement it is destined to be carried out.

We have done much to introduce honesty into trade. We have yet to establish honesty in industry. The adulteration and overcharges in provisions are as nothing to the adulteration of workmanship, and under payment of wages. We who have done so much to stop the higgling of the market, have now to arrest the higgling of the workshop. The cheating in trade can be avoided by intelligent buyers—the cheating in labour no man can avoid, whose wages are regulated by his destitution. The hired hand must do fraudulent work if he is so ordered by his employer. The workman is under hourly espionage. Mr. Schloss has shown in his book on 'Industrial Remuneration' that the competitive workshop is a daily conspiracy by the employer to get from the worker the largest amount of labour for the lowest amount of pay. Are we going to conduct a movement for the consumer only, and do nothing for the labourer? Hard by here is the grave of Mr. Bright, who took a lion's part in destroying the monopoly in corn. But the corn monopoly was not half so baleful and disastrous to the workman as is the monopoly of profit by capital. The corn monopoly made bread dear—the monopoly of profit by capital makes wages low and keeps them low in every workshop in the land. This we know, since every man who has a larger income than he could obtain by his own labour, must derive it from the underpaid labour of others. Co-operation is intended—and if it be not a fraudulent thing it is pledged to put the fruits of work into the hands of the workers. It is intended to do what Mazzini told the Italian workmen co-operation could do—'Unite Capital and Labour in the same hands.' Addressing the artisans Mazzini said: 'You were once slaves—then serfs—then hirelings'—as workmen are now. 'The remedy,' he continued, 'is the association of labour and the division of the fruits of labour between the producers in proportion to the amount and value of the work done by each.' What hinders this division being general now? We are in the same position with regard to labour as the Americans were with regard to slavery. Their constitution declared 'all men free and equal,' but they drew the line at colour. Freedom was construed as applying only to white men, and it took a civil war to amend that infamous interpretation. So, with us, co-operative principles declare that division of profits applies not only to purchasers but to producers. Yet in our movement we see the official line drawn at labour. It will involve a long contest to efface that line, but it will be effaced. Two men in America—Wendell Phillips and Lloyd Garrison—effaced the line drawn against the equality of the coloured slave, and co-operation, in the name of equity, will efface the line drawn by capitalism against the white slave in our own country. Profit-sharing is opposed by precisely the same arguments and in precisely the same language as were used against the emancipation of slave labour in America. The subjection of the slave was defended by a pretended law of 'economic subordination.' That was the way the philosophers of

slavery put it at last. We have all heard this doctrine of capitalism and cupidity defended in our movement in the name of 'economic science.' Here Howarth and Smithies, Cooper and Kershaw plotted, and made countless speeches and journeys, to create for labour a better future than it knew in their day. They created the movement which we celebrate, though we may not live out its spirit. Lord Tennyson said—

> "'Our little systems have their day;
> They have their day, and cease to be.'

"But no; they do not cease if they are necessary and just. The Rochdale system of co-operation was the littlest, the obscurest, the most unfriended, the most disregarded, most contemned, the least hopeful, the least likely to succeed of any system ever devised by man. Yet it has not 'ceased to be.' On the contrary, it continues to grow, and it is even now the most prosperous system yet devised for the amelioration of the workers of England. How did the Pioneers bring this to pass? What was their inspiration? They had no learning of the schools, but they had that genius which enters the hearts of honest men. They knew as well as Archbishop Whateley that it makes all the difference in the world whether you put truth first or second. They put principle first and profit second, believing that principle was the foundation of all honourable profit, and the only honest source of it. It was not dividend which mainly inspired them, for they had never seen it, and they detested the competitive underhandedness by which they saw others acquiring profit. Like Diogenes, they went in search of honest profit by the light of principle, and they found it in honest co-operation. Let us keep to their methods and we shall see the day which they desired to see—when principle shall rule in this movement, when the humiliation of hired labour shall cease, when worker as well as purchaser shall share in the profits created, when the penury of the many shall terminate, and the scandalous fortunes of the few be impossible, under the co-operative law of the common interest, inspired by goodwill and governed by equity."

THE END.

INDEX.